CORPORATE PLANNING, HUMAN BEHAVIOR, AND COMPUTER SIMULATION

CORPORATE PLANNING, HUMAN BEHAVIOR, AND COMPUTER SIMULATION

Forecasting Business Cycles

Roy L. Nersesian

QUORUM BOOKS
New York • Westport, Connecticut • London

Library of Congress Cataloging-in-Publication Data

Nersesian, Roy L.
  Corporate planning, human behavior, and computer simulation :
forecasting business cycles / R.L. Nersesian.
    p. cm.
  ISBN 0-89930-458-3 (lib. bdg. : alk. paper)
  1. Business forecasting. 2. Corporate planning. 3. Human
behavior. I. Title.
HD30.27.N47 1990
658.4′03—dc20   89-37650

British Library Cataloguing in Publication Data is available.

Library of Congress Catalog Card Number: 89-37650
ISBN: 0-89930-458-3

First published in 1990 by Quorum Books

Greenwood Press, Inc.
88 Post Road West, Westport, Connecticut 06881

Printed in the United States of America

The paper used in this book complies with the
Permanent Paper Standard issued by the National
Information Standards Organization (Z39.48-1984).

10 9 8 7 6 5 4 3 2 1

TO DIANNE, JULIE, CATHIE, & ERIC

Contents

Preface

I served in various corporate staff positions for about fifteen years prior to my joining the ranks of academia. These positions were excellent perches from which to observe the making of business decisions. They also provided me a certain degree of noninvolvement in these decisions because the purpose of staff is to evaluate and recommend, but not make the final decision. The noninvolvement inherent in a staff position is not an aid in climbing the ladder of success. Line management is the route to the executive suite. But noninvolvement permits observations, and these observations are the foundation of this book.

I have always had an interest in the process by which management makes key decisions. Key decisions, such as what to produce over the next six months or what to invest in, require a forecast. Forecasting is an imprecise art, to say the least, yet the outcome of a decision depends on the forecast being correct in essence, even if it is lacking in accuracy. Some forecasts contain the assumption that the world that exists today is the world that will exist tomorrow. Others are slightly more sophisticated in that they assume that trends in existence today will continue in the world tomorrow.

The most sophisticated forecasting models are econometric models consisting of thousands of mathematical equations. Yet, from my perspective as an observer, the decision making process did not seem to rely on complex mathematical expressions, but rather on simple expressions of faith, or lack of faith, in the future. In other words, an element of human behavior enters into the decision making process that is not, and possibly cannot be, incorporated into complex mathematical equations.

The decision to build a new factory is partly quantifiable and partly non-quantifiable. The economic analysis on the rate of return of an investment in a new factory is part of the decision making process—a preliminary part of the process, a necessary first step that requires a forecast. The decision itself contains nonquantifiable elements. Any decision includes the feelings of the decision maker, be they noble or ignoble.

One can decide to build a new plant because of a feeling of confidence in the future and, therefore, a feeling of confidence in the validity of the economic analysis that indicates that operation of the plant will justify the investment. One can be altruistic and pretend that the plant is being built for the good of the community and the welfare of the workers. On the other hand, the decision can be motivated by greed, where the building of a plant is solely to make a fortune, or by fear, where not building the plant would place one in a disadvantageous position.

The result of many business decisions is what is called economic activity. If economic activity is influenced by the nature of decisions, and if decisions are based partly on human responses to such things as prices and costs and partly on human emotions, shouldn't the forecasting process itself incorporate human behavior? If human behavior, in turn, is influenced by such factors as prices, costs, incoming orders, outgoing shipments, warehouse inventory, and the general level of confidence in the future, shouldn't these be incorporated into the forecasting process?

The purpose of the book is to attempt to address these questions. A very simple island society is created for purposes of assessing the possibilities of a forecast containing within it the elements that might cause a change of consumer sentiment during the forecast period. A change of consumer sentiment during this period can have significant implications for the accuracy, or usefulness, of a forecast in the planning process.

The book is experimental in nature in that it does not provide the final solution to this question because the island society contained herein is too simplistic in comparison to the real world. It is the hope of the author that the methodology, and the underlying thought process, will be of value to others who are attempting to build a forecasting structure that would be more useful in the planning process of corporations than current methodologies are.

I would like to take this opportunity to thank the staff of Quorum Books, the faculty of Monmouth College, my family, and my friends for their support of my endeavors. All have contributed to the writing of this book. They should, however, not be held responsible if the purpose of this book is not achieved. That responsibility is mine alone.

CORPORATE PLANNING, HUMAN BEHAVIOR, AND COMPUTER SIMULATION

1

The Requisites for Forecasting

Forecasting of business conditions is a fairly recent phenomenon in the history of mankind. However, the seeking of advice concerning future events extends back to the dawn of human existence. Tribal chieftains sought a sign from the powers that be before leading their clans to victory or defeat. Roman Caesars and generals based decisions on whether to wage war on the prognostications of a soothsayer. The soothsayer would slaughter a chicken, slice it open, and let fall what may. He would observe the general layout of what fell out of the chicken's cavity and then interpret the meaning of the pattern of the entrails. The soothsayer had to be careful about what he said because he paid a fitful price if he was wrong. Naturally, this provided an incentive to ambiguously word the forecast of future events and deliver the message in as soothing a fashion as possible. Nevertheless, no matter how ambiguous the message, and no matter how soothing the delivery, the general, king, or emperor used the forecast to decide whether to embark on a campaign to extend an empire, or wage war to retaliate for a real or an imagined offense, or engage the enemy in a battle.

Here were two men. One had absolute control over the goings-on of an empire, a nation state, or an army. The other had a demonstrated history of surviving his own forecasts. Who ran things? The emperor, king, or general seeking the soothsayer's prediction of future events? Or the soothsayer interpreting the placement of the gizzard with respect to the liver? Or was the chicken actually controlling the situation? Or, perhaps, the chicken's gizzard was running the affairs of this world by how it decided to place itself among the viscera as the mess plopped on the ground.

Hopefully, none of this should have any bearing on forecasting of business conditions as a rational exercise. Some may contend, however, that business forecasters have about the same reputation for accuracy as the soothsayers of old or another popular forecasting service of the time: the priestesses of Delphi.

Hopefully, the methodology of modern forecasting techniques is far different. The gods and goddesses of old are not being asked for a sign. Modern-day forecasting of business conditions, in an organized, formal sense, is primarily mathematical in structure with some degree of intuitive discretion used in determining underlying assumptions, interpreting results, and reporting findings.

The less sophisticated forecasting models presume that existing trends will more or less continue "as is" into the world tomorrow. The more sophisticated of these models rely on statistical, or mathematical, relationships between and among various measures of business activity. If certain mathematical relationships exist today between different measures of business activity, and if these relationships hold true tomorrow, then one would expect a certain level of business for a given set of assumptions. If the mathematical relationships of today do not hold true in the world tomorrow, then it is back to the drawing board.

The mathematical approach to forecasting requires that we make one of two basic assumptions. In one case, the assumption is that the world tomorrow is more or less a straight line extrapolation from the worlds of yesterday and today. If the annual growth in the gross national product (GNP) was 3 percent a year ago and is now 4 percent, then next year's forecast may be on the order of 5 percent, depending on the forecaster's assessment of other pertinent factors. Regardless of the nature of the fiddling by the forecaster, the resulting forecast is essentially an adjusted extrapolation of a current trend that is expected to remain more or less intact over the forecast period.

For the other case, the assumption is that the statistical relationships of the world tomorrow will be essentially the same as those derived from examining the worlds of yesterday and today. If the observed growth in steel production was 1.5 percent a year ago when the GNP grew at 3 percent, and if this year's growth in steel production is 2 percent with a corresponding growth of 4 percent for the GNP, then the forecast for steel production, given a GNP forecast of about 5 percent, would be on the order of 2.5 percent. In other words, because the growth of steel production has been observed to be about one-half the growth of the GNP, it is presumed that the growth of steel production in the world tomorrow will remain about one-half the projected growth of the GNP. If the past relationship between the growth rates of the GNP and steel production holds true tomorrow, then the forecast of 2.5 percent is valid for the assumed GNP growth rate of 5 percent. If the relationship between the growth of steel and the growth of the GNP changes during the forecast period, then the reliability of the forecast will be adversely affected. If this change is of sufficient magnitude, then the forecast may become misleading, or spurious, or, the worst of all forecasting sins, wrong.

While this may be a overly simplified description of the forecasting process, these two assumptions are commonly incorporated into forecasting models. A person viewing the complex appearance and forbidding nature of the mathematical expressions of modern forecasting models cannot help but develop a sense of confidence that anything as forbidding and complex as these must work. And the forbidding and complex formulations would work if the world operated on straight-line extrapolations and unchanging statistical relationships.

The problem is that the world tomorrow is not a more or less straight-line extrapolation of current trends. The business cycle is noted for its ups and downs, not for its constancy in maintaining past trends. Forecasting on the basis of extrapolations is similar to looking out of the window, watching the rain fall to the ground, and forecasting that it will continue to rain. At some point, the rain is going to stop, with a forecast of continued rain still on the books. While continued rain is the safest forecast to make under the circumstances, it will be proved wrong at some point in time. The fact that a number of forecasts of continuing rain proved to be right will be forgotten the one time that it turns out to be wrong. A forecaster is remembered for his mistakes. Irving Fisher made many bullish predictions about stock market activity during the roaring 1920s, and he was right every time. But he is remembered for his forecast, made just prior to the 1929 Crash, that stocks had reached what appeared to be ''a permanently high plateau.'' For people who were following his forecasts, this was the worst of all possible times for Irving Fisher to be wrong. He is now part of the folklore of the Great Crash.

Assuming that past statistical relationships between and among various measures of business activity will hold true to form in the world tomorrow can be likened to building a house on a foundation of sand overhanging the edge of a cliff on an active fault line. As long as the wind doesn't blow too hard, as long as the rain doesn't fall too fast, as long as the ground doesn't shake too much, the house stands. The same fate awaits the forecaster when statistical relationships derived from past data are no longer relevant in predicting future business activity as awaits the occupant of the house when the wind blows too hard, or the rain falls too fast, or the ground shakes too much.

Forecasting is a tough business—ask any planner or forecaster. The essential problem with forecasting is that a forecaster is being asked to do something that transcends being a mere mortal. With rare exceptions, mortals cannot peer into the future. This is why the priestesses of Delphi were in such great demand. They were mortals who supposedly had contact with the gods who could peer into the future. Sometimes there may have been a little muddling of the conversations between the mortals and the gods, or between the priestesses and the generals and kings, that added an element of confusion, or drama, to a forecast. The king of Lydia decided to make war against the Persians on the basis of a prediction that a great power would fall if he went ahead with his plans. Was it the priestesses' fault that the king of Lydia failed to ask which power would fall?

Sometimes the gods changed their minds about what was to happen after they had given their solumn oath as to what was supposed to occur. Other times, the greater gods overruled the lesser gods. On other occasions, a lesser god appealed to the greater gods to change the course of supposedly predestined events, and sometimes gave birth to another god as a result of that appeal. Thus, the confusion of changing goals, objectives, and priorities was as common in the Olympian management team as it is in modern-day corporations. Nevertheless, it was comforting to seek the prognostications of those who were in contact with those who knew the future. Unfortunately, managers of mundane businesses operating in a free market economy are forced to forecast without the benefit of a tax-deductible side trip to Delphi. Of course, considering what happened to the king of Lydia, maybe it is to their benefit that they can't.

One way around the challenge of having to do a forecast is to try to avoid forecasting. Dodging this challenge certainly does add to the challenge of running a business. What does one tell production about what products to make, and how many of each to make, without a forecast? What does one say to marketing about how to conduct its activities without any thought on the future volume of sales? And how does finance plan to pay the bills with little thought as to the future cash flow of the firm? Without some kind of a forecast of business activity, it is difficult to run a business. It is difficult even to imagine operating a company with little thought about the future. Rare must be the company with a product to sell in a competitive environment that operates without one iota of thought on the future volume of sales of its products. Forecasting can be accomplished without any formal mathematical basis and without the formulation of one statistical relationship. A forecast of sales, profits, cash flow, or what-have-you can consist of nothing more than a single number written on the back of an envelope. This type of forecasting, based on a gut feeling for future business activity, is the most common form of business forecasting. It is called a judgmental forecast.

The process of obtaining a forecast, whether judgmental or quantitative, follows a common pattern in most companies. Using a manufacturing company as an example, the first step for the businessman-forecaster in assessing the future volume of sales is to take a close look at the present business environment, with a prolonged peek at the recent past. These two points of observation provide the businessman with insight into existing trends in his business.

Because forecasting, in either its mathematical or its judgmental form, requires a bit of artistry, one can visualize the business forecaster following much the same as an artist painting a picture. Certainly, then, the backdrop of the painting of a forecast is the present and historic sales data and other measures of present and past business performance. The past performance of a company is so deeply rooted in a forecast that one could say that recent business experience is not only the backdrop of the painting but also the distinct outline of the painting itself. More than that: from this recent experience, one can clearly grasp the subject matter, the basic coloring that will be applied, and a sense of the technique that will be employed to complete the painting.

Superimposed on this backdrop and the visible outline of the painting is the perception of future business conditions. This perception of the future is usually addressed in terms of comparison with present business conditions. Are present business conditions going to improve, stay about the same, or worsen? The addition of perceived business conditions to the canvas backdrop of recent business experience completes the painting in the rough. It may not be ready for display, but it isn't far from it.

Mr. Jones makes widgets in his garage. Last week he made and sold one hundred widgets. In fact, he has been averaging about one hundred widgets per week for the last two months. He feels that there will be no change in the general business climate for consumers buying widgets over the next few weeks. What is his forecast for next week's sales volume and production level?

The painting is given further definition and coloring by considering where a product is in its life cycle. Whether a product is in its growth stage, maturity stage, or declining stage is melded into the unfinished painting made up of available and historic data superimposed on the anticipated level of business activity.

Mr. Jones is producing an item that has been totally outmoded by the development of a technically superior widget. From the point of view of the product life cycle, the Jones widget is about to enter its declining stage. An improved version of the widget has been announced, and new production facilities are being built. Mr. Jones' lease on life is that production of better widgets has not yet occurred. When the production of better widgets materializes, and when sufficient numbers have been produced, Mr. Jones may have to convert his garage back to its original use. He scrutinizes the trade magazines for signs that new widgets are appearing on the market. He watches for advertisements of the new widgets in newspapers. He walks downtown and peers into the windows of stores that sell widgets. Although none has yet appeared, he feels that consumers, in becoming aware of the new type of widget that will eventually make its debut in every store in town, may begin to postpone their purchases until the new widgets are available. Mr. Jones ponders how the threat of a new widget's debut in the months ahead affects the number of widgets he should produce next week.

Hues and shadings are provided by market strategic objectives of expanding, or retreating, in a particular market. Mr. Jones has not been entirely idle. He feels that there may be some residual market for the old-style widgets, and that he may be the one and only manufacturer of widgets in the nation not to convert to the new improved type. He has signed up to offer technologically obsolescent widgets close to the cost of production through a national mail order catalog service that specializes in selling outmoded items. He expects the old-style widget to be included in the catalog once the new style widgets begin to become available to the public. Mr. Jones has no feedback on potential orders. How does this affect his planned production for next week?

Final touches to the forecast might include adjustments in inventory holdings and seasonal influences. Mr. Jones has one hundred widgets piled high in his bedroom, and Mrs. Jones is very upset over this. How would keeping peace in his family influence Mr. Jones' production forecast for next week? And how would he be influenced by the facts that spring is the peak selling season for widgets and that winter is now in its waning months?

Of all the aspects of making a forecast on the future volume of sales, the most important is Mr. Jones' consideration of his present and recent past history of sales. This, tempered with the influence of anticipated business conditions on current business activity, completes much of his thinking about what to do next week. If he thought that business activity would become more robust, he would set sales and production goals at a higher level with respect to current levels. If he thought that general business activity would plunge, he would set sales and production goals at a lower level with respect to current levels. His sales and production goals would also be affected if business activity was sick, but was expected to improve, or if business activity was well, but was expected to catch a cold. Much of Mr. Jones' painting of his forecast is complete at this point. The finishing touches are applied when he considers the widget's stage in its life cycle, his marketing strategy with the national mail order catalog, adjustments to inventory, and the seasonal aspects of widget sales. This completes the thought process in deciding what to do about next week's production of widgets. The artist has completed his painting.

Regardless of what planners or managers think about forecasting, they are forecasting every time they recommend or make a decision about a future course of action. Forecasting of business conditions is not the proprietary exercise of businessmen. Forecasting is part of life. A person completing an academic degree program does so on the basis of a forecast of his or her future employment or career. Politicians are forever forecasting how their legislation will benefit the lives of their constituents. At election time, politicians become specialists in forecasting business conditions: if I'm elected, voters will prosper; if my opponent is elected, the world will end.

Nevertheless, having said all this, forecasting of business conditions is not a necessary function. Its necessity rests on the nature of the economic underpinnings of a society and on the productivity of its industrial base. If managers can dictate the nature of their products to the market, as is possible under a monopoly, forecasting is hardly a problem. If a firm has a monopoly on making clothes, what is the necessity of forecasting? The firm makes what it wants to make, in the quantity and sizes it selects, and charges what it feels like charging. A consumer has no real choice—he buys what is available at the price being charged, or he goes naked. A monopoly can be held by an individual with the sanction of the state, or the monopoly can be the state itself. A monopoly, however, does require coercion to maintain itself. The active involvement of the state is necessary to protect the exclusive rights of the monopolist, even when the monopolist is the state itself. Monopolies have a very low tolerance level for competition.

Some years ago, the people of mainland China all wore the same blue working-class uniform. Here, the monopoly was a state enterprise. Mainland Chinese managers of clothing factories did not have to perform forecasts. All they had to do was meet a quota assigned by a bureaucrat who was, in turn, told that all clothing would be uniformly uniform. Hong Kong Chinese clothing manufacturers did not have a monopoly on the market. They had to forecast clothing demands by size, shape, color, design, and type and texture of material. They also had to be reasonably correct in assessing fashions and fashion trends to stay in business. A wrong forecast meant a loss on the books, and several wrong forecasts meant the demise of the company. Meanwhile, the mainland Chinese clothing manufacturing manager was safely ensconced in his position, filling out quota sheets without a care in the world as long as the quota was satisfied. He was also confident that the state would not permit anyone else to make clothing of any kind—even regulation, uniform blue.

Business forecasting is also not necessary under conditions of scarcity. Regardless of the economic system in place, a business environment in which all one can make is sold hardly requires a forecast. The response to future planning is to make all that one can make because all will be sold. This condition can arise either from strong demand for one's product or from low productivity.

Low productivity was the hallmark of the making of goods before the Industrial Revolution. Much of what passed for manufacturing production was performed by peasants or serfs during the winter months or idle times during the growing season. Everything was made by hand, with the aid of simple tools, and each person completed the total product. Low productivity had nothing to do with individual effort. The people may have worked very hard. But the productivity of the cottage industry—that is, the output of goods made individually by hand—was low. There was no mechanization, no organization, no specialization. Whatever was produced was sold or traded. One might consider the lack of surpluses, or the improbability of production exceeding demand, as one of the hallmarks of the subsistence economy.

There were no recessions or depressions in the modern sense during the days of the cottage industry because there was no perch from which to fall. Recessions and depressions imply a fall in the standard of living. If the standard of living is basically at the subsistence level, measured in material things, it becomes quite a feat to fall from a perch that is already lying on the ground.

In the days of the cottage industry, each man had his cottage, his land to till, his position in society. Living standards, measured by the amount of goods one possessed, were low. This does not necessarily mean that the peasant was unhappy. In fact, some maintain that affluence in the form of material plenty may have a greater impact on unhappiness and social disintegration than those who pursue economic progress as the end-all and be-all of human existence might care to admit. Leaving happiness and other philosophical considerations aside, if the peasant spent his winter weaving baskets by hand, he did not set up a stand at the village fair in the early days of May to sell thousands of baskets. He actually had few to sell, or trade for other goods. He most probably was able to dispose of whatever he made. If, on the other hand, not all the baskets weaved the previous winter could be sold or traded, the peasant did not live with the fear of being thrown into the unemployment lines with a mortgage hanging over his head and three kids in college. He still had his cottage; his means of feeding, clothing, and sheltering his family; his position in the community. The chances were, however, that he would be able to eventually dispose of the surplus baskets because relatively few were made, and there was an overall scarcity of baskets, along with everything else. Under these conditions of scarcity and low productivity, there was hardly a need to put much effort into performing a forecast.

The need for a forecast of business conditions requires three conditions. One is a free market in which competition makes life uncomfortable for management. The second is the possibility of producing goods far in excess of demand. Third is the potential for a change in business conditions. This means that bad times may follow good times, and good times may follow bad times. There must be a fall in living standards between good and bad times to distinguish between the two. An economy that cannot distinguish between good and bad times is already in bad times in terms of possession of material goods.

Bad times are often referred to as recessions and depressions, depending on their severity. The common reaction of managers at the onset of a recession or depression is to cut production and reduce the availability of services. The common measure of distress is unemployment, which is a direct repercussion of the decision by managers or owners to cut production and the availability of services.

The need to cut production results from the fact that the goods currently being produced are not being sold and inventories are being piled up to the ceiling. Mr. Jones will be forced to stop producing widgets once the bedroom is filled with widgets, regardless of the personal satisfaction he gets from making widgets. To do otherwise would lead to his liquidation once he has transformed all his cash reserves into widgets—to say nothing of Mrs. Jones' objections.

The need to cut services results from the fact that the current level of services is not being utilized by customers. If Mrs. Jones runs a hairdressing firm with five hairdressers and if there are only enough customers to keep one busy, Mrs. Jones will be forced at some point in time to lay off a few hairdressers, no matter how reluctant she may be to throw her workers, who might include her mother and daughter, into the unemployment lines. To do otherwise would lead to her eventual liquidation once she has exhausted her cash reserves keeping her establishment open with too many employees for the number of customers. When business is conducted in a free, or quasi-free, market environment—in which the production of goods and services can exceed that which the market can absorb and in which the cyclical nature of business fluctuates between good and bad times—business forecasting becomes a necessity.

The more or less free market environment in which firms compete and the capacity of firms to overproduce goods with respect to the ability of the marketplace to absorb such goods are partly responsible for the existence of business cycles. These are the political and physical aspects of business cycles. The human aspect must be added—and that is the characteristic of people, as producers and consumers, to think alike under a given set of circumstances.

Business cycles are partly the result of seemingly independent decisions by owners and managers on what, and how much, to produce based on the profitability of various items. Because profitability is the common signal to all businessmen, it is not unusual for businessmen, each seemingly making his own independent decision, to look at the same data base of prices and costs and arrive individually at the same conclusions on whether to expand or cut production. The herd instinct to expand production collectively and to cut production collectively, as the end result of free-will decisions of many individuals, is a repercussion of the economic thinking of Adam Smith. However, it is not the herd instinct per se that spawns business cycles; rather, the herd instinct, coupled with highly efficient means of production, is responsible, in part, for the cyclical nature of business activity.

The herd instinct of people as producers—be they entrepreneurs, businessmen, managers, owners of factories, or owners of capital—is not entirely to blame for the existence of business cycles. The herd instinct of people as consumers is just as important. The degree to which people spend their salaries on goods and services in good times as compared to bad times is a powerful force that affects the behavior of people as producers. The spending habits of people were vastly different before and after the Crash of 1929. The propensity to spend, and, indeed, overspend, prior to the Crash contributed to the good times; the propensity to save, and, indeed, oversave, after the Crash contributed to the prolongation of the bad times. There is a chicken and egg situation between the respective roles individuals play as either producers or consumers in the boom and bust of business cycles. The blame for laying off thousands of workers cannot be laid solely at the feet of the managers of enterprises if millions of consumers cease buying their goods. The blame for millions of consumers ceasing to buy goods and putting away as much as they can in their savings accounts cannot be laid solely at their feet if they see thousands of their numbers being laid off. Who, then, is responsible for good times changing to bad times? People acting as producers, or people acting as consumers, or people acting as humans?

If the conditions for business cycles require an economy in which individuals can make decisions based on the profit motive and a productive plant capacity that can create unmanageable surpluses of goods, then, perhaps, a few words ought to be dedicated to those who played key roles in setting the stage where forecasting business conditions becomes a necessity.

Despite the growth of "isms" of one sort or the other, much of the Western world still has an economic system steeped in the thoughts of Adam Smith. To the degree that individuals have the right to form firms, and to the degree that these firms are forced to be dissolved or liquidated if they are unsuccessful, then the basic tenets of Adam Smith's free market economy can be regarded as valid and pertinent to the times. The right to form firms means that no one company can achieve a monopoly on the production of any product. The threat of bankruptcy ensures that a firm must respond to the demands of the marketplace in an efficient manner.

There is a strong voice of opinion that Adam Smith's free market economy does not apply in the world of Big Business. Most industries in Europe, North America, and the Far East are dominated by a half dozen giants that through mutual cooperation, overt or covert, intentional or not, supposedly control the market. Breaking into the old boys' club requires a great deal of financial muscle and intestinal fortitude. The sheer size of a new operation in an already developed industry acts as a barrier to new entries. Therefore, the basic tenets of Adam Smith's free market economy would not apply for Big Business because a few existing firms, forming an oligarchy, can set up a barrier to prevent real competition from making a stage appearance. With Big Business able to protect itself against competition by throwing up barriers against new entrants, and with so much of the total production of goods and services falling under the purview of Big Business, very little of the economy of a nation is exposed to the "invisible hand" of Adam Smith.

As an example, it may be difficult to open up a new automobile company in a nation in which one company may already dominate the market. The sheer size of the investment in a new automobile company and the numerous hinderances that can be thrown up by the ensconced firm to maintain its position provide an effective barrier against new entries into the market. These barriers hindering the opening up of a new automobile manufacturing plant may prevent the workings of the free market as set forth by Adam Smith.

However, it is difficult for the managers of even a sole automobile manufacturing company to control the automobile market in the host nation unless the company can induce the government to ban automobile imports. The workings of a free market require a number of competitors to ensure the game is played fairly. There is no requirement that the competitors be local firms. The existence of free trade ensures that no one company can dominate the market as long as consumers can freely purchase automobiles made in other nations. In a nation that has only one automobile manufacturer, free trade creates an economic environment with a number of real competitors. This applies even when there are real barriers to entry of another automobile manufacturing firm in that nation, such as a government edict prohibiting the formation of a new automobile company. The possibility of consumers' purchasing foreign-built automobiles has the same effect on the behavior patterns of the managers of the auto maker as if there were competitive plants located a few yards down the road.

As long as managers are held accountable for performance measured in terms of generating profits or, on the other side of the coin, performance measured in terms of controlling costs, the legacy of Adam Smith remains intact. Despite all sorts of government interventionist policies, consumers still have a real choice of products to purchase, and managers rise and fall on their selection. Individuals are free to form new firms, and unsuccessful firms, those that cannot successfully compete for the consumer's dollar, are eventually consigned to the scrap heap of corporate has-beens. Whether the consumer is an individual purchasing a sweater, or a company purchasing a computer, or the government purchasing a missile is immaterial. Success in satisfying the market gives the firm the right to exist until such time that it fails to satisfy the market and is liquidated by impatient creditors. Even government-subsidized industries have found out that a creditor in the form of an agency of the state can run out of patience.

Each firm in a given industry pretends that it is making its own independent decision about its future course of business. In fact, all the managers of the same industry are making the same decisions at the same time because they are all experiencing the same business conditions, and they all have the same essential feelings about the future course of business conditions, and they all do their economic analysis the same way, and they all refer to the same data base on prices for goods and services. While they may differ on costs for making goods or providing services, if their costs are near parity, then their business decisions will be nearly identical. This almost mechanical response to the relationship of prices and costs on the part of owners and managers, coupled with the freedom to control the output of their highly productive factories, is vital in understanding one side of business cycles. Understanding the consumers' behavior patterns is the other side.

Once one accepts the basic tenets of Adam Smith that the free market is the most productive mode of manufacturing goods and the most effective means of enhancing the living standards of the population, then the existence of the business cycle becomes inevitable. That inevitability has to do with human behavior characteristics and human reactions to a common data base. For people as producers, the common data base may include prices and costs, and anticipated changes in prices and costs. For people as consumers, the common data base may include the state of the job market, and anticipated changes in the number of those standing in unemployment lines.

The economic thinking of Adam Smith is woven into the political fabric of much of the free world. This might explain the use of the words "political economy" in his writings. In fact, one may make the argument that Adam Smith is more alive today than ever before. In a global economy, competition is expanding. The manufacture of automobiles is now a world business. A few decades ago, American consumers had a choice of automobiles from the Big Three manufacturers; now they select from a score or more of manufacturers that are oriented not to their national market but to the world market. The Big Three have learned a painful lesson: they cannot dictate the nature of their product to the American public. The cost of that lesson was a loss of about one-quarter of the domestic market, the near-bankruptcy of one of the Big Three, and a restructuring of the industry including restyled management-union relationships, production techniques, and products.

Even the hypothetical illustration of a single automobile company in a nation would not necessarily mean that the owners of that company would seek protection against imports to protect their market. Outside of the United States, most automobile companies depend on exporting a portion of their products. Thus, the hypothetical single automobile company may sell a significant portion of its output to neighboring countries. Banning imports by one nation is an open invitation for retaliating nations to ban the buying of the exports of the offending nation. The single automobile company may be worse off by gaining a monopoly in the domestic market if the consequence of its success is the loss of its international market.

The possibility of trade wars has become somewhat more remote in recent decades because the overwhelming number of international agreements on the books promote free trade, with more awaiting ratification. The world well remembers the repercussion of the Hawley-Smoot Tariff Act of 1930. Its high tariffs managed to shrink world trade to a trickle, thus adding to, and prolonging, the Great Depression. The memories of the Great Depression and the sinister political forces that it fomented are still vivid in the minds of policy makers. In fact, much of the driving force behind political and economic policies today is the desire to avoid a repeat of the 1930s.

Because politicians and economists are attempting to avoid falling into the abyss of a depression, and because technological improvements in communication, data processing, and transportation, have increased dramatically, the world is fast becoming economically integrated. Europe is well on its way to total economic integration in the same sense that the various states of the United States are economically integrated. Business is conducted on a global scale between the principal industrialized areas with remarkably little interference by government agencies—at least as compared to former times. Europe, North America, Japan, and other Far Eastern industrial nations are moving rapidly toward, or may have already arrived at, a sort of quasi–one world economy. One can argue over how quasi it is, but not over the fact that the interests of much of the industrialized world are already integrated in an economic and financial sense, if not yet in a political sense.

Yet the political structures of most nations of the industrialized world, which usually take the form of a democracy with power shared by two or three major parties, have many more similarities than differences. Political leaders meet fairly regularly to discuss matters of common interest. They are followed by finance ministers who attempt to coordinate economic and financial policies around a general framework of a global economy with minimum barriers to free trade. The industrialized world may not be politically integrated in the sense that one voice is speaking for all, but it is integrated in the sense that all the voices are speaking the same message.

All of this means more, not less, competition for the consumer's dollar, despite the existence of barriers set up by Big Business to make life comfortable for themselves. Free trade has made a mess of this corporate club, and the members must continue to compete for the consumer's dollar. The recent experiments in the Soviet Union and China, in which people organize themselves to provide consumer goods and services with profit as a motive for individual effort, is more of a vote for Adam Smith than for Karl Marx. There is talk in these nations of ending state subsidies to chronically sick companies, of making the factories responsive to the market by letting them go out of business if they don't produce goods that people are willing to buy, of letting prices rise to cover costs, of decentralizing control over what and how much to produce, and on and on. None of these principles is found in the writings of Karl Marx, but they certainly are part and parcel of the writings of Adam Smith.

Recessions and depressions also require a highly productive society. Machines are required to change the output of an individual from fifty baskets per winter season to fifty baskets per hour, eight hours a day, five days a week, fifty weeks a year. Although the list of individuals who contributed to the efficiency of modern-day production capacity is quite long, the collective achievements of many individuals can be summed up in the accomplishments of two: Eli Whitney and Henry Ford. These two individuals were selected because their contributions transcend invention, technological innovation, and enhancement of efficiency. Were it not for individuals such as Adam Smith, Eli Whitney, and Henry Ford (and there were many others), there might not be a need to forecast demand. The statement can be made more forceful: were it not for these individuals, there would be no need to forecast, probably be no business cycles to worry about, no need to consider changing levels of business activity in the forecasting process, and no need for this book.

2

Adam Smith, Eli Whitney, and Henry Ford

ADAM SMITH

To appreciate the contribution of Adam Smith, one has to look at the workings of industry, or what was called industry, before Adam Smith. Business was conducted within a feudal structure, and international commerce was governed by what Adam Smith called *mercantilism*. This was a world of certainty—or what passed for certainty. In a world of certainty, there is no need for forecasting.

The son of a candlestick maker in Venice might desire to be a glass blower. He may have been born with a hefty set of cheeks to blow and shape liquid glass into the most exquisite shapes. Yet his desire to become a glass blower—to shift occupations, so to speak—would be frustrated. This is an understatement because frustration implies the existence of a possibility. If frustrated at first, try and try again. In the tradition of Horatio Alger, success would simply be a matter of redoubling one's efforts.

In feudal society, the candlestick maker's son could try and try again, but it would be to no avail. The feudal system was not ready for, nor could it accommodate, Horatio Alger. To become a glass blower in Venice under the feudal guild system, one had to be invited to join the guild, and invitations were usually given only to sons of bona fide members of the glass blowing guild. Perhaps, under unusual circumstances, invitations to membership might be extended to sons-in-law. This might offer an opportunity for the candlestick maker's son to switch professions.

The son of a candlestick maker had limited access to joining the glass blowers guild because the feudal guild system had total control over its membership. Not only was the candlestick maker's son prohibited from joining the glass blowers guild, but also he would, in fact, be forced to join the candlestick makers guild by virtue of the fact that not joining might mean starvation. Not starvation in the literal sense, but starvation in the economic sense of not having any real alternatives of making a living as a craftsman in another trade.

The rules of the guild exerted total control over one's position within the guild and, therefore, over the nature of the individual's output. The beginning position was that of apprentice. As an apprentice, one's work was limited to what an apprentice is supposed to do: watch, go'fer things, and clean up. Through a progression of steps, each of which required the approval of guild members, one became a journeyman and, after some number of more steps, a master. The thirty-two degrees of the Masonic Order to become a Master Mason are modeled after the feudal masonic guild.

And what was the chief purpose of being a master glass blower? It may have been blowing glass; but that was done between approving the listing of new apprentices, controlling their progression through the ranks, and determining the nature of their output. The guild members controlled every aspect of their membership, the output of the guild, and the selling price of goods. Who needs to forecast demand when one has complete control over what will be stocked on the retailers' shelves?

The son of the candlestick maker was simply born to the wrong family. Primarily by accident of birth, he must make candlesticks—unless by intention of marriage, he could join the glass blowers guild. Against his inclination, he is making candlesticks.

Suppose that he is making copper candlesticks. As people buy his candlesticks, they voice their opinion that glass candlesticks would be preferable. The candlestick maker begins to think in terms of offering candlesticks made of either glass or copper. He thinks in terms of gearing his production to the demand for glass and copper candlesticks as determined by the buying public. If the buying public has a growing penchant for glass over copper candlesticks, the candlestick maker could adjust his production accordingly, shifting personnel and material resources from the making of copper candlesticks to glass candlesticks.

If he found that he was having trouble keeping up with the demand for glass candlesticks, he would hardly be blamed for raising the price of glass candlesticks to enhance his profits and, incidentally, discourage demand. If he found that copper candlesticks were beginning to fill up his place of business, he would lower the price of copper candlesticks to encourage sales and reduce what he perceives to be an excessive inventory of copper candlesticks, even if it means sustaining some degree of financial loss.

One would not consider it unusual behavior if the candlestick maker enhanced the productive capacity of glass candlesticks by taking the incremental profits and expanding his workshop. He might attempt to recruit glass blowers from the glass blowing guild, or he might provide incentives for the makers of copper candlesticks to learn the glass blowing trade. If the public swing from copper to glass candlesticks is too rapid from the point of view of making a smooth transition with the resources at hand, he might consider pooling his resources with those of his friends, family, and fellow workers to add significant capacity in his workshop for the manufacture of glass candlesticks. This might entail taking the funds thus acquired and buying an existing glass blowing establishment. He might even consider converting his workshop to a factory dedicated entirely to the making of glass candlesticks by throwing away all the tools associated with copper candlestick making and laying off all his remaining and unconvertible copper candlestick makers.

If glass candlesticks are a real market winner, the son of the candlestick maker would be expected, in a normal human reaction to success, to open up new market outlets for his products. He might open up a store in London and sell his glass candlesticks, using advertising and promotion to encourage the public to purchase glass candlesticks. The reception of glass candlesticks in London might cause him to open outlets in Vienna and other commercial centers. He might have to offer stock to the public to acquire the necessary funds to vastly expand the productive capacity of his Venetian factory to satisfy the burgeoning demand created by his international marketing activities. All of this is what we would expect the candlestick maker's son to do. This behavior pattern would be normal in today's world. It simply was not done in the pre–Adam Smith world.

Besides introducing to the world the concept of free choice in what Adam Smith called *political economy*, he also attacked mercantilism. If the budding glass-candlestick-making entrepreneur was a good mercantilist, he would convert all the earnings from selling glass candlesticks in foreign markets (less local expenses) into gold and ship it back to Venice. Mercantilism promoted the concept that the purpose of international trade was to build up the gold reserves of a nation. With that definition of success, a moment's worth of thought would show that it is impossible for all the nations of the world to be successful world traders. If anything, such a policy would not encourage, but rather discourage, world trade because each nation would be very reluctant to disgorge whatever gold had already been hoarded. Thus, a nation would not run what is today called a *deficit trade balance*, even if it were transient in nature, because it would have to give up part of its hoard of gold. This mind set of being a winner at all times in the arena of world trade, with the tally of winners and losers emblazoned on piles of gold, does not foster common economic interests beyond national borders.

Adam Smith's contribution to giving mercantilism the kiss of death was the idea of the Venetian glass candlestick maker taking his excess earnings in England and converting them into something that the English excelled in making and that was in demand in Venice. Maybe that something was woolen capes. Maybe the Venetians were not good at making woolen capes, whereas the English were. Maybe the English were not good at making glass candlesticks, whereas the Venetians were. Therefore, it would enhance the economic well-being of all for the Venetians to specialize in making glass candlesticks and the English to specialize in making woolen capes, and for the two parties to exchange or trade what they were good at making. Thus, the purpose of international trade was not to collect the largest hoard of gold, but rather to enhance the standard of living of the citizens of the trading nations. Adam Smith was a proponent not of autarky (national economic self-sufficiency) but of free trade, both within and without a nation, to promote the material well-being of humankind.

Adam Smith lived from 1723 to 1790. He wrote the *Inquiry into the Nature and Causes of the Wealth of Nations* around 1763. His title for Book I, "The Division of Labor, Value and Distribution," says much about his feeling that increasing the productivity of labor requires, above all else, specialization. The specialization of labor, or its "division," is the key to economic progress because "the annual labor of every nation is the fund which originally supplies it with all the necessaries and conveniences of life." Because the pool of labor is fixed, anything that increases its productivity enhances the living standards of the people. In Adam Smith's world, labor should do what it does best, and the excess output should be used to trade for whatever else is needed. Specialization applied to the products made by a community and to the tasks necessary to manufacture those products. The cottage industry, in which each community made everything it needed, with each member of the village making the entire product, was not part of Adam Smith's world. Rather, each village would make what it was best at making, with each member specializing in that function he was best at performing. Then each village would trade products—not so much by bartering as by using a medium of exchange. And the medium of exchange would be money—principally, but not necessarily limited to, gold and silver.

The demand for any article of manufacture would be reflected in the price people are willing to pay for it. The greater the demand with respect to supply, the higher the price. The higher the price, the greater the profits. The greater the profits, the greater the incentive to expand production. On the other hand, the greater the supply of an article with respect to demand, the lower the price, the smaller the profits, and the less the incentive to expand production. At some point, the diminished profits become losses, forcing production cuts in order to restore the balance between the supply of and the demand for a particular article. Price, based on the relationship between the supply of and the demand for an article of manufacture, would be the key factor in determining the level of production. Price is ultimately controlled by the willingness of consumers to purchase the article and the capacity of producers to manufacture the article— not by an edict or decision made by a government body or a guild association. Adam Smith laid the foundation of a capitalistic, free market society in which human progress, and presumably happiness, was to be measured in the possession of material things.

Adam Smith attacked what he called the mercantile and feudal guild systems at their very roots. He declared as anathema any restrictive regulation, any monopolistic institution, practice, or privilege, any "system either of preference or of restraint." These systems "being thus completely taken away, the obvious and simple system of natural liberty establishes itself of its own accord."

What did Adam Smith have in mind as items of preference or restraint which should be shoved into the dustbin of history? Adam Smith wanted free choice of occupations by the removal of apprenticeship restrictions—in other words, the abolition of the guild system. He attacked the duties imposed by, and the monopolistic privileges, of chartered companies. Implicit in this was the principle of free formation of corporations, or associations, for the pursuit of business. In the world of a landed gentry, he wanted free trade in land by abolition of primogeniture—that is, the transfer of all land to the eldest son, which entails the legal prohibition of land transfer other than through inheritance. There were to be no barriers to trade within a nation and no barriers to trade between nations other than in those special circumstances in which free trade between nations would cause considerable unemployment for a particular industry.

The role of government would be limited to furnishing defense, administering justice, and providing other amenities associated with civil government. The government would also be responsible for public works, such as the construction of an internal transportation system and the education of the people. Public works would be self-funding to the maximum practical extent. Tolls on roads and bridges would self-liquidate the government's investment in building them. This is the essence of what is called *laissez faire economics*: hands-off policy by government authorities and civil associations such as guilds, allowing economic decisions to be made by individuals in their roles as entrepreneurs, businessmen, owners of companies, and owners of capital.

Though never mentioned as such, laissez faire economics lies deeply imbedded in the Constitution of the United States. The freedoms extended to those who are involved in commerce and trade are pure Adam Smith, and that mysterious phrase "pursuit of happiness" has an Adam Smith ring to it. The American Revolution itself was a revolt, in part, against mercantilist doctrines that required the colonies to supply the mother nation with raw materials and to be the market for its manufactured goods. The requirement that all commerce be transported in British flag vessels was to ensure that the colonies were exporting only raw materials and that all their manufactured goods came from Britain. One purpose of the presence of the British army in the colonies was to enforce "Made in Britain" on all manufactured goods by making sure that there were no manufactured goods bearing the label "Made in America." On this subject Adam Smith wrote in *The Wealth of Nations*:

All systems either of preference or of restraint, therefore, being thus completely taken away, the obvious and simple system of natural liberty establishes itself of its own accord. Every man, as long as he does not violate the laws of justice, is left perfectly free to pursue his own interest his own way, and to bring both his industry and capital into competition with those of any other man, or order of men. The sovereign is completely discharged from a duty, in the attempting to perform which he must always be exposed to innumerable delusions, and for the proper performance of which no human wisdom or knowledge could ever be sufficient; the duty of superintending the industry of private people, and of directing it towards the employments most suitable to the interest of the society.

As every individual, therefore, endeavors as much as he can both to employ his capital in the support of domestic industry, and so to direct that industry that its produce may be of the greatest value; every individual necessarily labours to render the annual revenue of the society as great as he can. He generally, indeed, neither intends to promote the public interest, nor knows how much he is promoting it. By preferring the support of domestic to that of foreign industry, he intends only his own security; and by directing that industry in such a manner as its produce may be of the greatest value, he intends only his own gain, and he is in this, as in many other cases, led by an invisible hand to promote an end which was no part of his intention. Nor is it always the worse for the society that it was no part of it. By pursuing his own interest he frequently promotes that of the society more effectually than when he really intends to promote it.

There it is—the philosophical underpinnings of the free market economy; of the narrow pursuit of the buck to bring about the greatest good; and of the inherent virtue of entrepreneurs, businessmen, industrialists, and owners of physical and monetary assets alike in opposing the shackling of their hands by government bureaucrats.

Two of Adam Smith's observations ought to be discussed because events subsequent to his life may not have supported their initial inclusion in his work. Adam Smith believed that the natural price of things would, in the long run, be the competitive price determined by the cost of production. Profit is the compensation for risk and in an economic environment of free competition, profits would fall to a minimal level. The more an economy moves toward what Adam Smith called a "stationary" economy, the smaller the profit margins would be. However, in the short run, prices are determined by the relationship between the supply of and the demand for a particular item.

A stationary economy implies one in which there is little change in terms of products and little change in terms of consumer preferences. While this might have been possible in the days of the cottage industry at the time of the writing of *The Wealth of Nations,* a stationary economy has not been with us since the start of the Industrial Revolution. In fact, there is an enormous amount of effort put into preventing the development of a stationary economy. It is in the introduction of new products and services that there is the potential for the greatest profitability. A stationary market in potato peelers exists when every household possesses a potato peeler. Money is not made when there already is a potato peeler in every house. There is little excitement in a mature market for a product when replacement is the primary incentive to buy—or, in Adam Smith's terminology, in a stationary economy. In that respect, he is correct. The profit margin in the potato peeler replacement market is slim when the primary incentive for buying a potato peeler is that the old one has been worn out from peeling too many potatoes.

Money is made when a better potato peeler is invented. Then everyone wants one. A stationary economy cannot exist as long as billions of dollars are being poured into research and development for new products and new processes to more efficiently make old products. When a new product is brought into being, millions of dollars are spent advertising the product to make its existence known to the buying public and to induce them to buy it. With so much effort being devoted to preventing the development of a stationary economy, a pricing mechanism based on costs and a slim profit margin is uncommon, except in relatively rare cases such as that of potato peelers. More often than not, the price over the long term is nothing more than a continuing series of short-term prices, set primarily by the relationship between the supply of and the demand for a particular product.

Adam Smith also concluded that wages for workers would be always near the subsistence level. He believed that employers, or combinations of employers, held a stronger bargaining position than did workers in determining wages. As such, the workers would be in the unenviable position of working primarily for a wage that barely keeps them alive. And certainly the early history of capitalism, which is synonymous with the early stages of industrialization, would bear out the truth of Adam Smith's observation. Adam Smith did not view the dealings between employers and employees through rose-colored glasses. He did not place his faith in the goodness of heart of the owners of capital.

The early British textile mills were living testimony to Adam Smith's assertion that the workers would barely be allowed to subsist. The British textile mill owners, the capitalists of the day, knew that to maximize profits, one had to both maximize revenues and minimize costs. Every dollar, or pound, saved by reducing costs would go straight to the bottom line as profit. What were the principal costs of operating a textile mill? How about machinery (looms), raw material (cotton or wool), and labor? Labor was treated as equivalent to a bale of wool—a cost item to be minimized. To this end, the British textile mill owner fulfilled Adam Smith's prediction to the fullest. The workers lived in hovels, they worked long hours under the most deplorable conditions imaginable, and they were entirely at the tender mercies of the owners. With the exception of Robert Owen, who both cared for the workers and ran a profitable textile mill, there was little in the way of mercy to be found. The workers were truly at the subsistence level—and even below the subsistence level because starvation occurred from time to time. Most importantly of all, the workers wore rags for clothing.

Why is this point so important? Take another look at the situation. The owners were maximizing their profits by minimizing their costs. They were eminently successful in minimizing the cost of labor. That could be demonstrated by the fact that the workers wore rags. But there is another part of the profit maximizing equation that the manufacturers had to deal with—maximizing profits means more than minimizing costs. It is also necessary to maximize revenues. At the barest minimum, the textile owners had to sell the output of their factories at some price above the cost of manufacture. To whom, then, do the owners of the textile plants sell the textiles? Their workers? Some market that is. The workers can barely feed themselves; that is why they are wearing rags. Because the manufacturers could not maximize their revenues by selling to their workers, they turned to the government and urged it to acquire colonies. The colonies would be the market for the manufactured goods. And how would the colonies pay for the manufactured goods? By supplying the factories with raw materials. How did they enforce such a policy? By controlling the shipping and by stationing an army.

Does any of this sound vaguely familiar? It should. Grade school history books state that Britain's purpose in seeking colonies was to satisfy the demand of the industrialists to obtain a market for their manufactured goods and a source of supply for their raw materials. What these same grade school history books fail to point out was that these industrialists had to promote imperialism as a result of their success in minimizing labor costs. Adam Smith missed the inverse relationship between success in impoverishing the working class and success in generating profits. An impoverished work force does not have the purchasing power necessary for the factory owners to maximize their revenue. The British textile mill owners thought that the answer to this imbroglio was in Britain's acquiring colonies. Neither they, nor Adam Smith, recognized that there was a better solution to this problem much closer to home. In fact, the solution was sweating it out in their workshops.

Although Adam Smith dug the philosophical grave for the feudal guild system in the economic sense, much of its essence still exists. In the legal, accounting, medical, consulting, and other professions, there is a graduated sequence for advancement. In the legal profession, one starts out as a law clerk, an apprentice, and becomes a journeyman by taking on the less complex cases. With time, and with peer observation, an individual becomes a full partner, or master lawyer, so to speak. Advancement through experience and peer review was not the reason for Adam Smith's criticism of the system. He criticized the fact that the guild controlled the number of those entering the system, the nature and the output of their work once in the system, and the price of the product or service. Today, anyone can become a lawyer who has the proper education and can demonstrate the required level of proficiency by passing a bar examination. Although some may maintain that lawyers do create their own demand and do try to control the market, the fact that many lawyers are not in the mainstream of six-figure incomes suggests that their control over the situation is less than complete. As for those lawyers who do command huge salaries, all that Adam Smith requires is that this group be penetrable by anyone who wishes to enter and who is capable of entering therein. As long as the lawyers guild, so to speak, cannot prohibit budding lawyers from entering the more lucrative areas of the legal profession, then, with time, the invisible hand can apportion lawyers in a more equitable fashion.

ELI WHITNEY

Eli Whitney (1765–1825) was a mechanical wizard. While traveling in the south, he became acquainted with the problem of removing the seeds from cotton. Enormous numbers of slaves were employed pulling the seeds out by hand. Eli

Whitney spent a whole two weeks on this challenge and invented the cotton gin. He patented the invention and went on to capitalize on his invention by opening a factory to make cotton gins. It ended in bankruptcy.

The failure of Eli Whitney to make his fortune on the cotton gin was due primarily to the very simplicity of the design of the machine. Once the initial shipments of Whitney's cotton gin arrived on the cotton plantations of the South, entrepreneurial individuals pried off the top and peered inside. What they saw was eminently copiable—and copy they did. The Patent Office in Washington wasn't eager to send agents into the South to enforce Eli Whitney's patent rights, and he couldn't obtain legal redress in the court system, so he eventually walked away from his invention.

Business students, in common with all students, are told not to copy. Copying is dishonorable and deserving of dismissal. They graduate and enter a world in which copying is endemic. A new idea is not the property of its originator because everyone copies in all areas of business. If a firm discovers a more efficient way of doing something, it will be copied. If a firm discovers a more effective way of marketing a product, it will be copied. If a firm discovers a more efficacious way of financing its expansion, it will be copied. Copying is critical in understanding the nature of the business cycle. Copying contributes to the ups and downs of the business cycle by directing larger investments into new areas than would occur if copying were not so endemic. The building of a greater number of factories than is necessary is a consequence of copying that helps to keep the good times good.

On the other side of the coin, copying can cause businesses to dedicate too much productive capacity to new products. When all the investments are completed and the combined productive capacity of a thousand and one copyists is brought to bear on the market, all the copyists have for their efforts are huge unsold inventories and excessive productive capacity. Then they copy one another again by collectively slashing production to try to keep inventories in line with sales. This type of copying helps to turn good times into bad.

One might expect that patent protection should limit copying. However, if what is being copied is a strategy for marketing or making financial deals, there is no patent infringement because an idea cannot be patented. Even copyrights on computer software have been difficult to enforce because a program can be essentially copied by rewriting it with minor editorial changes, such as calling something X that was called Y in the original program. Patents on products and processes are enforceable within a given nation, but they are more difficult to enforce in the international arena. Thus, a firm can spend millions to develop a new product and find itself in the position of not being able to recoup its research and development expenditures because copies are being imported from foreign copiers that do not have to price the goods on the basis of recouping the initial R&D expense. The globalization of manufacturing facilities and free trade have proved to be a boon for copyists.

The simplicity of the cotton gin, the ease of copying it, and Whitney's sad return on his investment in his invention are of interest in understanding the role of copying in the business cycle. But the real point of this discussion is Eli Whitney on the comeback trail. Whitney obtained a government contract to make ten thousand muskets. The contract presumed that he would make the muskets in the way that all muskets, and everything else, were made. In the cottage industry of the day, a musket was assembled by an individual who made a barrel, a stock, a flintlock, a trigger, and the other mechanical parts. As each part was made, it was filed to fit the rest of the components making up the musket. The result of this mode of production was that each particular part of a musket was unique. A flintlock made for a musket could not be removed and interchanged with the flintlock of another musket and be expected to work. The parts were not interchangeable without further filing because they were not uniform in design and would not fit together properly. Each musket was, in effect, tailor made to its own set of specifications.

To fill his contract with the government, Eli Whitney built a factory near New Haven, Connecticut, in 1798, that was unique in several respects. Water-powered machines were designed to replace human effort as much as possible. The machines were dedicated to the manufacture of the individual component parts of a specified design, rather than each part being individually handmade. In other words, Eli Whitney was substituting machine labor for manual labor, thereby increasing the productivity of labor.

In Whitney's factory, the parts produced were of sufficiently close tolerances to be interchangeable. Quality control was introduced to ensure that the flintlock of one musket would be interchangeable with the flintlock of another with no additional filing. Eli Whitney's "uniformity system" had at its core the idea of manufacturing ten thousand barrels, ten thousand stocks, ten thousand flintlocks, ten thousand trigger mechanisms, ten thousand whatever, all of sufficiently close tolerances to be interchangeable without additional filing. The parts were manufactured first, and the completed musket was assembled later. Whitney's uniformity system was the forerunner of today's assembly line.

Eli Whitney gave to modern society the most productive means of manufacture known to mankind. There are those who can point to the fact that he did not originate the idea, that it had antecedents in Europe. That is true and bears about as much weight as the fact that Christopher Columbus was not the first European to discover America. Leif Ericsson may, or may not, have been first. Even if Ericsson was first, what does that do to take away from Columbus' achievement? It was the discovery of America by Columbus that counts. The nations of North and South America owe their existence to Columbus' explorations, not to Ericsson's.

The same holds true for Whitney's uniformity system. More than any other individual, he popularized the idea of Adam Smith's specialization of labor. Eli Whitney vastly increased the productivity of his specialized labor force by replacing tools with machines and by introducing quality control measures to ensure that the interchangeable parts were indeed interchangeable. His water-powered factory in New Haven was the progenitor of many such plants in the northern states.

Eli Whitney affected the course of the development of the United States in two quite unintentional ways. The removal of the cotton seeds by the cotton gin rather than by a slave's fingers had a dramatic impact on the profitability of growing cotton in the South. One might conclude that the price of slaves would fall with the invention of the cotton gin because the labor required to remove the seeds from the cotton was nearly eliminated. Were there no other impact, that might have turned out to be true. But the cotton gin made cotton growing much more profitable because the slaves could dedicate more of their time to planting and harvesting the cotton rather than to removing its seeds. Nothing did more to spread the growing of cotton in the South than did the cotton gin. As new areas of the South were brought under cultivation, there was a greater demand for slaves. The price of slaves increased, and the institution of slavery, which was actually waning at the time of the invention of the cotton gin, was given new life. The South embarked on a path of agriculture based on slave labor.

In the North, just the opposite occurred. Whitney's factory in New Haven was a cause of the North's embarking on a path of industrialization, based, as some would assert, on wage-slave labor. As in the South, Eli Whitney himself had no pretensions of embarking on anything. He invented the cotton gin and tried to make a buck from his invention. When that failed, he devised the uniformity system to make a buck out of a government contract. Nevertheless, the social repercussions of his contributions to technology had a significant impact on the history of the nation.

HENRY FORD

Henry Ford (1863–1947) did not invent the automobile. In 1769, a Frenchman by the name of Nicholas Cugnot made a three-wheeled "steam carriage." It was large and cumbersome. Its principal contribution to the development of the automobile was popularizing the idea of a horseless carriage. In the 1880s, two inventions gave enormous impetus to the development of the automobile: the gasoline-driven engine and the air-filled rubber tire. The first successful automobiles were built late in the nineteenth century by Gottlieb Daimler in Germany and by the Duryea brothers in the United States.

Henry Ford did not invent the assembly line. He got his idea for the assembly line from watching a meat packing plant in operation. The workers stood still, and each performed a specialized task as the carcasses moved through the plant on a conveyor belt. An assembly line does require interchangeable parts, but Eli Whitney gave birth to that idea. So what did Henry Ford do? Well, he expanded the concept of the moving assembly line to a manufactured product: an automobile. As no one before him had done, he standardized processes and products, integrated supplying industries, and organized manufacturing around the continuous flow of product components to a moving assembly line. At this point, one can conclude that Henry Ford made significant contributions in improving existing production technology and in managing the operations of the assembly line in a far more comprehensive manner.

Ford did something else. He reduced the price of the automobile to enhance sales. Considering the mentality of capitalists to maximize profits, this must have appeared to be heresy, and lunacy, to the capitalists of the day. But Henry Ford was interested in maximizing profits. By decreasing the price of an automobile, more people could then afford to purchase a Model T. This increased the volume of sales and allowed Ford to build larger plants with improved production efficiency. The resulting lower cost of production on a per unit basis permitted him to reduce the price of the automobile again, and he would repeat the cycle. By going around the same circle again and again, reducing the price of the car from over \$800 to a little over \$300 over a twenty-year period of time, Henry Ford expanded assembly line operations on a scale that had never been envisioned by anyone.

The degree of expansion required that a new term be coined to adequately describe its magnitude. It became known as *mass production*. So one can conclude that Henry Ford made significant advances on Eli Whitney's work in terms of producing huge volumes of products. True—but it was not simply a mechanical improvement. Henry Ford's idea of maximizing profits by lowering profit margins on a per unit basis was the spark of original thought behind Ford's ability to introduce mass production.

Lower profit margins meant lower prices. This created more sales. A greater volume of sales created more profits. The incremental profits supported the building of larger and more efficient production facilities that could produce more automobiles at a still lower unit cost. The lower unit cost permitted a further lowering of prices and another jump in sales. Then Ford would take another turn on his price/volume merry-go-round by building a bigger and better assembly plant that again lowered the per unit production cost.

Is this the extent of Henry Ford's contributions to the workings of modern-day industry? Not quite. Even with all these accomplishments, Henry Ford did something in 1914 that confounded the world. Henry Ford sat down with his chief accountant and, without changing the price of a Model T, began to increase the pay of his workers in increments of twenty-five cents per day. That doesn't sound like much until one realizes that the 1914 base pay was \$2.30 per day for the average worker. Each time he increased the base pay by what amounted to a 10 percent increment, the accountant would calculate the new profit per automobile. Naturally, it was less than before. This process kept going until the pay was up to \$4.90 per day. The accountant concluded it was time to stop. Henry Ford felt that the dramatic impact of \$5.00 per day outweighed the economic consequences of increasing the pay by another ten cents. He was right; the world could not believe what he had done. It is said that the Russian peasant knew far more about Henry Ford on the eve of the Russian revolution than he knew about Karl Marx.

Why did Henry Ford do this? Remember the problem of the British textile mill owners. Behaving in the tradition of Adam Smith, they had reduced the wages of labor to the subsistence level. However, they now had no domestic market for the textiles. If the bulk of the working population was living at the subsistence level, to whom could the British textile mill owners sell their wares? To the rich? Certainly, but the rich and those others who could afford to buy the products of the British textile mill owners amounted to a small portion of the population. Their response to the lack of a market was to call on the government to go out and fetch them some colonies.

Henry Ford recognized the market as being his own work force. If his own workers could not purchase the Tin Lizzie, who could? The rich? The rich preferred the hand-crafted Pierce Arrow, not a standardized black automobile, the chief design criterion of which was ease of production. And the Tin Lizzies were pouring out of the Ford plants by the thousands. Where was the market? Ford recognized something that was missed by Adam Smith. Creating a pauperized work force barely able to eke out a living is not in the interest of the profit seeking capitalist. Henry Ford found a simple solution to the problem of creating a market for his thousands of Tin Lizzies. He created it out of his own workers. To mass production, Ford now added mass marketing. Like the cotton gin, the elegance of the solution was in its simplicity.

To be sure there were critics. Some said that turnover in Ford's assembly lines was so great that only high pay could keep a man working in such noisy and dirty conditions, doing the same monotonous task over and over again. Others maintained that, irrespective of pay, the dehumanizing aspects of mass production were not worth the advantage of enhanced productivity. Perhaps so, but it must not be forgotten, for better or for worse, that Ford sold tens of millions of the Model T, and its successor the Model A, and put America on wheels.

Ford made one other contribution in addition to giving modern society the means to produce on a scale that had never been envisioned by anyone before Ford did it. That contribution was the vivid demonstration that the market is servant to no one, not even Henry Ford.

Since World War II, General Motors, not Ford Motor Company, has dominated the American automotive scene. Why not Ford? Henry Ford certainly started out a winner with the Model T and Model A dominating the U.S automotive business. Unfortunately for Ford, Alfred P. Sloan was busy during the 1920s building up what came to be known as General Motors. Sloan's success, going beyond his business ability to organize and manage a large corporation made up of a collection of smaller ones, was his ability to sense the desires of the consumer. Ford thought he could dictate the market just as he dictated the operations of his company. If he had had monopolistic powers to control all automobile production, he could have realized his aims. And, presumably, we would still be driving Model Ts.

But Adam Smith's world of free enterprise would not permit a monopoly to be given to Ford. The government was prohibited from protecting Henry Ford from competition. More importantly, it was not in the American nature to even think about doing this. Sloan ran General Motors on the basis of satisfying the needs of the market. Ford wanted people to start their cars by turning a crank. Sloan discovered that people preferred to start their cars inside the car by pushing a button. Sloan put starters in his cars, and Ford didn't. Ford thought it was right and proper for the driver and the passengers to have to dress warmly in winter to ride in his cars. Sloan discovered that people really did not like to freeze while driving a car. Sloan put heaters in his cars, and Ford didn't. And so it went.

The dispute over who controls the market, the consumer or the producer, was resolved over who had the right to select the color of a car. Sloan discovered that some people liked yellow cars, while others preferred blue. Ford liked black. General Motors started producing cars of various colors and began attracting more and more customers at Ford's expense. The executives of Ford watched with dismay and, finally building up their courage, broached the subject with Henry Ford. His retort, "Give them fourteen shades of black," was a milestone in arrogance that knocked Ford Motor Company out of its preeminent position in the manufacture of automobiles and settled the dispute over who controlled the market.

The point of this discussion is not to explore the character of Henry Ford, but rather to illustrate certain characteristics of the free market. First and foremost, the market has a short memory. People are not going to buy Ford automobiles because they remember that Henry Ford made the product at a price that put it within reach of the working class. People are not going to buy Ford automobiles because they remember how he doubled the pay of his workers. Maybe Henry Ford thought the public should buy his cars in remembrance of his contribution to bringing the automotive age to America, but he wasn't making the purchase— and more importantly, he could not force the purchaser to buy a Ford. He lacked the coercive power of the government to enforce his ideas of what a car purchaser should get for his money.

Second, capitalists serve the market and not vice versa. The free market determines what a capitalist should do. Henry Ford apparently did not understand the dynamics of a free market. Alfred Sloan did. Sloan gave the market what it wanted. If the market—really the individual consumers making up what is called a market—wanted red polka dots on a canary yellow top with a pink stripe around an aquamarine body, and if the market was large enough to justify producing this color scheme, Alfred Sloan would give it to them. If he had thought this height of tackiness was too much for his tastes, then another automobile manufacturer would have eventually stepped forward and filled the demand.

However, the buyers were not that tacky. They just wanted a choice of basic colors. Sloan was the faithful servant of the market, catering to its whims and wants. While Sloan gave the market what it wanted, Ford gave the market what he thought it should have. That almost cost him the existence of his company.

What does all this mean? Adam Smith provided the economic philosophy of the free market system—a system that works with a minimum of outside constraints, restraints, and interference. The free market, by virtue of its several competitors and no legal impediment to others becoming competitors, coupled with the existence of free trade, ensures that the whims and wants of the market ultimately control the decisions of owners of productive resources. That is, every owner, no matter how great a tyrant when dealing with his employees, is a cringing, slithering, slimy sycophant when dealing with his customers. If he does not give his customers what they want in terms of product, price, and service, his competitors will. Nothing chastises an owner of a business more than losing a piece of business to his competitors.

The business cycle requires a meaningful standard of living from which to measure a recession or depression. It is hard to imagine a recession when the general population is already at the subsistence level. The chief reason why Adam Smith saw little in the way of a business cycle when he wrote *The Wealth of Nations* was that, from an economic point of view, there was no step down. A system of agriculture supported primarily by manual labor which absorbed a huge portion of the population, coupled with a method of manufacture that was primarily geared to whiling away the winter months, could hardly suffer the consequences of a depression. The society was already there—although the people were neither aware of it nor particularly unhappy about the state of things. It is difficult to be unhappy about something that has never been experienced, and a relative plethora of material things was experienced by only a few privileged individuals prior to the Industrial Revolution.

Many people made contributions in bringing about the Industrial Revolution. No slight is intended to James Watt in not detailing his invention of the steam engine. Nor to Thomas Edison for the light bulb, the record player, the movies, the electric generating industry, and many other contributions. As an aside, Thomas Edison and Henry Ford were close friends. Edison also suffered from the Henry Ford syndrome of wanting to control the market. Hollywood was founded by entrepreneurial producers and directors trying to escape from Edison's attempts to monopolize movie making. At the start of the movie age, movies were made in the metropolitan New York region, and Edison had plenty of hooligans in his hire to make life uncomfortable for newcomers to the business. So the budding producers and directors headed west to get away from Edison, and Hollywood was as far west as they could get.

Adam Smith gave Edison and Ford a political and economic philosophy through which their geniuses to invent and produce could germinate and flower. Adam Smith also prevented them from monopolizing their inventions because this same political and economic philosophy encouraged the germination and flowering of competitive firms.

While thousands of others have advanced the technological frontiers of knowledge, Eli Whitney and Henry Ford were selected for reasons beyond technological advances. In the area of production, they provided the means by which living standards could be raised to a level from which one could measure a fall. Unfortunately, the means of production generated a social setting in which that fall could be very painful. The cottage industry had an inherent safety net in that a peasant who could not dispose of all his baskets still had a roof over his head, fields in which to grow crops to feed himself, and a well-defined role in the community that was not affected by unsold baskets. Modern methods of production born from the inventive geniuses of Whitney and Ford place the worker and manager, blue-and white-collar, entirely at the mercy of the system—a system not particularly noted for mercy. Unemployment means, eventually, the inability to feed oneself or to keep a roof over one's head. Assembly lines and mass production may be far more productive in terms of output, but they lack the security provided by the cottage industry. Many of the "isms" of the nineteenth and twentieth centuries were born from the insecurity of employment inherent in modern methods of production. These "isms" are attempts to replace the safety net of the cottage industry that was lost when society industrialized itself. Yet, at the same time, the lack of incentives for individual initiative of some of these "isms" are causing some to revert to the thinking of Adam Smith, without, of course, admitting it. Most, if not all, of the "isms" are counter-productive in terms of supplying people with goods and services. A short tour of Eastern European nations would make it abundantly clear that the "ism" of communism has not produced an abundance of goods and services.

Adam Smith still points the way for a society to enhance its productivity. It is up to the society to best deal with the seemingly conflicting desires of the people to have the best of all possible worlds. Everyone wants the material plenty of the good times during the upward swing of the business cycle. They also want the safety net of the cottage industry to protect them against the bad times during the downward swing. These expectations are understandable in the human context. Dealing with them within the human context is a different matter.

3

The Pig Cycle

For those in the business of raising swine, there is a very interesting and, in its own way, intriguing book entitled *Swine Production* written by Drs. J. L. Krider, J. H. Conrad, and W. E. Carroll. As the title suggests, the subject matter is the production of swine for those learning the fundamentals of the business or for those desiring to enhance the efficiency of their pig factories. However, several references are made to the economic aspects of the business of producing pigs-on-the-hoof. While these remarks on the economic facts of life of the pig business are not the primary focus of the book, selling pigs does have a place in the scheme of things when one is running a pig factory. The observations made by the authors on the marketing aspects of pigs-on-the-hoof lend themselves well to the purposes of this chapter. (All quotes in this chapter are taken from the fifth edition of *Swine Production* published in 1982 by McGraw-Hill Book Company.)

PRICE DETERMINES OUTPUT

In a free market economy, price is the indicator used by producers of goods and services to establish production goals. Rising prices for goods and services are the common signal to all to expand the supply of goods and services. Price, in turn, is established by the relationship of the supply of and the demand for goods and services. Moreover, anticipated changes to that relationship also affect prices. And, finally, as any businessman knows, price is essentially unpredictable, and being in business is a risky undertaking. The fact that the goods are not packed in boxes, but walk on their hooves, makes no difference: "The wide and largely unpredictable day-to-day price variations that occur on the hog market increase the hazard of the hog business" (pp. 37–38).

The pig cycle, as measured by the price of pork or the price of pigs-on-the-hoof, has been observed for well over one hundred years. It has been studied extensively because the ups and downs of the pig cycle have wrought havoc on pig producers. Actually, the downs in the pig cycle have wrought havoc—pig producers enjoy the ups of the pig cycle. That's one reason why they are in the pig business. One can maintain that a businessman is in business to make a living. True. One can also maintain that he also lives for the day when the level of business generates income that exceeds what is necessary to feed his family. There is much more fun than work in raising pigs when the price of pigs-on-the-hoof is skyrocketing to new heights. Unfortunately, what goes up also has a tendency to come down. That takes all the fun out of the game. Our reference source on swine production—which, it must be admitted, avoids the use of the word "pig" to the maximum practical extent—has a few words to say about how the volatility of the market comes to be a concern to those in the pig business.

Certain price movements have come to be recognized as characteristic of the hog market. After the market is observed carefully for a few years, an understanding of these movements is developed. . . . Close students of the market also become fairly expert in sensing conditions responsible for day-to-day and short-time price changes. However, many of these changes are entirely unpredictable and, even after they occur, appear to have lacked adequate justification. These are genuine market hazards with which the swine enterprise has to cope (p. 38).

These price movements, which have come to be recognized as characteristic of the hog market, can probably be described as follows: the prices for pigs-on-the-hoof are sometimes up, sometimes down, and sometimes in between being up or down. How students of the market can become fairly expert in sensing the conditions that result in day-to-day price movements when many of these changes are unpredictable and cannot be justified, even in hindsight, is left to the imagination of the reader. If one could become an expert in sensing conditions responsible for day-to-day price fluctuations for hogs or porkbellies, he might not be found slopping the hogs in the pig pen. Instead, he might be found sailing the Caribbean in a yacht with a satellite telecommunications tie-in with the hog and porkbelly trading pits in Chicago.

What matters in all this is that, over the years, the pig producers have had difficulty dealing with the hazards of the market. The complaints from those in the pig business whenever the price of pork cannot justify raising piglets have been duly registered with the politicians, and the problem has been duly studied by government agricultural agencies for over a century. In fact, the problem has been studied, and studied again, without finding any real solution to protect the pig producers from the bad times that follow the good. Quoting again from our reference source on raising pigs (or, as the authors prefer, swine and hogs) concerning the potential solution to the problem of volatility of prices in the pig business: "No satisfactory solution to the problem has been developed; perhaps there is none" (p. 38).

However, some ray of hope is given to the reader: "The marketing of swine is discussed in more detail in Chap. 23" (p. 38).

In the intervening twenty-odd chapters, every aspect of the raising of pigs from an operational and cost point of view is covered in thorough detail. Topics include the location of the enterprise (the pig factory), the connection between the number and kind of swine and the production costs, and the various breeds of swine and their comparative advantages and disadvantages in terms of the nature of the product (fat versus lean pork, greater or lesser degrees of bacon) and in terms of environmental matters (some breeds grow better in the tropics, while others prefer more temperate climates). Other chapters discuss genetic and physical selection, performance testing (to ensure the pigs are gaining weight as expected), the proper ratio of boars to sows for happiness to reign, and the reproduction cycle and breeding practices for procreating litters galore. The remaining chapters deal with cost management and the details of raising hogs from weaning to market, including housing, equipment, nutrient requirements, parasite and disease control, and other matters that fall under the control of the pig factory owner.

And that is the point of this discussion. The book vividly illustrates exactly what is under the control of those in the pig business. The perhaps 90 percent or more of the book that is dedicated to proper management and cost control practices covers only one-half of what is required to make a living in raising pigs. The other half is revenue. Revenue consists of two elements: the volume of pigs sold by the pig factory owner and the price of a pound of living pig. Even on this side of the equation, the pig producer has absolute control over the output of his enterprise. However, on the matter of price—the cents per pound for a living pig-on-the-hoof—the pig producer is entirely at the mercy of the market. There is no way that he can dictate the price that the market is willing to pay for his pigs. Having no impact on price, other than reacting to it from the point of view of how many pigs are to be sent to market, the pig factory owner has no control over revenue. Ergo, his profitability becomes a throw of the dice each and every day of his existence. That something more that Chapter 23 is to offer on the key subject of marketing can now be divulged. "That the price at which hogs are sold influences the profits which are realized from raising them is so obvious as to require no explanation; the higher the price, other things remaining equal, the greater the profit" (p. 631).

And as critical as prices are to the economic welfare of the pig producer, his control over prices is nil, particularly if he insists on operating as an independent businessman. The only hope for the thousands upon thousands of independent businessmen who own pig factories is to unite.

Uniting, however, is not as easy as one might expect because one reason a pig factory owner is a pig factory owner is to be lord and master over his domain. A pig producer is similar to all independent businessmen in desiring the self-fulfillment of being one's own "man" or "woman." One cannot be master of his domain and have the output of his pig factory controlled by an outside authority. That being the case, there really is little incentive to get up at five in the morning to slop the hogs. The psychological impact of uniting adversely affects productivity because the illusion of independence is gone.

And what does control the price of pigs?

The market price of hogs at any given time and place appears to be determined by a free interplay of (1) the prevailing price level of commodities in general; . . . (2) the current supply of hogs, including hog products (storage) as well as the prospective supply in the immediate future; (3) the ability and willingness of consumers to purchase pork and pork products; (4) the number of consumers; (5) the weight, grade, and quality of hogs offered for sale; (6) conditions which are peculiar to the particular market on which the hogs are offered for sale; and (7) the supply and price of competitive red meats, especially beef (p. 632).

Offering a somewhat simplified interpretation of this, the price of pork is related, to a large extent, to the monetary measure of the cost of production. If it costs forty cents per pound to raise a pig, one should not expect to see the price of pork as low as one cent per pound or as high as twenty dollars per pound. A price of thirty-five cents per pound is sufficient to sharply reduce the slaughter of pigs because each slaughtered animal would represent a true loss to the pig producer. True loss means a cash loss on a variable cost basis. When the pig producer stuffs $150 worth of grain down the pig's throat and receives $100 for his efforts, that is a cash loss. Businessmen understand cash losses on a variable cost basis. They sometimes forget to value their time, or to depreciate their investments, or to take into account overhead expenses in determining their breakeven points. However, they are keenly aware of the breakeven point based on the variable cost of production.

On the other hand, a price of forty-five cents per pound is sufficient to sharply increase the slaughter of pigs because each slaughtered animal would represent a true profit to the pig producer. Again, true profit means a cash gain between what a pig producer receives and what he has spent on raising the pig on a variable cost basis. If $150 has been stuffed down the throat of the animal, and if someone pays $200 to stuff himself with the animal, that's $50 of cash profit. Businessmen understand $50 in cash. The fact that the $50 has to be spent on keeping the farm and machinery in good condition and on feeding his family and for the value of his time might escape his economic calculation. Nevertheless, the free market economy, in which price controls production, works very nicely around the price that represents the variable cost of production.

Although price will have some relationship to costs in monetary terms, what really matters to a businessman is whether the price is above or below costs. This is his signal when planning his level of production. Whether price is above or below costs is determined by the relationship between the the supply of and the demand for pork. The supply is mainly determined by the current inventory of pork and the perceived number of pigs in transit to the slaughterhouses. The demand for pork is primarily determined by the population of consumers, their total meat intake, and their pork intake. The last determinant is affected by the relationship of the price of pork to the prices of other meats—particularly beef and, to a lesser extent, poultry. In addition, there are other idiosyncrasies in the market that affect price, such as the differentials reflecting different grades, or cuts, of pork and other details of that nature.

All of this can be summed up even more succinctly. The price of pork is determined by the relationship of the supply of and the demand for pork and the anticipated changes in that relationship.

Of just under seven hundred pages of good advice on the subject of swine production, nearly all are dedicated to the guidance necessary for one to become an efficient and productive independent businessman in the pig growing business. The size of the operation, the number of pigs being raised for market, and all the operational aspects of running a pig factory fall entirely under the purview of the independent businessman. An independent businessman has total control over costs and output and has no control over price. Hence, his control over revenue—which is his output multiplied by the price per unit of output—is nonexistent. He cannot effectively plan his future output of pigs because he cannot predict the future price of his product.

He has no control over price as long as he insists on maintaining his individuality as an independent businessman. And as long as he does maintain his individuality, he is not beholden to any outside association of other individuals in the pig business or to government authorities as to the level of productivity of his pig factory. Thus, the independent decisions of many independent businessmen establish the level of supply of the product to the market. Consumers, by their purchases of his product, determine demand. The relationship between the supply and demand for the product pork determines price. If the price of pork is above the cost of production, selling pork generates a profit. Profit maximization is achieved by increasing the output of the pig factory—sending more pigs to market. If the price of pork is below the cost of production, selling pigs generates a loss. Loss minimization is achieved by decreasing the output of the pig farm. This terse bit of advice on the economic aspects of swine production is given to the hog grower, emblazoned as a heading to a paragraph: "AIM FOR HIGH MARKET" (p. 271).

What is meant by "independent businessman" in a free market environment? An individual in the pig business is independent in the sense that he alone decides how to operate his factory for a given price of pork as it is translated to the price of pigs-on-the-hoof. In that sense, he is independent. However, the key decision to be made by an independent businessman on managing his enterprise is determining its output. That key decision is controlled, in turn, by price, over which he has no control.

Price is leading those in the pig business by their proverbial noses. And the price of pork, in relation to the cost of production, causes all owners of pig factories to behave in an identical way. If price is above cost, the human reaction is to increase production. If price is below cost, the human reaction is to decrease production. These human reactions are essentially mechanical in nature. The decision to expand or contract can be viewed as an essentially mechanical response based on whether there is a positive or negative difference between price and cost in sending a pig to market. This question may be more philosophical than anything else: are independent businessmen truly independent in how they make decisions, or are they simply organisms responding to an outside stimulus called price?

THE PRODUCTIVE OUTPUT OF A PIG FACTORY

Pigs eat almost anything. Indeed, one of the advantages of pigs in human society is that the inedible processed remains of producing food for human consumption can be fed to pigs. The pig then transforms something unfit for human consumption into something that can be eaten by humans, barring cultural or religious prohibitions against eating pork. Pigs can eat, and thrive, on a balanced diet of table scraps, bakery waste, culled or unmarketable vegetables and fruits, and moldy grains. Somewhat more palatable feeds include the residue of grains after being used to produce alcohol, vegetable oils, and the residue from making sugar. Other appetizing delicacies found in pig cuisine include ground fish and fish residue from fish processing plants; meat, bone, and blood meal residue from slaughterhouses; the residue from milk product and cheese processing plants; and that all-time favorite, feather meal.

The most common source of feed grain for pigs is corn. Most pigs in the United States are raised on corn-growing farms where the proprietor can select the ratio of corn sold to the market in the form of corn to that sold in the form of pork. In other words, the typical pig producer is a corn grower with excess production of corn in comparison to what can be devoured by his pig herd. Thus, the typical owner of a pig factory is a corn grower playing the odds in two markets: corn and pork. If the profitability of selling corn direct without converting it to pork is greater, one would expect this behavior, even though the price of pork represents some degree of profitability. Bearing in mind that nearly half of U.S. corn production is consumed by pigs, one can see that the corn and pork markets are truly intertwined.

Meat is a concentrated form of nutrition. One mouthful of meat is worth several mouthfuls of grains, vegetables, and fruit. As one might expect, to generate one pound of meat standing on four hooves, what is standing on those hooves must consume several pounds of grain. Approximately four pounds of grain are required to produce one pound of live-weight pig. A 200-pound live-weight pig on his way to the slaughterhouse has consumed about 700 pounds of corn and about 100 pounds of protein supplement of one form or the other since his birth. Of course, not all of what walks on the hooves is edible. A 200-pound squealing pig is transformed into about 120 pounds of saleable pork (trimmed of fat) by means of a number of slices of the knife.

In a weak market for pork, the typical pig farmer runs a segregated operation. Boars and sows are kept apart, but the breeding stock is maintained in a state of readiness. When demand for the boars' services is low, perhaps a few more aged males are sent to the slaughterhouses than one would expect if the market were more robust. When the sows grow older and are approaching an age when their reproductive capacity may not be what it used to be, some of these go to market. Therefore, the breeding of litters is basically intended to maintain the capacity of the breeding stock to reproduce when better times come. The pig factory-owning businessman is maintaining his pig factory in good working order in terms of both the number and age of sows and the requisite number of boars to service the sows. He is, however, in the very worst of times still sending a few pigs to market.

The boars, however, are bored. Everything is on hold; even the nutritional content of the diet is adjusted to slow down the rate of weight gain. However, when the price of pork increases to a level at which the productivity of the breeding stock is to be taxed to its fullest, the following facts are of utmost importance in understanding the dynamics of the pig business:

1. A sow can give birth to her first litter when she is about one year old.
2. A sow can give birth to two litters per year when in full production.
3. A sow can produce nine to twelve piglets per litter, with an average of about eleven piglets per litter during her most productive five years of life.
4. By adjusting the nutritional value of its diet, a piglet can achieve a ready-for-slaughterhouse weight of 200 pounds in as short a time as five to six months. This is a full two months off the time required for raising a piglet to this weight in less auspicious times.

There is a mathematical exponential function working in pig rearing. By the time a sow is giving birth to her second litter, the first litter is on its way to market with a combined live-weight of a ton or more (two hundred pounds per pig with an average litter size of eleven piglets). Because this can happen twice a year, a typical sow can produce upward of two tons of pig-on-the-hoof per year. Record holders have more than doubled that. On a more realistic level, and without much in the way of special care or effort, and taking into account infant mortality, one sow can easily produce one-and-a-half to two tons of living, and marketable, pigs per year. This is full-tilt production from a zero starting point. As an economist might say, there is a great deal of elasticity of supply in the pig business.

THE PIG CYCLE

A cycle means that the price moves up and down and that, over time, these price movements repeat themselves. The cyclical movement in the cash price for hogs during the early 1980s shown in Exhibit 3.1 is based on data extracted

Exhibit 3.1
The Pig Cycle

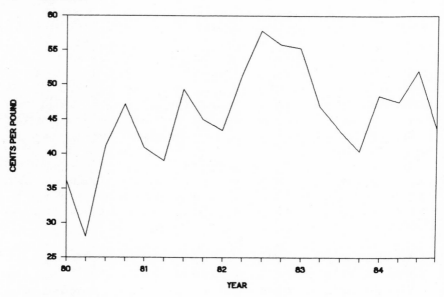

from the 1985 *CRB Commodity Yearbook* published by the Commodity Research Bureau, Jersey City, N.J.

Over the indicated period of time, businessmen in the pig industry have experienced several market cycles. Although cycles are repetitive by definition, and although the characteristics of the various phases of a cycle are quite similar from one cycle to the next, no two cycles are the same. In other words, the cyclical nature of prices is repetitive, but not predictive. Knowing the price of pork at one phase of the pig cycle is of limited use in predicting the price of pork at the same phase of another pig cycle.

Moreover, the volatility of the cash price for hogs is considerable on a day-to-day and a week-to-week basis, and these fluctuations are not shown in Exhibit 3.1. What is shown are the broad market movements over quarterly periods of time. This means that a speculator in hog futures can be right in judging the broad movement of the hog market and still be wiped out by short-term fluctuations. Speculators operate in a world in which guardian angels fear to tread.

The general phases of the pig cycle can be entitled Times of Depression and Despair, The First Rays of Hope, Honeymoon Motel, The Expectation of Riches, The Achievement of a Balance, The Swamping, The Deluge, and Times of Depression and Despair. As the titles suggest, the last phase of one cycle becomes the start of the next.

Times of Depression and Despair

A description of a cycle has to start somewhere. Times of depression are the troughs of a business cycle, or a pig cycle. Inventories of pork are at record levels. How inventories reached these levels will be explained shortly. The point is that inventories are too high. The price of pigs is low because the slaughterhouses have their freezer capacity jammed with pork. There is no incentive to slaughter more pigs. And it does not matter how low the price of pig-on-the-hoof falls in relation to the price of pork in the meat counter; there is no more freezer space. Under conditions of minimal or nonexistent demand for slaughtering pigs, the price drifts lower—there is certainly no reason for it to drift higher.

The lack of demand for slaughtering pigs causes the price of pigs to become so low that it does not pay to raise pigs. Every pig sent to market represents a loss. The pig factory owner is better off selling his corn than feeding his corn to his pigs and then selling the pigs. Under these circumstances, a businessman in the pig business essentially stops breeding his sows, and segregation by sex is strictly maintained. The only pigs going to market are sows who are advancing in age and boars who are getting bored from having nothing to do. The only litters being raised are replacements for the breeding stock to ensure the potential breeding capacity is maintained. The pig factory, though essentially idle, is maintained in good working order for the better days to come, whenever they occur. As any good businessman worth his salt knows, better days will come—that's the nature of a cycle. The argument is one of timing, not eventuality.

One may reason that the pig producer might be better off economically if he got rid of his breeding stock and sold his corn rather than using a portion of his corn production to maintaining a breeding stock that is breeding only to maintain itself. That may be true. However, selling the breeding stock also takes him out of the game. If the price of pork goes up, how is he going to participate in the party? He cannot go out and buy breeding stock under these conditions because the price may be very high, if breeding stock is even available. The pig factory owner is optimizing his long-term profitability potential by taking a marginal, though real, loss on his corn income to maintain the breeding stock.

The demand for pigs-on-the-hoof is at a very low level because the slaughterhouses are attempting to liquidate excess inventories. Furthermore, the supply of pigs going to market is very low because pigs being sold for slaughter represent a cash loss. These are very bad days for the pig producers. This is the time when their cries for government assistance in one form or the other reach a fever pitch.

However, not everything is negative in the pig business. The demand for pork is climbing because pork is cheap. The consumers of America, looking at a roast of beef for $2.79 per pound and a roast of pork for $1.09, are doing what is expected of them in a free market environment. They are doing what is in their best interests. Their interests are best served by having a roast of pork for Sunday dinner rather than a roast of beef. They are buying pork from the slaughterhouses' freezers at a faster pace than the slaughterhouses are slaughtering pigs. The high inventory levels are gradually being eaten up.

The First Rays of Hope

Although prices of commodities are volatile and unpredictable, there is one time when predicting prices is less impossible than at other times. During times of low prices and huge inventories, speculators focus on the liquidation of the overhanging inventories. Because the price of the commodity is below the variable cost of production, new supplies are at minimal levels. Regardless of whether demand for the commodity has increased because of its low price, one can be fairly confident that there is no hope of a price increase until the inventories are reduced to manageable levels. When inventories are reduced to manageable levels—or when the expectation that inventories will be reduced to manageable levels within the foreseeable future gels in the minds of speculators, investors, and consumers of a commodity—then price increases in the commodity are as close to certain as one can get in a free market environment.

These price increases are, to some extent, predictable by observing the size of the inventory and its rate of liquidation. Any commodity speculator worth his salt knows this, as does every commodity producer. The ray of hope for those in the pig business comes when consumers are well on their way to devouring the excess inventories of pork. The slaughterhouses, seeing a few empty meat hooks in their freezers, decide that they ought to slaughter a few more pigs to replenish their stocks of pork. Their increased purchasing of pigs provides the first signs of a recovery. The price for pig-on-the-hoof makes its first upward move.

Honeymoon Motel

Businessmen, in any endeavor, are not fools. They know exactly what is going on in their area of business. As for the businessmen in the pig growing industry, they know the demand for their product is up because pork is cheap compared to beef. It is simply a matter of time before slaughterhouse freezers have more empty hooks than hooks with split halves of pig. The price of pigs-on-the-hoof is increasing because the slaughterhouses don't like so many empty meat hooks. Because the price for pigs-on-the-hoof is still below the cost of production, there is hardly an incentive for the pig producers to send more pigs to market. It isn't any more fun selling a pig for a small loss than it is selling it for a large loss. The slaughterhouse call for more pigs is going largely unanswered. Price cannot drift down under these circumstances—it drifts slowly upwards.

Businessmen are excellent trend extrapolators. The demand for pork from consumers is at a high level. *Trend extrapolation*: the demand for pork will remain at a high level. The supply of pigs-on-the-hoof is down because each pig sold represents a cash loss. *Trend extrapolation*: the supply of pigs appearing at the slaughterhouses' doors will remain at a low level. This means that the flow of pork into the freezers will also be at a low level. The amount of pork in inventory is falling because pork is being consumed faster than it is being replenished. *Trend extrapolation*: inventory levels of pork will continue to fall. The price of pigs-on-the-hoof is rising because slaughterhouses need to replenish their pork inventories, and pig factory owners are reluctant to sell their wares because they cannot yet recoup the variable costs of production. *Trend extrapolation*: the price for pigs-on-the-hoof will continue to rise.

The question at this point is not what the pig growing businessman would do. The question at this point is what you, the reader, would do under these circumstances. The business cycle, or the pig cycle, cannot be studied in isolation from the behavior patterns of human beings. Why? Because the business cycle, or the pig cycle, is the net result of thousands of business decisions by independent producers on what to send to market and thousands of purchasing decisions by independent consumers on what to buy. If the human motivation behind these decisions is not taken into account, one ends up with a peculiar understanding of what is called economics. Economics is the study of human behavior—or, to be more exact, the consequences of human behavior in the material realm of things.

An economy does not stand in isolation from the population that makes up that economy. There is a reason why no one has written a best-selling study on economic activity in Antarctica. Could it be that there is no permanent population in Antarctica to make up a society that, in turn, can exhibit those attributes to which the word *economy* can be ascribed?

Nor can an economy be studied in terms of regression equations and differential calculus equations devoid of an understanding of human behavior. An economy is made up of the physical aspects of producing goods and services, the human aspects of transforming raw materials into goods and services, and the rules of conduct of a society that influence the way human decisions are made with regard to producing and consuming the end products. Therefore, it appears reasonable to incorporate the human behavior patterns of the people making up a society—particularly the ways humans respond to the rules of conduct established by that society—in an economic study of that society. The rationale for doing so is based on the absurdity of not doing so.

The times of depression and despair have been painful. Yet, through it all, you, dear reader, have maintained your breeding stock. Your sales have been limited to sows that were getting too old and boars that had too little to do. Each time you sold one, you took a loss with respect to the corn and care invested in the animal. Yet you persevered through it all because the pig business, as any business, requires an expertise that you have acquired. You are reluctant to give up that expertise because, by giving it up, you will have to learn another. Giving up on pigs and going into chickens cannot be easily done. All the tricks of the trade have to be learned, and these lessons can be very painful for a novice. Career changes are generally avoided, if at all possible, because there is no escape from having to experience the oftentimes painful lessons necessary to gain the expertise associated with a new career.

Would there not be a temptation at some point, as the price of pigs-on-the-hoof drifts upward, for you to consider the possibility of not selling the older sows, but keeping them on the hunch that the extrapolated trend of upward prices will materialize? Consider the nature of the picture as you see it. Pork is still cheap in the food market. Empty meat hooks are appearing in the slaughterhouses' freezers. Pigs-on-the-hoof are still being sold for a loss, but that loss isn't nearly as large as it once was.

The price of pig-on-the-hoof is a subject near and dear to you and all your friends, and the narrowing gap between the price to sell and the cost to produce is a popular topic of conversation. Nothing on the business horizon is going to break the extrapolated trend over the foreseeable future. Therefore, it is only a matter of time before the price of pigs-on-the-hoof will be going through the breakeven point, and there will be profits to be made in selling pigs.

As life will have it, there is a time lapse between deciding to expand production and actually experiencing the effects of the expansion. There is a lag between the time the sow is bred and the time the litter is born. Then it takes another five or six months for the litter to mature to marketable weight. Would it really be premature to create a little excitement in the boar pen by breeding a sow or two in the expectation that there are better days ahead in the pig business? Is it really unwise to slowly start the process whereby a sow can be on her twice-a-year litter bearing schedule that will bring her up to her full capacity to produce something of the order of one-and-a-half to two tons of pig-on-the-hoof per year?

The only problem with your thinking this way is that there are thousands of others thinking the same way. Your strategy of holding back on selling the older sows to the slaughterhouses to optimize your position when better days arrive in the pig business has been copied by thousands of others, who are looking at the same data base and coming to the same conclusion.

As you hold back on selling your older sows, and perhaps begin breeding them in response to the increasing price of pig-on-the-hoof, you may also have a tendency to hold back on selling the old boars because their services may once again be in demand. You are not alone. All pig raising businessmen are copying you because they have all extrapolated the same trend from the same data base, and they have all come to the same conclusion.

What is best for each individual is to hold back from the market some of the old sows and boars because this might be the start of a new upward swing of the pig cycle. Of course, after the times of depression and despair, one cannot be absolutely sure that a new day is dawning. The rays of hope are very faint. With time, they become not quite as faint as they were. Perhaps it is time to give the old sow and the old boar a new lease on life.

The upshot of you and thousands of others thinking and acting alike is that the supply of old sows and old boars to the slaughterhouses does not increase with the increasing price for pigs-on-the-hoof, but perversely decreases. The slaughterhouses must now scramble to bid on the few pigs that are coming to market. Naturally, the price of pigs-on-the-hoof continues its upward ascent, passing through the breakeven point at which time raising pigs once again becomes a profitable enterprise. Pork prices in the supermarket are going up because pork supplies are falling, and replenishment is becoming more expensive. Whether higher prices for pigs-on-the-hoof or higher prices for pork are leading the price parade is academic: they are both going up.

As soon as it is clear that the price of pigs-on-the-hoof is above the cash breakeven point, the behavior of pig businessmen, no pun intended, takes on a universal change of character. It is a complete metamorphosis from caterpillar to butterfly. It is no longer a sow or two being wooed by the boars. Any female who is old enough is old enough to replenish the pig pen. And at eight, ten, or twelve piglets per litter, replenish it they do. The pig sty has become a honeymoon motel. Would you, as an individual, do otherwise?

The Expectation of Riches

The problem, again, is one of timing. There is a lag between the time the boars sow their oats and the time the sows reap the harvest. Then the litter has to mature on its richly enhanced protein diet of pig slop. Meanwhile, the slaughterhouses are scrambling for pigs. The price of pigs is going through the roof as the slaughterhouses compete with one another for the few pigs coming to market. The slaughterhouses raise the price of pork to cover the expense of paying more for pigs-on-the-hoof. Consumers see the price of pork going up and think twice about buying the loin of pork at $1.59 per pound.

At this point it doesn't really matter how much pork is being purchased because relatively few pigs are being slaughtered. Pigs are either producing more pigs or in the process of growing up to make the final trek to the slaughterhouses. Under these conditions, the price of pork keeps rising, as does the price for pigs-on-the-hoof.

Every morning, you eagerly awaken at five and rush down to the pig pen. During the night, perhaps, a litter has been born. As you slop the hogs with the best possible nutritional mix for the fastest possible growth, you perform the following calculation.

Recall the number of pigs that you had last week, and estimate the average weight for all the pigs. Multiply the two, and that is your total weight of pigs-on-the-hoof one week ago. Take the price per pound for pigs-on-the-hoof for last week, and multiply the total weight by last week's price. That was your pig worth last week.

Now the fun begins. Take the average weight gain for the herd of pigs over a period of a week and add that to the overall weight. Then add in any new litters. Now redo the calculation using the current price of pigs-on-the-hoof, which is higher now than what it was a week ago. That is your pig worth this week.

The best is yet to come. Subtract how much you were worth last week from what you are worth this week. That is how much richer you are just for staying alive for a week. Now isn't it fun to get up at five in the morning and slop the hogs?

You are not alone in doing the net worth calculation with every shovelful of slop. Everyone else is doing it. You look at your truck—ninety thousand miles and falling apart. Time to buy a new one. A pig shed needs repairing. Perhaps, another pig shed should be added while this one is being repaired. Maybe a new plow, or a corn husker, or even a tractor is in order.

Money? Money to pay for all this? What money? The pigs are too young to be sold. Go borrow the money. The collateral is there. All the banker has to do is walk around the pig factory, and he sees the collateral, he hears the collateral, he smells the collateral. There is no problem in getting the money. It is a question of what options you want on the truck, the corn husker, and the tractor. These are the good times. These are the times you have been waiting for through all the bad times. Bad times? What bad times? There is no shorter memory on earth than a businessman's memory of the bad times.

The Achievement of a Balance

The first pigs-on-the-hoof to hit the market are those that were bred earliest during the days of the first rays of hope. The slaughterhouses swallow them up as though there is no tomorrow. As time goes on, more and more pigs-on-the-hoof make their appearance at the slaughterhouses' doors. All these are immediately welcomed because freezer capacity has been far too empty for far too long.

Unfortunately for the pig producer, demand for pork is also way down. These are the days when a loin of pork is going for $2.99 per pound and beef may be at, say, $2.29 per pound. Consumers are again doing what is in their best interests, and their best interests are served by having a roast of beef for Sunday dinner, not a roast of pork.

Wave after wave of pigs-on-the-hoof, each one greater than the preceding one, shows up at the slaughterhouses' doors. In a relatively short time, the price of pork stabilizes in the meat market, and the inventories of pork have been restored to Warren Harding's concept of normalcy. Once the number of empty meat hooks has been sufficiently reduced, the slaughterhouses' welcome is not as warm as it once was.

The Swamping

Wave after wave of pigs-on-the-hoof, each one greater than the preceding one, keeps on showing up at the slaughterhouses' doors. The price of pork at the meat counter begins to decline as new supplies are exceeding demand. The slaughterhouses are unwilling to expand their inventories, and they are unwilling to pay more for pigs-on-the-hoof than the declining netback price from the meat counters can justify. Thus, the price that slaughterhouses are willing to pay for pigs-on-the-hoof begins to decline.

Again, what would you do, dear reader, under these circumstances? While slopping your hogs at five in the morning, you quickly run through the net worth calculation and find out that your net worth this week—despite taking into consideration your normal weekly weight gain for the herd and new members of the pig population—has slipped a bit below your net worth of last week. Would this make slopping the hogs any less fun than it was a short while before?

And while you are at it, you may as well go through the trend extrapolation exercise. The inventory levels in the slaughterhouse freezers are satisfactory. *Trend extrapolation:* the demand for pigs to restore inventory levels is, and will continue to be, nil. Consumers still consider the price of pork expensive in comparison to the prices of beef and poultry. *Trend extrapolation:* the demand for pigs in the form of a pork roast on the dinner table will continue to be weak. More and more pigs are marching off to market. The supply of pork is increasing with respect to demand. Pork prices are decreasing. *Trend extrapolation:* the price of pigs-on-the-hoof is going to continue to decline. As the price for pigs-on-the-hoof continues to fall, there will be a greater incentive for pig factory owners to send more pigs to market. *Trend extrapolation:* things are going to get "worser faster." You look at your spanking new truck, your spanking new corn husker, and your spanking new tractor with its spanking new set of plows; you watch the workmen building the nicest looking spanking new pig shed in the whole neighborhood. You have barely started making any payments on all this. What are you going to do?

The Deluge

If you were the only one thinking this way, the deluge would not occur. The problem is that thousands of independent businessmen are thinking the same way. The faster one can get his pigs to market, the better it will be for him. Each businessman believes that he, and only he, has arrived independently at the decision that the best thing he can do to optimize his returns, his profits, and his personal financial worth is to ship his pigs to market as fast as his new truck can deliver them. And delay in shipping the pigs to market will only cut into his net worth all the more.

Because this behavior is being copied by thousands of other independent businessmen, and because the slaughterhouse owners are not so stupid as to take on the mounting waves of pigs without severely cutting the price for pigs-on-the-hoof, panic seizes the pig businessmen, again no pun intended, en masse. Their worst fears become a self-fulfilling prophecy as they dump on the market not only their rapidly maturing piglets, but also the mommas and the poppas and the aunts and the uncles.

The deluge is caused by the widespread acceptance of conventional wisdom that you must get rid of as many as pigs as you can as fast as you can because to delay means that you will get an even lower price tomorrow. To act is more lucrative than to temporize. In fact, to temporize is folly. The wisest course of action is to get your pigs to market before your neighbors wake up to the reality of the situation. There's nothing wrong with this line of reasoning—other than thinking that your neighbor is not thinking the same thing.

The managers running the slaughterhouses, anticipating a floodtide of pigs coming to market, slash the price for pigs-on-the-hoof far below the netback value from the pork being sold in the meat counter. At the time, this appears to be a good deal for the slaughterhouses and induces them to expand their inventories far beyond normal levels. The process stops when the freezers can't hold any more split halves of pig and/or when the price of pigs-on-the-hoof plunges below the breakeven point. The time difference between these two events is probably quite small; in fact, they may well occur simultaneously.

There is nothing much for the businessman in the pig growing business to do now but to segregate the boars from the sows, and watch the price of pork decline at the meat market. Three things he knows for sure. As the price of pork declines, the demand for pork will increase. *Trend extrapolation:* the demand for pork will increase. As the freezer space at the slaughterhouses is filled to capacity, the demand for pigs-on-the-hoof will be minimal. *Trend extrapolation*: the price of pigs-on-the-hoof will remain very weak. The supply of pigs-on-the-hoof will be small because the proceeds of the sale do not cover the variable costs of raising a pig. *Trend extrapolation*: the supply of pork will be less than the demand. Because supply is less than demand, inventories of pork will begin to fall. *Trend extrapolation*: at some point in time, things will get better. Your recommended course of action? Convince the bankers that this is so before they take away the new truck, the new corn husker, and the new tractor and plows and foreclose on the farm because you haven't paid for the new shed.

Any industry or business that is oriented to the consumer market, in which there are a number of competing firms and relative ease of entry, could have been selected to describe the business cycle. Real estate would have been a superb example for describing the cyclical nature of business activity. However, there is something about pig raising that lends itself particularly well to the description of the business cycle. What that is, is left to the imagination of the reader.

One might say that there is an element of hyperbole in this description of the business cycle, that the description of the booms and busts in the pig business is exaggerated, and that the supply of pigs drying up as prices begin to improve is an idiosyncrasy of raising pigs and has nothing to do with manufactured goods. In the manufactured goods industry, as soon as prices begin to improve, factories can immediately increase their production of goods and respond in a positive fashion to the market demand for greater output.

Dealing with the latter point first, most factories are not very busy during depressed times in their respective businesses and are able to react rapidly to the first signs of greater demand for their products. Therefore, there is no drying up of supply just when it is appropriate for supply to be increased. And as long as there is spare capacity in the system, there is little in the way of lag between the decision to increase the production of goods and the realization of that increased production. Because added supply can be felt more quickly in the manufacture goods market than in the pig market, price volatility would be considerably more dampened in the manufactured goods market than in the pig market. This point is well taken and need only be incorporated in a forecasting model by ensuring that supply increases, or decreases, as appropriate to the early stages of increasing demand.

There have been some noteworthy exceptions to the general observation that the supply of goods increases with the growth in the demand for goods. One was the backbone of the industrial world from its inception to about the 1960s: steel. One needs only to gaze at a picture of a steel mill to realize that the construction of a steel mill consumes a great deal of steel. There have been times in the history of the steel industry when building steel mills has been the second largest single source of demand for steel.

During the building of the nation's railroads, there were times when it was necessary to build more steel mills in response to the increased demand for more steel rails. What happened to the supply of steel needed for making steel rails when new steel mills were under construction? At the very time when there was heightened demand for steel for manufacturing rails, the supply of steel shrank as steel was being diverted to the construction of more steel mills. It does not require a great deal of imagination to guess what the impact was on the price of steel while new steel mills were being built. How much different is this from the fall in the supply of pigs going to market during the time when the pig producers are attempting to increase the supply of pigs by breeding everything that walks on four hooves?

Another example of the sometimes perverse relationship between supply and demand is congested ports that become even more congested as a consequence of the port authorities' decision that it is time to expand port facilities. Port facilities require material for their construction, which, when shipped in, adds to the congestion of the port. It is true that port congestion will be relieved once the supply of new facilities becomes operational; nevertheless, during the time of construction, port facility construction adds to the demand for port services, not to the supply of port services. And as a final example, the Thanksgiving 1988 issue of the *New York Times* contained an article on the decreasing supply of copper, with prices climbing to record highs, caused, in part, by labor disruptions in the important copper producing nations of Peru, Zaire, and Zambia.

The point is not whether supply responds in a positive or a negative manner to the first signs of a recovery in an industry. The point is that a business forecast of what is happening in an industry does have to take into consideration the nature of the response, be it negative or positive. The essentially negative response of supply in the steel and pig industries to increasing demand adds to the volatility of prices. Whether the added volatility in prices will affect the degree of capacity being added to the industry—which, in the end, determines the degree of damage caused by the deluge—depends on how the participants react to the volatility in prices.

On the other hand, the immediate and positive response in the manufactured goods industries, in being able to quickly increase the supply of goods at an early stage of the business cycle, reduces price volatility, dampens the urge to increase capacity, and, in the end, lessens the degree of damage from the deluge. Business forecasting should take into consideration the nature of the response of the supply of goods to the demand for goods during the upswing of the business cycle.

The purpose of forecasting the general business environment is not to extrapolate current trends, but to search the business horizon for signs of a turn in the economy. The turns in the business cycle are marked by certain physical happenings. In the pig cycle, bad times come when each succeeding wave of pigs arriving at the slaughterhouses' doors can no longer be accommodated. The turn occurs when humans, as businessmen, react to the first sign of falling prices. Instead of reducing the supply of pigs coming to market, they increase the supply, each thinking that he is alone in sending more and more pigs to market. The collective actions based on thousands of supposedly independent decisions become a tidal wave of pigs, flooding the system and bringing on the bad times as a self-fulfilling prophecy.

The difference between the pig and steel industries lies in the number of players. There are thousands of pig businessmen because the investment necessary to open a pig factory is not very great. There are very few steel companies because there are real barriers of entry for new participants. And the participants have a habit of banding together to reduce the number even further—and with good reason.

Why are industries usually organized around a half dozen major companies within each nation of the Western world? Could it have anything to do with the fact that the investments in these companies would be jeopardized if the free market economics of Adam Smith were given free rein? It should be remembered that Adam Smith, by dying in 1790, never lived through a business cycle during the industrial era. The elegant simplicity of having price determine output loses some of its luster after a few nineteenth-and twentieth-century treks though the troughs of the business cycle as thousands were thrown on the breadlines, banks closed, and firms folded up forever without even a farewell party. Even so, the system of Adam Smith still has its faithful followers, and for good reasons:

"The functions of a market are to establish prices and to allocate supplies. The market that prices commodities nearest their true value and allocates them most equitably is the best market" (p. 631). However, the system is not without its faults. The forces behind prices are uncontrollable in the pig business because of the way the system is structured. The grower simply cannot influence the market forces generated by the system unless he acts in concert with other swine growers.

These points are relevant in understanding the structure of Big Business. Thousands of independent businessmen in the pig industry cannot be organized so as to act in concert. However, it is relatively easy for a dozen or so steel companies to unite into a smaller number and still act in concert to control the forces that control price. The amalgamation of companies into what is sometimes called Big Business is an attempt to get control over the rate of capacity addition.

The first annual report of U.S. Steel is a model of candor in communications between management and shareholders. In its message to shareholders, management admitted that one of the benefits achieved in amalgamating the five or so steel companies into one behemoth known as U.S. Steel was that they could scrap about three major additions in steel making capacity. These additions were approved prior to the formation of U.S. Steel by independent managements, all desiring to fill the same gap between the supply and the demand for steel. The new management of U.S. Steel readily admitted that had these expansions taken place, the steel industry would have been plagued with excess capacity for years to come. By controlling supply, they could maintain price. The reader of this annual report might be surprised to read that once the supply of new steel capacity was under control, management decided not to raise steel prices because the corporation was making plenty of money at the current prices. The pig emotion was not showing itself as fully as critics of Big Business might prefer—except that management successfully translated all sales to cash on the barrel head at the time of purchase. This can be easily recognized by any purchaser of material goods as a form of price increase.

As to the earlier self-inflicted charges of hyperbole and exaggeration, perhaps some amount assimilated itself into the description of the various phases of the pig cycle. Then again, perhaps, one ought to be in business to experience the emotions of being in business. One reason for the existence of the pig cycle is that pig factory owners exhibit one behavioral pattern that bears some semblance to what they are raising: greed. The other emotion shared by both the producer and the product is fear.

Neither of these emotions should be interpreted as an insult to those who operate in the free competitive market. Rather, it is simply an admittance that the business cycle is marked by two human emotions: greed and fear. Greed transforms a tranquil pig haven into a frenzied honeymoon motel, the output of which, in aggregate with all the other thousands of pig factories, will eventually swamp the market. Fear of further price erosion causes the massive slaughtering of pigs that deluges the market and makes trend extrapolation of further price declines a self-fulfilling prophecy.

A forecast of business conditions should also include the organizational mechanisms in place to control the degree of capacity addition during good times by subduing the human emotion of greed to expand, expand, expand. On the other side of the coin, measures taken by government and industry to counteract the human emotion of fear during business contractions should also be taken into account in forecasting business conditions.

Thus, forecasting of business conditions has to reflect the physical, emotional, organizational, and social realities of the conduct of business. The physical reality deals with the magnitude of productive capacity of the manufacturing plants, the state of training and the size of the work force, the level of inventories with regard to sales, the state of inventory liquidation or accumulation, the relationship of price to cost, and changes to each of these parameters.

Forecasting requires an evaluation of the nature of the emotional response to these physical stimuli. How people react to the stimuli of prices and costs depends on the nature of organizations and on the rules enforced by society. The rules people play by in reacting to the physical aspects of changing business conditions are part of their society and, thus, are different in the United States, England, Sweden, Japan, and the Soviet Union.

Although the reactions of the people in these various nations are different, their motivations are the same. The reality of life is that people will respond on the basis of one single motivation: what is best for me rules over all. The free market economy, with its hope of making a killing, no matter how remote that possibility, is the most productive in the sense of inducing people to get up at five in the morning to slop the hogs. One might say that this is the carrot. The free market economy is its own whip for inducing a superior level of performance because a businessman must run his operation efficiently, or at least perform at a level comparable to that of his competitors, or he'll eventually be forced out of business.

A comparative analysis of productivity shows that societies that espouse a set of rules for the game based to some degree on the free market have been most successful in squeezing the most production of goods and services out of available resources. A comparative analysis of the consequences of business downturns would probably show that a system similar to the one espoused by Adam Smith would suffer more than those organized in the fashion of Big Business.

Many independent businessmen in a given industry place no limitation on the rate of adding capacity. Left to their own devices, businessmen will invariably add too much capacity; in fact, they will continue to add capacity until the price structure has been destroyed. By then, it is far too late to do anything about the excess capacity except either wait for demand to rise to absorb the excess supply of capacity or wait for excess supply of capacity to decay to the level of demand.

The challenge facing businessmen in a free market environment is how to survive until better days come. Many don't.

In "less in accordance with Adam Smith" economies where Big Business or governmental-industrial combines prevail, there is more control over adding capacity and more control over the general level of production, which ameliorates the worst of the instability inherent in laissez faire economics. This is not to say that Big Business or governmental-industrial combines always work. They don't. It is clear, however, that the incentive behind their establishment is the instability experienced in a laissez faire economy when many individual businessmen busily copy the actions of one another to their mutual detriment.

It should come as no surprise that the forecasting of a business environment is taking on added dimensions. There are the physical aspect, the emotional aspect, the way industry organizes itself to control capacity addition during good times and to deal with falling prices during bad times, and the rules set by society for playing the economic game of life.

Every individual on earth is doing what he thinks is best for himself, even if he is living a monk's life: in that case, the individual is maximizing his worth in the life hereafter rather than in the life here-at-hand. A citizen in the Soviet Union maximizes his worth by being a watcher and regulator of doers rather than by being a doer. This brain and talent drain from the doers to the watchers and regulators of doers explains much of the low productivity of that society. Government interventionist policies in England and Sweden concentrate on making a softer landing when the bad times come, while government involvement in industrial decisions in Japan is keyed to keeping the economy running with the minimum of ups and downs.

The role of government in controlling or influencing the behavior patterns of businessmen, the type and nature of the safety net that is placed under business enterprises during bad times, and the actions taken by government to avert the bad times when the signs of bad times make their first appearance are important factors in assessing future business conditions. In fact, if a government, or a combination of government and industry, could devise a workable method of averting severe downturns in an economy, then forecasting could be reduced to extrapolating current trends. This is an important point to bear in mind because it is the cyclicality of business that makes forecasting such a hazardous occupation. Reducing the degree of cyclicality eases the burden of forecasting.

Is the task of forecasting business conditions impossible? Yes.

That does not take away from its necessity. In a free market environment, production planning requires a forecast. In fact, all planning requires a forecast. The first step is to examine the current situation in light of the recent past. The next step is to assess future business conditions.

The objective of forecasting business conditions is not to establish a current trend and then to forecast on the basis that the trend will continue over the forecast period. If the history of business cycles proves one thing, it is that current trends don't last very long. The objective of forecasting is to attempt to get a handle on the turning points in the business cycle. This is an admittedly impossible task because this requires peering into the future: a treat denied to mere mortals. However, it is possible to identify the signs that suggest a turn in business conditions may be in the cards.

In the pig cycle, a turn in the cards from good times to bad can be called by considering the size of the pig population being readied for market and the ability of the market to absorb the onslaught, an onslaught that can be predicted by the maturation period of a piglet. A turn from bad times to good can be called by considering the rate of inventory liquidation and estimating when inventories will be restored to manageable levels. These forecasts are not infallible with respect to timing. Speculators have been ruined over their inability to forecast the precise timing of a turnaround. This does not necessarily mean that they were wrong in expecting a turnaround. And that will be the objective: to determine the signs one can look for that will indicate a turn in the business cycle during the forecast period.

Forecasts that are tuned to changes in the climate for conducting business have an inherent superiority over those forecasts that look at favorable trends in a business and extrapolate that good times will last forever and over those forecasts that look at unfavorable trends in a business and extrapolate that bad times will last forever. The one thing that is clear from viewing the pig cycle is that it is cyclical: good and bad times do not last forever. Exhibit 3.1 shows that things are either moving up or down and that things don't move in a single direction forever. Another aspect of Exhibit 3.1 is that the cyclical movements, although unpredictable because of their irregularity, aren't all that irregular. There is a rhythm to the irregularity that may ruin a speculator, but sustain a pig farmer over the long haul. One might also be audacious enough to conclude that the pig cycle might even be understood in terms of human behavior with regard to the cost of making and the price of selling a pig, the dynamics of pig production, and the number of players in the game. And dreaming the impossible, there may even be the slightest possibility of predicting changes in the pig cycle—predicting changes in the price of pigs not for the purpose of playing a fancy game in the hog futures market, but for knowing when to reserve rooms at Honeymoon Motel.

4

Man as Consumer

Because forecasting business activity requires incorporating the behavior of man, a few words must be spent on behavior characteristics. One side of man's behavior is what he does in a store. The behavior patterns of man as consumer determine overall demand for goods. Potential changes in his behavior patterns over the forecast period affect the results of the forecast.

THE NEGATIVE SIDE OF A CONSUMER

There is a negative connotation associated with being a consumer. A consumer is oftentimes viewed as an individual without spirituality. A consumer prowls the aisles of material things without any purpose other than spending every penny he has on his person, and then some. Thus, it behooves those in marketing to ingeniously package the worthless trinkets to induce the impulsive consumer to purchase Brand X over Brand Y. Man as consumer is a spiritual empty shell, a degenerative form of life whose appearance on the stage of history signals the end of an age.

Indeed, there may be an element of truth in this. To some, a shopping mall is paradise, a secular temple where one explores every niche and corner in search of inner happiness. And when happiness is found, an offering is made to the gods in the form of a plastic card.

The word *consumerism* carries with it the implication that a consumer can exist in society without that person participating in any way in the production of goods and the offering of services. To some extent, this is true. Society can tolerate a small segment of its population consuming without producing goods or offering services. Problems arise when large segments of the population feel that they have a right to a free ride. The separation of a consumer from a producer of goods or a supplier of services has even become engrained in political thinking.

The word *entitlement* is usually construed to mean that a person has a right to the possession of goods by virtue of the fact that he breathes.

Societies have always provided for the young, the sick, and the aged. Historically, this was done through the family. A productive society can afford to provide some level of support to a nonproducing segment of the population independent of the reasons why the recipients cannot participate. However, the questions that modern society has to address are those associated with the requisites for ''entitlement'' and the level of support for those who are deemed ''entitled.'' Few would seriously argue that the young, the aged, the sick, and the handicapped are not entitled to some measure of support.

Others feel that consumerism has become an end unto itself. For some consumer advocates, the purpose of life is to consume goods. The workings of modern civilization are to be dedicated solely to satisfying the whims and fancies of consumers. Owners of factories who sell goods for anything more than cost and whose products fail during the lifetime of the consumer are to be dealt with severely unless they provide a double-your-money-back, lifetime guarantee on their product. Consuming becomes a patriotic duty because, without consumers, the whole system of making things to satisfy the insatiable appetite of consumers falls apart.

THE POSITIVE SIDE OF A CONSUMER

A consumer need not be viewed in such negative terms. The most upright citizen in the most civilized setting is a consumer unless he has learned to live without food and to be dressed without clothes and to be sheltered without furnishings. Being a consumer does not mean a denial of the spiritual side of man; like it or not, there are spiritual and material sides in the nature of man. The spiritual side is within man and defines his relationship with the eternal. Whether or not the eternal exists and what form that relationship takes are not particularly germane to how man behaves as a consumer. When a man enters a department store, his belief in the eternal does not detract from his being a consumer. While he might be less apt to buy the frivolous if his thoughts are geared to an eventual face-to-face meeting with the eternal, he is still a consumer. Relatively few believers in the eternal deny themselves material things and, as consumers, can barely be differentiated from those who doubt the existence of the eternal.

This point is being brought up because of the negative connotation associated with the word *consumer*. One connotation is that a consumer is someone who neither produces nor contributes to the workings of society. A consumer is a sponge whose function in life is to absorb the output of the factories. The other connotation is that a consumer is purely of this world and does not have any interest in life other than to accumulate material possessions. A man of the clothe seen purchasing an automobile obviously cannot be a true man of the clothe.

This form of thinking carries over to man as producer. A man standing by a machine stamping out parts cannot possibly have a spiritual side to his personality. This nonsequitur is central in the writings of Karl Marx. Apparently, in the world according to Marx, a society cannot hope to stamp out goods unless it first stamps out the spirituality within man. Why this spiritual emptiness is a kind of condition precedent, necessary for a society to produce goods or consume goods, makes little sense. As a matter of fact, it makes no sense at all. There isn't a shred of logic connecting spiritual emptiness with material plenty.

The most consumer-oriented society on earth has ''In God We Trust'' emblazoned on its currency. The Protestant work ethic intertwines the spirituality of redemption and the performance of useful tasks in a material world. ''Redeem the time for the times are evil'' is taken to mean that one is to pursue his vocation to the utmost of the talents given to him by the eternal, while refraining from all forms of evil. Vocation is not confined to the spreading of the word. Vocation is any honorable occupation, including the ownership and management of legitimate businesses. The last thing one does under the Protestant work ethic is live a life of idleness while waiting for redemption. One shows his worthiness by what he does while he is redeeming his time.

The logic of the Protestant work ethic goes one step farther than what one might conclude from reading Scripture. Financial distress—or the inability to be a consumer—is interpreted to mean that the individual is out of sorts with his Maker. While there are statements in Scripture that support such a view, these statements should be balanced with those about distress in life being the testing and proving grounds for untested and unproved souls. An even better balance can be obtained by taking cognizance of other statements that suggest that the richness of material goods in this life is compensation for the poverty of the reward in the next.

Strict regimens are part of monastic life. Those in pursuit of a life of idleness do not line up to volunteer for the rigors of the monastaries. However, it has to be admitted that those living the monastic life are not apt to be selected as a target audience for a promotional campaign for trinkets and gadgets. Then again, these individuals do not make up a significant part of the population. This is not to imply that civilization is better off because so few individuals live the monastic life.

Man can be a consumer of things, and a producer of things, and can maintain his spirituality or dispense with it, as he sees fit. His behavior as a consumer does not depend on his feelings toward the eternal. Except for a relatively few individuals living the monastic life in or out of a monastery, man is a consumer of material things, regardless of what he thinks in the spiritual realm. It is merely a bit of irony to note that production and consumption of goods in societies that subscribe to the Protestant work ethic far exceed production and consumption in those societies that subscribe to Karl Marx's dictum that material goods are the end-all and be-all of existence. Nor have Far Eastern nations, which do not subscribe to the Protestant work ethic in the sense of being a Protestant, found it necessary to abandon their religious affiliations as they progressed in raising the standard of living of their people.

Spirituality in man is not the subject under discussion. On the other hand, spirituality certainly has not been ruled out from the makeup of man by focusing on his behavior in acquiring material goods. The business cycle does not depend on what a man thinks about his relationship with the eternal. It does depend on how a man reacts to changing conditions that affect his decisions on how much to spend and how much to save. An individual's decisions about how much to spend and how much to save are personal and independent of what he feels about the spiritual side of things. The only connection between the two might be that a person expecting to have a face-to-face meeting with his Maker might tend to be less frivolous in his purchases. Maybe.

SPENDING OUTWEIGHS SAVING

Generally speaking, man's wants exceed the capacity of the society to produce goods. For some, this is the result of a curse placed on mankind for disobedience in the Garden of Eden. For Karl Marx, believer in scientific materialism (whatever that is), this curse has no meaning because it never occurred. Mankind can organize itself to produce all the goods that are necessary for happiness. In Karl Marx's view of things, ultimate happiness is achievable when there is a chicken in every pot.

There is another view on the nature of man as consumer. That view, independent of spiritual considerations, is that man is acquisitive of material goods and that there is no ultimate sense of personal satisfaction or achievement of happiness in the acquisition of material goods. As a society progresses in the sense of being able to produce more goods, man as consumer merely develops a larger appetite for material goods. His idea of being poor, his concept of poverty in terms of the possession of material goods, keeps pace with the advancing productive capacity of a society. In fact, his expectations may exceed that which a society can physically provide in terms of goods and services. There are those who believe that the flashpoint for social unrest is the beginning of real economic progress in raising the standard of living of a people. The population, sensing the improvement but not yet benefiting fully, becomes impatient. The rest is subject matter for the history books.

For the most part, man does not reach the saturation point in the possession of material things. The fact that a consumer possesses more goods does not translate itself into happiness. The most common response to a larger paycheck is a greater predilection to acquire more goods. While it is true that there might be a point at which mankind would be saturated with goods and would not desire more goods, even if more purchasing power were given to him, it is clear from viewing the world that this is not worth serious consideration. The world around us is a world of scarcity, a world of limited resources, a world in which relatively few consider themselves well off. Even among the relatively affluent, most would increase their material possessions if given the chance to do so.

This does not necessarily mean that everybody is discontented. One can be quite content with a certain minimum level of material possessions. There are many who are happy with virtually no material belongings. These people have accepted what others would deem abject poverty with equanimity. Perhaps it is their way of dealing with the general lack of hope that things will get better in their lifetimes. General misery is more tolerable if all one's friends, neighbors, and relatives are in the same predicament. Who, then, is in a position to complain? Besides, material possessions are not a precondition for human happiness, as even the most casual observer can see. Affluence itself may be the greatest impediment to achieving some degree of happiness and satisfaction in this life.

Regardless of the connection between happiness and affluence, give a person a thousand dollars, and it will probably be spent in short order. For the poor, the money may go for food and clothing. For the affluent, a person in the process of purchasing a new car might spend the thousand dollars on buying a better equipped model. Give that person another thousand dollars, and the living room couch, which was in fine condition yesterday, although perhaps a bit worn at the edges, may no longer be considered to be in such fine condition. In other words, there is always something in the back of the mind of man as consumer which, if given one thousand dollars, would rapidly move to the front of the mind.

That something may not be for his personal consumption. A son or daughter may be recently married and in need of almost everything. The money might be spent for a dining room set for the newlyweds. Or it might be spent for a hearing aid for an aged parent. It does not matter if the money is spent on someone else—the point is the money is spent.

THE UNCERTAIN WORLD OF THE CONSUMER

On the other hand, not all the money may be spent. Some may be saved. Savings are important to an individual because he lives in a world of uncertainty. The uncertainty aspect that worries him most might be death, but a close second is unemployment. Unemployment is a consequence of a free market environment in which employers not only are free to dismiss, lay off, or in other ways terminate employees but also are forced to do so by the workings of the free market itself.

If a factory makes a product, and if for any number of diverse reasons that product cannot be sold, at some point the factory owner or manager must reduce the factory's output. If he does not dismiss any workers, the factory owner or manager is paying for workers who are producing goods that are not being sold. This is a cash outflow at the same time when he is not selling his product. Consequently, there is no revenue from sales to generate a cash inflow to counterbalance the cash outflow. What is his choice with regard to laying off his workers? Does he even have a choice? The answer is no.

He does have a choice as to how he lays off his workers and the circumstances surrounding the layoffs. He can tell them to pack up and leave in ten minutes, or he can provide advance warning that unless business conditions improve, there will have to be layoffs. He can counsel the workers and give them as much severance pay as he can afford. Nevertheless, the factory owner is dealing with *how* he will dismiss the workers, not with *whether* he will dismiss them. He can delay the inevitable, and he can make the inevitable somewhat less harsh by how he addresses the issue, but he cannot avoid the inevitable. The inevitability of a free market environment is that workers have no assurance of full time employment. The free market system has no way of assuring workers lifetime employment, even if those running things from within the system desired to do so. If the workings of the free market do not provide a guaranteed level of revenue to a company, how can the company provide a guaranteed level of wages to its workers?

A worker does not appreciate being dismissed. However, he can understand his being dismissed for cause. He can understand being terminated if his work habits are slovenly, if his work skills are inferior to others, and even if the product made by his factory is inferior in quality, or has been outmoded, and is no longer desired by the buying public. These are reasons for dismissal that the worker can understand—not that he appreciates the finer points of not being able to feed his family.

What a worker does not understand is the loss of his job when he is a conscientious individual with superior skills making a product that the public desires to buy. He cannot understand his dismissal when he is fulfilling his side of the moral obligation to give a fair day's work for a fair day's pay. This form of dismissal is difficult for a worker to accept because the worker cannot identify any course of action that he might have taken to avert the loss of a job.

This occurs, of course, when the business cycle takes a turn for the worse, when good times become bad times. And to add to the difficulties this represents to individuals, good times change to bad times in a relatively short span of time and are usually unexpected. By definition, good times are when things are looking up. When things are looking up, everybody is looking up. When a person is looking up, he may not see the chasm opening up below him.

THE PURPOSE OF SAVINGS

Thus, savings are necessary to provide some sort of cushion, a security blanket, a nest egg for the bad times. Savings are an individual's safety net to protect himself when things turn against him. People do not save, and, indeed, have no reason to save, if all their needs are guaranteed to be satisfied. Furthermore, savings are not necessary to provide funds to finance the expansion of industry. The free market system can continue to function, although less smoothly, without any savings on the part of the population during the good times of a business cycle.

Some people believe that the savings of individuals are needed by industry as a source of funds for expansion. The implication is that if no one saved, there would be no savings accounts within the banking system to fund this expansion. Thus, savings are viewed as absolutely indispensable for the workings of an industrial society in a free market environment.

This is not so. A shortage of productive capacity is defined as the situation in which the supply of goods is less than the demand for goods. With demand outstripping supply, factory owners are in a position to raise prices. At some point, prices for goods exceed costs, and the difference is profits. Profits can then be used to finance the building of more capacity. If a society has adopted fractional reserve banking (as all industrialized societies have in one form or the other), the banking system can respond to the capital needs of industry by simply creating the credit necessary to satisfy the demand for funds.

The good time side of the business cycle does not require savings on the part of individuals. Profitability can finance expansion—and a great deal of profitability is not required if a nation has a banking system capable of creating credit that can accommodate the needs of industrial borrowers. As soon as banks see that the relationship between the cost to make the product and the price to sell the product is sufficient to make them feel comfortable that the credit can be repaid out of the future earnings of the new factory, then the credit becomes more than available for building new plant capacity as one bank competes against the other for the business.

The purpose of savings is to provide a safety net for consumers when times get tough. Saving a portion of the paycheck is a personal decision made by individuals to deal with uncertainty in the material realm of things. In order to have some cushion for the bad times, savings have to be put aside during the good times.

The bad times side of the business cycle does depend on savings. Economic recovery from the bad times cannot occur until overhanging inventories of finished goods have been liquidated. Liquidation of excess inventories means that they must be sold. The timing of an economic recovery depends on individuals' continuing to consume after they have lost their jobs. The only way this can be accomplished is if unemployed workers have saved some money prior to their loss of employment. If disposal of excess inventories is necessary before the business cycle can turn the corner for better times, then consumers must have a source of funds to "buy themselves out" of a recession or a depression. That source of funds is savings. The free market system does not flounder because of insufficient savings during the good times to fund the expansion of industry. On the other hand, the system is in trouble if unemployed workers have insufficient savings in the bank to withdraw during the bad times to maintain their status as consumers.

SAVINGS IN A SOCIAL SETTING

Savings have little to do with the running of a communist society. The economic philosophy behind communism is that the state will take on all the burdens of an individual such that he is never exposed to risk of any kind. Housing, food, medical care, education, you-name-it—these are all the responsibility of the state. All the state requires in return is that an individual be happy with his assignment. Happiness is man married to machine. The goal of materialistic evolution is for the highest form of living matter (man) to be busily tending to the highest form of nonliving matter (machine), producing all sorts of material goods that will bring about universal happiness for man and machine alike.

The communist system does not expect that an individual has to save, as he would in the free market system, because all aspects of personal security are guaranteed by the state. However, it must be noted that individuals in communist nations do save. Sometimes it is to accumulate the funds necessary to make a major purchase, such as an automobile. Sometimes the act of saving is a default condition in that there is nothing on the shelves that a consumer wants to buy. Saving then reflects the inability to spend. Perhaps this best illustrates the fundamental difference between the two economic systems. In one, a consumer saves because of the inability to guarantee a secure income. In the other, a person saves because of the inability to be a consumer.

The philosophic underpinnings of the free market system assume that man is basically an unhappy and dissatisfied individual who abhors work. People work for one basic reason: if they don't, the alternative is to starve to death in a dark, cold room. Relatively few people find satisfaction in work. Most work is tedious, repetitious, and boring. The primary incentive to man a machine is to earn some money to feed one's family, keep clothes on their backs, provide a roof over their heads, and keep the rooms lighted and warm.

In a laissez faire environment, if a consumer wants to buy goods, the consumer had better be part of the system of producing goods. And if that consumer is not part of the system of producing goods, then the basic attitude of the society is that the consumer is not deserving of the benefits derived from spending eight hours of a day as part of the system. Adam Smith and Karl Marx had a basic disagreement over the nature of man.

The participation of a consumer in the workings of the free market goes far beyond standing by a machine stamping out parts, and beyond assembling the parts into a finished product, and their distribution, sales, and service. Participation includes providing public services such as education, medical care, transportation, waste disposal, police and fire protection, and defense of society from invasion or intrusion by other societies, and the administration and management of private and public enterprises. The system includes satisfying the more frivolous side, and the seamier side, of human nature.

In the free market system, a paycheck is continguent on making a contribution to society. The paycheck supports a family unit. For survival in a material sense, at least one member of a family unit must have a job. There are those who are mentally and physically handicapped and cannot contribute to the running of the free market system. Others lack basic education in reading, writing, and arithmetic and training in basic skills. There are still others who might be described as attitude handicapped. These people do not have the proper attitude to be trained for a job, nor do they possess the inner discipline and the sense of responsibility necessary to function in a production or service setting.

In the world of Adam Smith, these people are deserving only of what charity is willing to provide them. Charity is the free-will donations that those with paychecks are willing to share with those without paychecks. Charity has its way of sorting out the deserving poor from the undeserving poor. The money offered to charity is voluntary, and considering the state of the recipients, the money is spent, not saved. Charity is the voluntary transfer of money to be spent from one individual to another.

The welfare system is an involuntary transfer of funds to the deserving poor—and, as some critics maintain, the undeserving poor. The money is taken away from workers in the form of taxation, and considering the state of the recipients, the money is spent, not saved.

The role of government in taxation determines what amount of after-tax money is available for spending by those receiving paychecks. What the government does with the money taken from one class and given to another has to be taken into consideration in the general scheme of things. The question that matters is whether taxation is a form of saving or merely a redirection of spending from one group to another. To the degree that the government taxes individuals for the purposes of building up the resources of the nation, one could argue that this is a form of saving. To the degree that the government taxes individuals for the purpose of transferring income from those who receive paychecks as part of the productive system to those who do not, then taxation is simply a transfer of spending. The latter case usually prevails.

Because the very nature of the free market system hardly inspires confidence in the future, man as consumer saves a portion of his pay for a rainy day. The amount that he saves varies from individual to individual and depends on a number of issues. Among these are the extent of his present savings, his possession of material things, the general direction of prices, the relationship between the interest he receives on his savings and the effect of inflation on the price of goods, and his confidence in holding onto his job. While these are the more important considerations one takes into account in determining how much to save, one consideration overrides all others. That consideration is confidence.

CONFIDENCE

Confidence in the future is the greatest influence on man as consumer. The more confidence that he has in the security of his position, the greater the portion of his pay that will be spent. The less confidence that he has in the future, the less that will be spent. What a consumer does not spend is saved. Savings are important in understanding the business cycle. Under normal circumstances, savings may help to stabilize the cyclical nature of business activity. Savings may help to reduce volatility in prices. Savings, in fact, may be highly desirable; nevertheless, savings are not necessary to the working of the free market economy during the good times because profits and fractional reserve banking can provide the necessary funds, in the form of cash or credit, to support the expansion of the productive capacity of an industrial society.

The saving of a part of one's paycheck is considered a virtuous act. The spendthrift is the individual who is condemned by society as a malefactor. The free market can survive the actions of spendthrifts, even though spendthrifts themselves may not survive their excesses. There is, however, another side of saving that is not commonly mentioned in banking commercials. The virtue of saving can take on an ominous aura.

The viability of a free market economy can be threatened by both insufficient savings on the part of individuals and too much savings. Insufficient savings may add to the volatility of prices, to the magnitude of the swings of the business cycle, and to the sufferings of prolific spenders when the bad times come. Insufficient savings may prolong the bad times of the business cycle when unemployed consumers have too little residual purchasing power to liquidate excess inventories. On the other side of the coin, too much savings on the part of individuals have a negative impact on spending. What man as consumer spends is crucial in understanding the free market economy because what one consumer spends is another consumer's income.

The point can be made by considering the consequences of everyone saving his entire paycheck. By definition, no one is spending a cent. Some might consider this more desirable than a nation of spendthrifts. However, the consequences are far from desirable. Stores open up for business, and no one shows up. Because nothing is moving off the shelves, stores do not bother to replenish their goods; indeed, there is nothing to replenish.

Wholesale distributors see no orders from retailers and, therefore, send no orders to factories to replenish their stocks. There is nothing to replenish; the wholesalers' shelves are full of goods. Factories see no orders and have nowhere to send the goods piling up in their warehouses. With no goods being sent to distributors, there are no invoices being written. With no receivables on the books, revenues fall to zero. With no cash coming in, and with the workers expecting to be able to cash their paychecks, even if to deposit the entire paycheck into a savings account, there is no choice but cease operations. All the workers have to be laid off, and the system grinds to a halt. A total halt—a total depression that will never end.

Oversaving is a calamity of the first order—in the great scheme of things, saving all of one's paycheck may be a worse sin than spending all of one's paycheck. Spending all of one's paycheck may be a personal calamity for the spendthrift when the bad times come. Spending all of one's paycheck may add to the volatility of the business cycle. However, the virtual failure to spend by a large segment of the population cannot be described by any term other than national calamity—or perhaps Great Depression. Rather than acting as a safety net for the individual, total saving guarantees universal unemployment. No one needs to worry about the volatility of the business cycle under these circumstances. Excessive saving reduces the inherent volatility in the business cycle to zero. In fact, there is no cycle; there is nothing but an endless depression.

EXTENT OF PRESENT SAVINGS

Savings are a safety net for the individual. The size of a safety net depends on the individual's degree of insecurity. The safety net required by a person working on a steel girder three feet above the ground is quite different from what one would like to see if the girder is three hundred feet above the ground. If the nature of the volatility of the economy is such that bad times occur frequently with severe unemployment, one will have a certain concept of the size of the nest egg necessary to get him through the bad times. If the business cycles are mild without severe bouts of unemployment, the nest egg need not be so large. If society provides a safety net in the form of unemployment benefits, then the extent of these benefits will also have an influence.

The safety net is not absolute. If an individual perceives that there is no possible risk of unemployment facing him, and if there is no possible expense that concerns him unduly, then he does not need a safety net, and savings are superfluous. On the other hand, if the workings of society are such that he has a great deal of uncertainty, his idea of an adequate safety net or nest egg is going to be substantially greater.

One thing should be made clear. Savings reflect the decision that each individual makes to ensure his financial survival when bad times strike. During the good times of a business cycle, the economic system will continue to operate with, or without, savings.

However, the bad times of a business cycle are more sensitive to the degree of savings. The degree to which a consumer cuts his spending when he loses his job is dependent on the size of his personal nest egg. If the general population enters into the bad times with very little in savings, then, as people lose their jobs, their spending is essentially reduced to nothing. If their savings were more substantial, then their spending would not be cut to such a great extent. Continued spending by the unemployed, although at a lesser scale than the employed, is critical in liquidating excess inventories, a precondition to the resumption of good times.

The amount of savings has a significant impact on the extent and severity of the bad times of a business cycle because it determines whether the unemployed can still maintain their status as consumers. The act of saving during the good times does have an impact on moderating the volatility of prices, but its chief virtue is that the money saved can then be spent during the bad times.

POSSESSION OF MATERIAL THINGS

The desire to possess material things influences spending habits. If a person feels that he is behind, so to speak, on the possession of material things with respect to his peers, he will have a general tendency to spend more, even if his personal nest egg isn't large enough to support a sparrow. This is the Keeping Up with the Joneses syndrome. The behavior is particularly marked after a person has been unemployed for some time. Once employed, everything is spent in a feverish attempt to restore his standing with his peers in the realm of material possessions. The individual will not think of saving, even with virtually nothing in the bank, until he feels that he can hold his own when a comparison is made between what he and his neighbor possess. This is catch-up time.

This behavior pattern of Keeping Up with the Joneses is part of the good times. Good times are marked by rising employment. When people see the unemployment lines getting shorter and the want ads for jobs becoming more common, their attitude toward spending becomes more positive. Good times begin as soon as unemployment rates start decreasing. Even with continued high unemployment, the fact that things are getting better permeates the thinking of consumers. If unemployment rates are decreasing, and if one has a job, then the chances of being laid off are nil. The worst is over, and it is time to forget the bad times. Declining unemployment means that the security associated with a job is going to be much greater than during times of increasing unemployment. One can afford to be a bit more profligate than during less auspicious times.

Catching up with the Joneses may have resulted from a previous loss of employment. During times of unemployment, a person is hardly in a position to acquire much in the way of goods. The aging of his stock of goods is probably the primary reason why he finds himself at the lower end of the material possession scale. After regaining a job, the individual has to go through the process of building up his inventory of material things. Once he is again able to walk around the neighborhood with his head held high, he may take the time to reflect on the fact that he was unemployed at one point in the past. He may even go so far as to have a desire to build up a nest egg so that the trauma of losing his job won't be so severe the next time around.

If his savings rate is sufficiently high, and if the good times last long enough, the individual may achieve his objective of having a nest egg of sufficient size, at least in his eyes, for him to survive the next downturn in business. From here on out, his desire to save becomes nil, and most of his income is spent. He may begin to spend a portion of his savings if his nest egg is large enough and if prices of goods are going up faster than the interest he is earning on his savings. Withdrawals from savings, or dissavings, are common in inflationary times when postponing purchases means real higher prices—that is, the interest on savings does not compensate for the higher prices for goods. An individual in the dis-saving mode of behavior is actually spending more than he earns. He is not trying to keep up with the Joneses. He is now the Jones who is setting the standards for others to emulate.

The degree of confidence, the amount of material possessions, and the size of the nest egg are all intertwined. The discussion up to now has been primarily about the good times side of the business cycle. The bad times side is quite different. As unemployment lines lengthen and distress in the economy shows itself, fear grips the employed. All of a sudden the nest egg doesn't look very big. Spending patterns change dramatically. People become more cautious. Purchases of big ticket items, like homes and automobiles, are on the front lines of the cutback. Spending is cut back, and savings benefit. There is only one small thing wrong with this type of thinking. What is best for the individual is the worst thing that can happen to overall business activity.

As the economy falters because sales are collapsing, fear of losing one's own job makes one more cautious in his spending habits. This is in the best interests of the individual—spend less, save more, and add to the nest egg in case things get even worse. And they do get worse because the collective impact of everyone saving more has a direct adverse effect on sales revenues. This fosters more layoffs, which, in turn, creates more feelings of fear and insecurity, which, in turn, encourages a greater degree of saving, which, in turn, cuts back more on sales.

This is sometimes referred to as a *positive feedback system*. The word "positive" sounds comforting, but positive feedback systems are far from positive, or comforting. The classic example of a positive feedback system is the microphone squeal. A little background noise is picked up by the microphone and is amplified in the speaker system. The microphone then picks up the amplified background noise and rams it through the speaker system again. In short order, all one has is a penetrating background squeal.

Thus, to a large degree, the start of the bad times generates the climate for the further spread of the bad times. Bad times, once started, can be compared to a snowball starting an avalanche, which is another example of a positive feedback system. To a large measure, bad times are a self-fulfilling prophecy, once the mechanism starting bad times has been triggered. This is the nature of positive feedback systems—yet can one blame an individual for becoming more conservative in his spending habits once the bad times begin?

An individual pursues his selfish interests, and his selfish interests are best served by drastically trying to build up his nest egg at a time when it is apparent that he is going to need the nest egg. No one can be expected to step up his purchasing activity at the very time that his fitness for financial survival may well be tested.

THE GENERAL DIRECTION OF PRICES

The general direction of prices has an impact on the amount of a paycheck that is saved as compared to the amount that is spent. A consumer's best interests are served, in times of rising prices, by making a purchase before there is another price increase. Inflationary times provide an incentive to purchase goods. The incentive to purchase goods sooner, so to speak, than normal means less savings. The greater activity in purchasing means more dollars chasing the same amount of goods, which spurs further price increases. One cannot blame the consumer for this behavior pattern. His interests are best served in speeding up his purchases before retailers increase the price of goods again. Individuals cannot be expected to pursue the interests of others. As a result, the collective action of many consumers pursuing their best self-interests in spending more of their paychecks to beat price hikes creates, in turn, more inflationary pressures for further price increases. The collective action of many causing further price hikes is just another example of positive feedback, the nemesis of stability.

During times when prices are falling, a similar cycle sets in, which has about the same pernicious effect as when prices are increasing. Decreasing prices indicate deflationary times, and it behooves the self-interested consumer to postpone purchases for as long as possible. A purchase postponed long enough to ensure a lower price is to the benefit of the consumer. Deflationary times encourages saving because by postponing a purchase, one is de facto increasing his savings rate. Usually deflation is associated with bad times in that falling prices mean a lack of demand. As prices fall, consumers defer their purchases, which, in turn, reduces demand. As demand falls, retailers get anxious over the goods on their shelves and lower their prices to reduce their inventories. As prices continue to fall, consumers have even more incentive to defer their purchases. Factory owners, watching prices fall and sales remain sluggish, start another round of layoffs. Another example of positive feedback. Another self-fulfilling prophecy comes to pass.

INTEREST RATES, WAGE RATES, AND PRICE CHANGES

Consumer behavior is also influenced by the relationship among interest rates, wage rates, and price changes. For instance, if wage rate increases more or less match the rate of price changes, then the incentive to beat inflation may not be as strong as when wage rates lag inflation. If inflation exceeds the rate of interest on savings, there may be an incentive to reduce the amount of savings. If one's nest egg is a little on the large size and the rate of interest lags the rate of inflation, the nest egg is losing purchasing power. Rather than standing idly by and watching the nest egg wither away in terms of purchasing power, there may be an incentive to dissave—to make a withdrawal from the nest egg and spend the proceeds. This behavior would be expected for those who consider that their nest egg is already adequate in size to meet unforeseen contingencies.

Although all these matters must be accounted for in one form or the other, they are secondary, if not tertiary, considerations. The most important consideration in the propensity to spend, or the propensity to save, is confidence. Once the confidence level has been established by the general business climate, then one can look at an individual with regard to the extent of his savings and the possession of material things in order to assess his spending and saving patterns. Then adjustments can be made as to the relationship among price changes, wage rate adjustments, and interest rates. All this can be simulated.

CONSUMER BEHAVIOR SIMULATION

If man as consumer has basically an acquisitive instinct with a predeliction toward a positive view of life, then good times will be marked by a distinct propensity to spend. Suppose that there is an island economy somewhere in the middle of a vast sea. Suppose that a sociologist with an economics background, or an economist with a sociology background, observed and interviewed a number of people. The findings of such a study might be summarized in a few succinct statements:

1. The good times mentality prevails whenever unemployment is decreasing, no matter how bad it may have been in the recent past.
2. The good times mentality prevails whenever unemployment is less than 5 percent, no matter if it is rising or falling within a band of zero to 5 percent unemployment.

During the good times, an employed consumer's spending habits follow these patterns:

1. If a consumer is in the lower third of the scale that physically measures material things, the consumer will save nothing. He will attempt to catch up with the Joneses as quickly as possible by spending everything he earns.
2. Once out of the lower third in terms of possessing material goods, an employed consumer will save a maximum of 10 percent of his paycheck under any circumstance. What he actually saves depends on various factors. If his nest egg is less than two months' pay, he will save the entire 10 percent. If his nest egg is between two and four months' pay, he will save 6 percent of his paycheck. If his nest egg is between four and six months' pay, he will save 4 percent of his pay. If his nest egg is larger than six months' pay, then his savings rate is a mere 2 percent.
3. If during these good times price increases are exceeding wage rate increases—that is, these are inflationary times in that the paycheck is buying less and less with time, even though the paycheck itself may be increasing—then the savings rate will be cut in half. If, at the same time, the interest rate on savings lags price inflation, there will be dissavings (net withdrawals) only for savings that exceed six months' worth of pay. The rate of dissavings is 5 percent of the difference between the amount of savings and six months' worth of pay.

Bad times prevail whenever the requirements determining good times are not fulfilled. It is a default condition of not having good times. Bad times are any times when employment is below 95 percent of the working population and has decreased, or remained unchanged, from the previous period. During bad times, the Keeping Up with the Joneses syndrome and the dissavings phenomenon disappear altogether. The propensity to save is a function of both the extent of unemployment and its change from the previous period.

The fear that grips people during bad times comes from two sources. One is unemployment in absolute terms, and the other is the worsening condition of unemployment, based on its rate of change from the preceding period. In other words, people are less fearful when unemployment is 30 percent this month versus 30 percent last month than if unemployment is 30 percent this month versus 25 percent last month. In the former case, if a person is among the lucky 70 percent still holding a job, with unemployment essentially unchanging, the chances are that he will keep his job. If unemployment is 30 percent, while it was 25 percent the previous month, then one has far less confidence that he will be able to keep his job. The situation is worsening. Fear will be much greater.

This can be modeled by the following set of rules:

1. The base savings rate during bad times is 20 percent of take-home pay for all employed people with savings of less than six months' worth of pay.

2. For those with savings above six months' worth of pay, the base savings rate is 10 percent.

3. If prices are increasing during bad times, the savings rate of employed workers will be reduced to 15 percent for those with less than six months' savings and to 5 percent for those who have more than six months' savings. This models the behavior pattern of purchasing goods before there are further price increases.

4. If prices are declining during bad times, the savings rate of employed workers will be increased to 25 percent for those with less than six months' savings and to 15 percent for those who have more than six months' savings. This models the behavior pattern of postponing purchases in hope of obtaining a better price.

5. The quantification of fear can be incorporated into the savings rate by implementation of the following rule: the base savings rate is to be increased by two times the difference in unemployment rates between the preceding period and the present period.

The following example illustrates the last rule. If prices are declining, and if unemployment during the preceding period was 25 percent and it is now 30 percent, then the propensity to save will be 25 percent (the base rate) plus two times the difference in the unemployment rates (or another 10 percent) for a total of 35 percent. If unemployment was 30 percent during the preceding period, and is still 30 percent, then the propensity to save would be 25 percent.

And to complete the picture, if unemployment was 31 percent in the preceding period and is now 30 percent, and if a person's material possessions are measured in the lower one-third on the scale, and if he is still employed, his savings rate will become zero. This may be considered a rather abrupt change from a savings rate of 25 percent.

Why is this so? This is the nature of man. He is acquisitive by nature and is looking for an excuse to get back into the good times mentality. He views life as one trip around and, irrespective of his spiritual side, realizes that shrouds have no pockets. Man as consumer wants goods and does what he can to avoid the bad times mentality. The only reason why he has the bad times mentality is because circumstances, such as growing unemployment, force him to think this way.

However, declining unemployment is a horse of a different color. Because man as consumer did not lose his job during the times when unemployment was growing, why should he lose his job during times when unemployment is shrinking? It could happen, but the odds are that it won't. So why continue the reign of fear? Particularly when every fiber in the consumer's body wants to abandon the reign of fear mentality, even though this may not be warranted from a more rational point of view.

That brings us to the final point. Does man act rationally, or does he act in what he perceives to be his best interests? Man, according to Karl Marx, is a rational animal whose behavior patterns can be improved by removing the temptation of gaining an advantage over his neighbor. One way to gain an advantage over a neighbor is to go into business and make a profit. Remove the possibility of making a profit, and man will no longer be tempted to gain an advantage over his neighbor.

Man, according to Adam Smith, is driven by his self-interests. If the pursuit of his self-interests falls into a category that can be described as being rational, then man is rational. Otherwise, his behavior is irrational. Man is not concerned with whether his behavior can be described in terms of rationality or irrationality. He is concerned with doing what is best for himself. Adam Smith designed an economic system that suited the pursuit of self-interest by human beings quite capable of irrational behavior. Karl Marx designed a rational animal that suited his version of a desirable economic system.

Because the twentieth century has seen the greatest progress made by mankind in such rational activities as technology, science, production methodologies, transportation, communication, and information processing in his history on this planet, it should be its most rational century. Few observers of the historical happenings of the twentieth century would subscribe to that conclusion.

A STEP CLOSER TO A SIMULATION

Consumer Behavior

The rules for consumer behavior with regard to how much of a paycheck will be spent and how much will be saved can be summarized in a question-and-answer format.

- Is unemployment less than 5 percent?
  If so, then the times are good.

• Has unemployment shrunk from the preceding period?
  If so, then the times are good.

If neither of these conditions prevails, the times are deemed bad. Bad times are
a default condition: if times are not good, then they have to be bad.

Good Times Behavior

• Does the individual fall into the lower one-third of the scale measuring material pos-
  sessions?
  If so, the savings rate is zero. This is the Catching Up with the Joneses phenomenon.
• Does the individual have less than six months' worth of savings in terms of the current
  rate of pay?
  If so, determine the savings rate from the following table:

MONTHS OF SAVINGS	PRICE HIKES LESS THAN WAGE INCREASES	PRICE HIKES GREATER THAN WAGE INCREASES
< 2	10%	5%
2–4	6	3
4–6	4	2

If not, then the individual has more than six months' savings, and the following question
must be asked.

• Is the rate of inflation of the price of goods greater than the interest rate on savings?
  If so, the consumer will take 5 percent of the excess savings above six months' worth
  of pay and spend it. This is dissaving in inflationary times.
  If not, the savings rate is 2 percent if price hikes are less than increases in wages, and
  1 percent if price hikes are more than increases in wages.

Bad Times Behavior

The propensity to save can be derived from the following table:

SAVINGS	PRICE OF GOODS		
	Declining	Steady	Increasing
Less than six months	25%	20%	15%
Greater than six months	15	10	5

Then add in two times the difference between the unemployment rate of this
period and the unemployment rate of the preceding period.

Regardless of good or bad times, for those without employment, the spending in any given month is equal to 7.5 percent of the total savings. This is a sharp drop in consumption as compared with the consumption rate of the employed workers.

To illustrate this reduction in consumption, suppose that a worker's pay is $1,000 per month. His savings total $6,000 if he has 6 months' pay in the bank. His spending equals 7.5 percent of $6,000, or $450, which is 45 percent of his normal pay, or a 55 percent reduction in spending, assuming that his savings rate was nil. The reduction in spending increases with each passing month of unemployment as his savings are being consumed. For those with less than 6 months' pay in the bank, the reduction in spending is even more severe.

An Example

A scenario has to be established to demonstrate the nature of spending and saving under various circumstances. Suppose that the island economy located in the midst of a vast sea consists of one thousand heads of households—that is, family units with one working person. For purposes of illustration, suppose that a sixty-month period of time is selected during which employment is initially 550 (45 percent unemployment). As shown in Exhibit 4.1, employment is increasing, achieving full employment around month 30. Good times exist until around month 45. Employment falling below 950, and continuing to fall, ushers in the bad times.

Exhibit 4.1
Employment (1,000 = full employment)

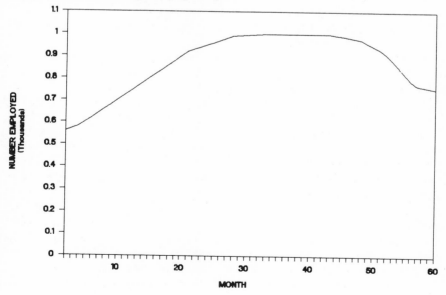

Exhibit 4.2
Monthly Pay

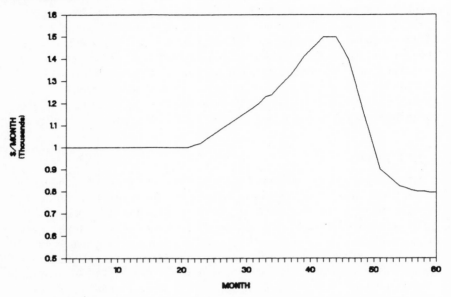

As shown in Exhibit 4.2, monthly pay begins at $1,000 per month and remains at that level until month 20. At that time, the labor market has tightened sufficiently to allow labor to increase its rate of pay, either because of negotiation or because owners of factories are bidding up the price of labor to keep their factories manned at the full complement for maximum production. Actually, the latter precedes the former, but that isn't critical at this juncture. The point is that wage rates are increasing.

All goes well for labor until the downturn starts at around month 45. Labor rates fall precipitously as owners lay off workers. The surplus, or unemployed, workers are eager to get back on the payroll at any wage. The owners of the factories simply fire a few more workers than they originally intended to and hire in lower-cost labor as substitutes. Wages fall in general because workers with higher-paying jobs are not eager to be identified by their higher wages as the next recipients of the pink slip. The wage rate falls quite sharply before it levels out after month 50.

Goods in this island economy are priced in terms of dollars per pound, regardless of their shape, size, or use. The base price for goods starts out at $6.50 per pound and begins to rise at around month 20 as business activity begins to peak. Prices triple around month 40, shortly before the bad times start. Thereafter, prices fall sharply as retailers, wholesalers, and factories attempt to get rid of their excess inventories as quickly as possible. As shown in Exhibit 4.3, prices level out at around $6.00–$6.50 near the end of the sixty-month period.

Interest rates start out at 4 percent per year until a little after month 20 and

Exhibit 4.3
Price per Pound of Goods

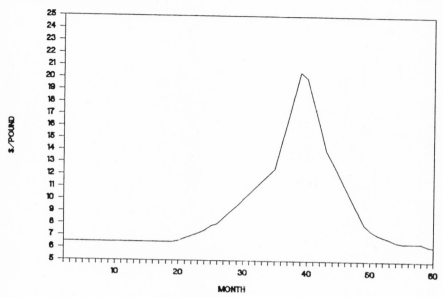

then start ascending as factory owners bid up interest rates in their search for funds to expand the productive capacity of their factories. Interest rates peak around month 40 and then, as shown in Exhibit 4.4, tumble as factory owners cancel further plans to expand productive capacity, causing the demand for funds to disappear.

This scenario of employment, price of goods, wages, and interest rates is arbitrarily constructed to illustrate the shifting savings rate of individuals under different economic conditions. Three individuals are to be examined. Individual A is shy in both savings and possessions, and Individual B is about average, whereas Individual C is relatively affluent. Savings are expressed in dollars, and the amount of possessions is expressed in pounds. It is presumed that those whose possessions weigh in at less than 3,000 pounds are in the lower third of the possessions scale. Those individuals who find themselves in this category will spend all they make in an attempt to catch up with the Joneses.

	SAVINGS IN DOLLARS	POSSESSIONS IN POUNDS
Individual A	$1,000	2,500
Individual B	$3,000	5,000
Individual C	$7,000	9,000

Exhibit 4.4
Interest Rate

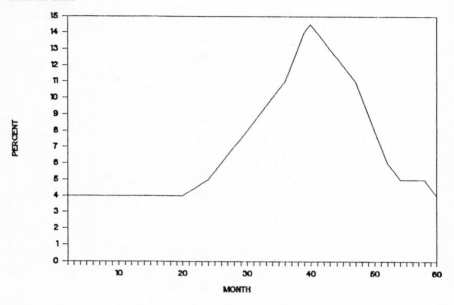

The appendix to this chapter contains the computer program used to generate the following exhibits regarding the behavior of each of these individuals with respect to saving. The program contains a few additional assumptions that have not yet been mentioned. Possessions of individuals are presumed to age, or deteriorate, at a rate of 1 percent per month. This, naturally, simulates the fact that all earthly possessions eventually turn to dust and ashes. Individual A, for instance, receives $1,000 per month and will spend all the money because he is in the lower third on the scale of material possessions. At $6.50 per pound, Individual A can accumulate about 154 pounds of possessions a month. If he possessed 15,400 pounds of possessions, these would decay at a rate of 154 pounds per month. Therefore, his net possessions would remain unchanged at 15,400 pounds per month. This is his equilibrium point in possessing material things. He cannot accumulate more than 15,400 pounds of material possessions, given his wage and the price of goods. In other words, his standard of living in terms of accumulating material goods is determined by the relationship between wages and prices.

Naturally, the higher the price of goods in relation to the basic wage, the lower the equilibrium amount of goods that an individual can accumulate. Suppose that labor managed to bid wages up to about $1,400 per month, and factory owners managed to price their goods at $14 per pound during the upswing of a business cycle. Now a month's salary can buy only 100 pounds of goods. This leads to an interesting situation where workers with higher salaries cannot buy the amount of goods that they could at the start of the cycle. If this condition remained stable long enough, the equilibrium amount of goods that an individual could accumulate would be about 10,000 pounds. One percent decay of 10,000 pounds of goods means that 100 pounds of goods are being consigned to the rubbish heap each month. This is compensated for by new purchases of 100 pounds of goods.

This may seem quite obvious, but there are ramifications that may not seem quite so obvious at this point. If both measures of wages and prices are applicable to full employment, then the society as a whole is producing the same amount of goods regardless of the wage/price relationship. If wages and prices change such that a person's equilibrium point in possessing goods falls from 15,400 pounds to 10,000 pounds, then his standard of living is falling with no commensurate change in the aggregate production of goods. One may ponder where all the extra goods are going that can no longer be purchased by the workers.

Another point to bear in mind is that the rules for savings have been set up in terms of current salaries. As the base monthly salary increases, the amount of savings required to accumulate the six-month nest egg increases accordingly. The worker is looking at his savings relative to his current salary.

Under normal conditions in a free market environment, it is difficult for workers to win pay increases during times of falling prices. Usually, the price of goods and the price of labor more or less coincide in their general direction of movement. If the worker is looking at the purchasing power of his savings in terms of the amount of goods it can buy, he will find himself in the position of having to increase his savings during the latter part of the business cycle to meet the objectives of his nest egg. This is true regardless of whether the nest egg is expressed in terms of a stipulated number of months of base salary at current pay scales or a stipulated number of months of purchasing power at current prices. Relatively simple programming changes can make the nest egg sensitive to either a stipulated number of months of base salary, as included herein, or a stipulated number of months of purchasing power, or a combination of the two.

Individual A

Exhibit 4.5 illustrates the savings rate of Individual A during the sixty-month period. Note that this and all other exhibits start with the second month of the simulation.

The savings rate is zero percent until month 5. Individual A is behind in material possessions. He has to reach 3,000 pounds before he advances beyond the lower third in terms of possessions. With his initial 2,500 pounds of goods decaying at an initial rate of 25 pounds per month and his acquisition of goods at around 154 pounds per months, his net gain is about 130 pounds per month. It requires four or so months for Individual A to cross the threshold of 3,000 pounds.

Up to this point, Individual A sulked with those other unfortunates who make up the lower third of possessors of goods. Now he can hold his head high with

Exhibit 4.5
Savings Rate: Individual A

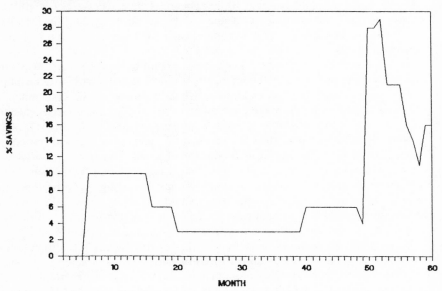

the upper two-thirds. His attention turns to the poor state of his savings, as illustrated in Exhibit 4.6. Note that the period of time covers eighty months. It is presumed that Individual A, and the others under scrutiny, lose their jobs in month 61.

Individual A's savings appear flat, although the money is earning interest, until month 5 when he starts to save 10 percent of his current salary ($100 per month). This continues for 10 months until his savings exceed $2,000. With 2 months' savings, his savings rate falls to 6 percent until month 20 when it falls to 3 percent. Under the established rules, one has to conclude that the increase in the price of goods in month 20 must have been higher than any wage increase. This would cause the savings rate to fall by half as workers speed up their purchases to beat future price increases. A review of the data base shows that month 20 is the first month of price increases. Wage rates are still $1,000 per month at that time.

This condition in which price increases are greater than wage increases persists until month 40 when savings go back to 6 percent. Again, a review of the data base shows that wages are now going up faster than prices. In fact, in month 40, wages are still going up as prices begin to decline.

Obviously, something big happened at month 50. Unemployment exceeded 5 percent for the first time, and the psychological impact of good times changing to bad times causes individuals to scrutinize their nest eggs and conclude that they are inadequate. The fact that the nest eggs were considered adequate a short

Exhibit 4.6
Savings: Individual A

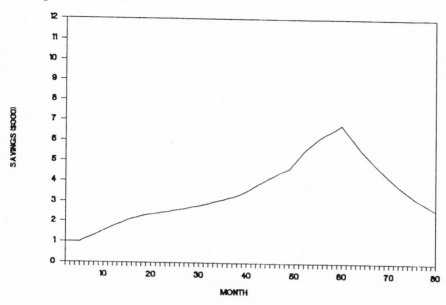

while before has no bearing on their change of perception. They are not adequate now as layoffs exceed what is deemed acceptable for a good times mentality. Uncertainty about future employment and fear of further layoffs rapidly replace the complacency and confidence of the good times. If one considers the change of attitude too abrupt, a transitional period of ambivalence can be built into the simulation. The purpose here is not to set up a final model but to illustrate the possibility of constructing a simulation of human behavior in terms of spending and saving.

The base savings rate for an individual with less than 6 months' savings during a time of declining prices is 25 percent. The additional fear aspect is two times the difference in unemployment between the present and the preceding months. In month 49, 960 were employed. Thus, the unemployed numbered 40, or 4 percent of the total population of one thousand. In month 50, 945 were employed. This works out to 5.5 percent unemployment. The difference between the present and the preceding months' unemployment is 1.5 percent, which, when multiplied by two, provides a fear increment of 3 percent. Added to the 25 percent this yields 28 percent.

For month 51, the calculation is similar. The unemployment is now 7 percent, compared to 5.5 percent in the previous month. The difference of 1.5 percent, when multiplied by two and added to the base savings rate of 25 percent, yields a savings rate of 28 percent. For month 52, the two respective unemployment rates are 9 percent and 7 percent. The difference, when multiplied by two and added to the base rate of 25 percent, yields a savings rate of 29 percent.

Increased saving starting in month 50 is apparent in Exhibit 4.6. Total savings are close to $6,000 by month 53. The monthly wage rate has fallen to $850 in month 53. Because the amount of savings is now in excess of 6 months' of current monthly pay, the base savings rate falls to 15 percent. Unemployment is 12 percent in month 53, and 9 percent in month 52. The difference is 3 percent, resulting in a fear factor of 6 percent. This, added to 15 percent, yields a savings rate of 21 percent for month 53. Another 3 percent rise in unemployment rates for months 54 and 55 yields two more months with a savings rate of 21 percent.

One can argue that the blind following of what appeared to be a reasonable set of rules doesn't seem to make a great deal of sense. The world is falling apart, and the individual cuts his savings rate because falling wages (or falling prices, had the model been set up that way) have increased the value of his savings in terms of employment (or, with appropriate programming changes, in terms of months of purchasing power). Would an individual actually cut his savings rate just because falling prices of goods have made his savings worth more in terms of purchasing power? Or would he watch the growing unemployment lines and shudder at the thought of increasing his purchasing activity, regardless of the growing purchasing power of his savings? Perhaps purely mechanical rules for describing human behavior are not entirely appropriate.

Anyway, continuing the process for month 56, prices are steady with regard to the previous month. The base savings rate falls to 10 percent. Unemployment is 21 percent in month 56 and 18 percent in month 55. Two times the difference is 6 percent, which, when added to 10 percent, yields a savings rate of 16 percent. Prices are still steady in month 57 with a difference of 2 percent in unemployment rates. This generates a savings rate of 14 percent. The same situation holds for month 58, except that the difference in unemployment rates is 0.5 percent. This, when multiplied by two and added to the 10 percent base rate, ends up with a savings rate of 11 percent. In months 59 and 60, unemployment continues to increase at 0.5 percent per month, but prices have resumed their decline. From the rules that had been established, the base savings rate increases to 15 percent, plus 1 percent for the fear increment, resulting in a savings rate of 16 percent.

Individual A loses his job at month 61. With no source of income, he begins to make withdrawals from his savings account at a rate of 7.5 percent of the outstanding balance. Bearing in mind that his last monthly paycheck was $795, of which he was spending 84 percent, or a little less than $670, his new spending pattern is shown in Exhibit 4.7.

The continuing decline in spending reflects the drawing down of Individual A's savings account. No dissavings, or withdrawals, took place during the good times prior to month 60 because he never exceeded 6 months' savings during that period of time.

Exhibit 4.7
Dissavings: Individual A

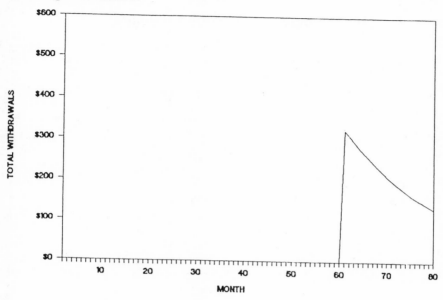

The savings rate in Exhibit 4.5 can be criticized for any number of reasons. One might not like the nature of the rules. However, there is little problem in changing the nature of the rules to fit the description of how people behave from the point of view of spending and saving. However, no matter what rule is adopted, for savings to remain exactly at 10 percent, or 3 percent, or any other arbitrary value, for relatively long periods of time with no monthly variation is quite unhumanlike.

A random factor can be easily built into the computer program to create variability of savings on a month-to-month basis. This could be viewed as introducing noise. A random number varies between zero and one, and the random factor is a random number applied to a factor of 2.5 percent. This is added, or subtracted, from the base savings rate. Over the period of months 6 through 15 when the savings rate was 10 percent, the month-to-month savings rate is permitted to vary between 7.5 percent and 12.5 percent. The average savings rate is still about 10 percent, but its month-to-month fluctuations reflect human variability in personal decisions on how much to spend and how much to save. The random factor in the program in the appendix varied with the base savings rate.

Individual B

Individual B is in better shape than Individual A. He starts out with $3,000 in savings and 5,000 pounds of possessions. With an initial base wage of $1,000

Exhibit 4.8
Percentage of Savings with Random Factor: Individual A

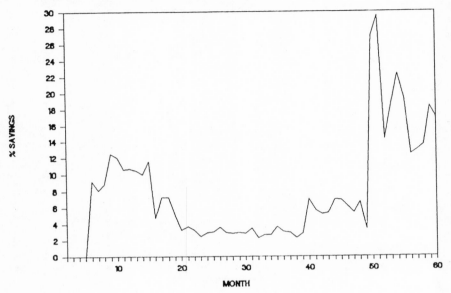

per month, he has the equivalent of three months' wages in savings. His initial savings rate is 6 percent, as shown in Exhibit 4.9.

This continues until month 16 when his savings, as shown in Exhibit 4.10, exceed $4,000, or four months' worth of wages. Then the savings rate drops to 4 percent.

The savings rate is cut in half to 2 percent in month 20 as prices begin to rise with flat wages. This condition persists until month 30. The wage level is increasing and reaches $1,160 per month at this time. Total savings are now worth less than four months' wages, and the savings rate would normally revert back to 6 percent. However, because prices of goods are rising faster than wages at this time, the savings rate is cut in half to 3 percent to reflect consumers' speeding up their purchases before the next price rise takes effect. The savings rate jumps to 6 percent at month 40 as prices are no longer rising faster than wages; in fact, prices are beginning to decline at this time. Then it is back to 4 percent in month 44 because savings are in excess of $6,000, which is equivalent to four months of present wages ($1,500 per month).

Both wages and prices are declining in month 49, but prices are falling faster than wages. Savings should actually increase because the incentive is to postpone purchases to take advantage of even lower prices with respect to wages in the future. Additional programming steps should have been inserted to compare the larger of two negative numbers to ensure that the savings pattern of consumers

Exhibit 4.9
Savings Rate: Individual B

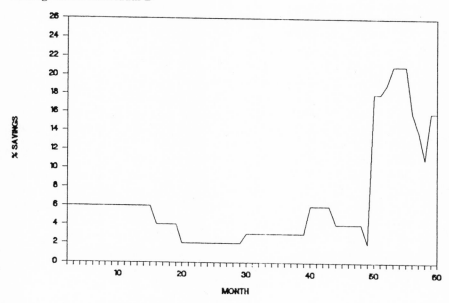

Exhibit 4.10
Savings: Individual B

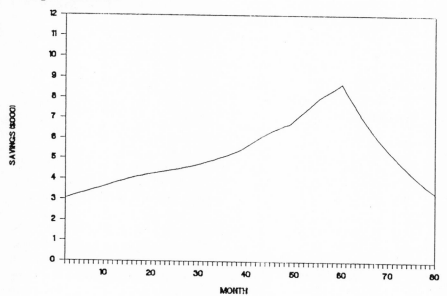

is consistently applied during times of increasing wages and prices and times of declining wages and prices.

This was not done for a specific reason. Although the rules appear straightforward, it should be starting to become apparent that it is difficult to justify their application under all circumstances. For instance, as wages increase, would people be expected to increase their savings rate as their savings, expressed in terms of months of current pay, fall below six months' worth of pay? Rising labor rates are usually prevalent in the latter stages of a business cycle. This is a time of general ebullience, which is hardly the time to increase the savings rate. Hence, one can rapidly find oneself on the defensive, attempting to justify what started out to be a straightforward, and sensible, set of assumptions on human behavior for each stage of the business cycle.

It is not the purpose of simulation to state categorically that humans behave according to a stipulated set of mechanical rules. If one wanted to cast human behavior into a hard and fixed set of rules, then that person had better be prepared to spend a great deal of effort attempting to justify the rules under every possible circumstance. Simulation does require that mechanical rules be set up to determine the general parameters of behavior, but care must be taken that these rules are not too rigid, or their structure too formal, as they are here.

To complete the picture, month 50 is the transition from good times to bad. Wages have already fallen to $1,000, and with something under $7,000 in the bank, Individual B has more than 6 months' savings. His base savings rate is 15 percent. The difference in unemployment between months 50 and 49 is 1.5 percent. Doubling that and adding it to the base rate of 15 percent yields the savings rate of 18 percent. The remaining savings rates can be derived in a manner similar to that used for Individual A.

Exhibit 4.11 shows the dissavings of Individual B. There are no dissavings during the good times because his savings did not exceed 6 months' worth of salary. Individual B's spending after losing his job in month 61 is higher than Individual A's because of the larger amount of money that had been saved.

Exhibit 4.12 shows the savings rate with a random, or noise, factor to simulate variations in savings on a month-to-month basis.

Individual C

Individual C is relatively well off with initial savings of $7,000 and 9,000 pounds of material possessions. His savings exceed 6 months' worth of wages. With flat prices and wages, his initial savings rate is 2 percent, as shown in Exhibit 4.13.

This continues until month 20, when the price for goods increases from $6.50 to $6.60. On a monthly basis, this is equivalent to 1.5 percent price inflation. On an annual basis, this is 18 percent price inflation, which greatly exceeds the 4 percent interest on savings. Thus, there is an incentive to dissave, or withdraw from savings, and turn the funds into tangible goods, the prices of which are

Exhibit 4.11
Dissavings: Individual B

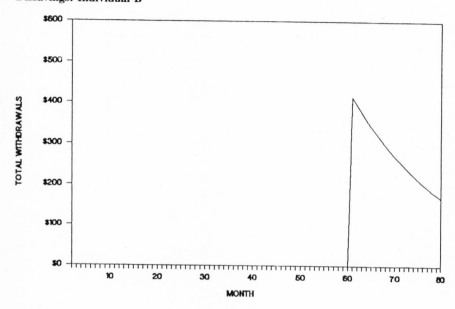

Exhibit 4.12
Percentage of Savings with Random Factor: Individual B

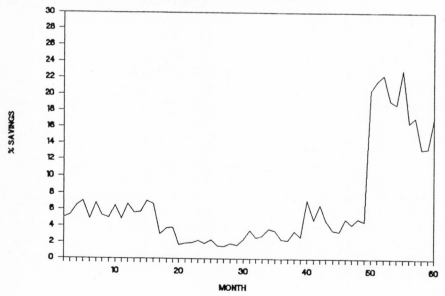

Exhibit 4.13
Savings Rate: Individual C

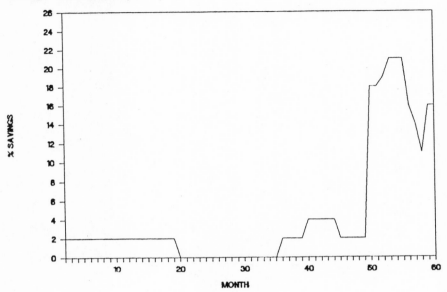

going up faster than the interest earned on the savings. Total savings, from Exhibit 4.14, is about $7,800 at month 20.

The basic wage scale is $1,000 at month 20. The difference between the total savings ($7,800) and 6 months' worth of wages ($6,000) is $1,800. Five percent of $1,800 is $90. Dissavings are illustrated in Exhibit 4.15.

Dissavings are reduced to nothing by month 36 by increases in the base wage, which increases the amount of savings that is equivalent to 6 months' pay. This reduces dissavings markedly and is the consequence of arbitrarily applying a mechanical rule. Dissavings can be seen by noting the declining savings in Exhibit 4.14 during this period of time.

Also at month 36, savings are no longer equivalent to 6 months' pay. The base savings rate is 4 percent, which is then cut in half to compensate for the fact that price hikes are exceeding the rate of increase of wages. Month 40 marks the beginning of price declines, and the savings rate reverts to 4 percent. Month 45 marks the start of declining wages and prices, as discussed before. The savings rates of both individual B and Individual C are the same after month 50 because both have more than 6 months' worth of savings. A comparison of Exhibit 4.12 with Exhibit 4.16 below shows that the random, or noise, factor does change the savings rates between Individuals A and B, although the average over many individuals would remain essentially unchanged.

Exhibit 4.14
Savings: Individual C

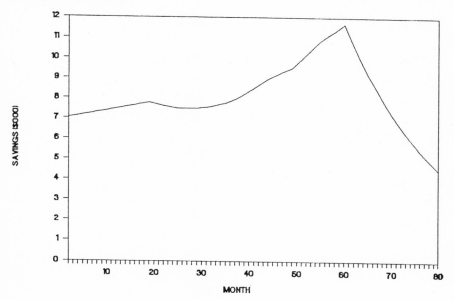

CONCLUDING REMARKS

The program used to generate the savings rates is illustrative as a means of creating saving rates for consumers under varying business conditions using mechanical rules. In some respects, the model is too mechanical. The addition of a random, or a noise, factor simulates the fact that no two individuals act exactly alike, even when the same mechanical rule applies.

The problem with mechanical rules is that they can give conflicting signals, or not easily justifiable conclusions, under rapidly changing conditions in the business cycle. This might necessitate additional commentary to justify the existence of the rules themselves. Another problem is that no two individuals follow the same set of rules in determining their savings rate, although in the aggregate, there may be similarities in behavior for groups of individuals.

In reviewing the exhibits pertaining to the savings rate with the inclusion of noise (Exhibits 4.8, 4.12, and 4.16), one is drawn to the conclusion that the mechanical rules can be relaxed, although not eliminated. It is apparent that the subtle nuances of how mechanical rules can be applied to shifting circumstances are being absorbed in the noise, or randomness, built into the model. Or to proceed one step farther, a better simulation might be one that is less rule oriented and more noise oriented.

Exhibit 4.15
Dissavings: Individual C

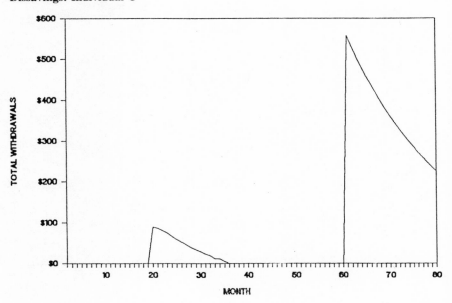

Exhibit 4.16
Percentage of Savings with Random Factor: Individual C

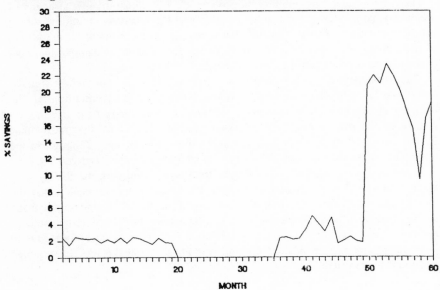

APPENDIX

The program listed was used to illustrate the nature of modeling the behaviorial characteristics of consumers. Statements 30–180 are an internal data base of total employment, monthly payscales, price per pound for goods, and interest rates, as illustrated in Exhibits 4.1 through 4.4. Statements 200–214 permit the entry of savings and possessions for Individuals A, B, and C. In statement 250, each month is examined as to whether good or bad times prevail. Starting in statement 260, each of the three individuals is examined to determine his savings rate.

Good times occur either when total employment is above 950 (statement 270) or when employment is increasing (statement 280). Statement 400 is the start of the good times section. If a person has less than 3,000 pounds of possessions, his savings rate is set at zero (statements 400 and 410). In statements 420–455, the savings rate as a function of the number of months' worth of wages saved is determined. Statements 460 and 465 compare the rates of increase of prices and wages. If prices are going up faster than wages, then the savings rate is cut in half in statement 470. Statements 480–490 handle the situation for dissaving when savings exceed 6 months' worth of wages and when the rate of inflation of goods exceeds the interest rate on savings.

Bad times are covered in statements 305–385. Statement 325 can be entered only if there are no price changes and if savings are less than 6 months' worth of salary. Statement 330 handles the situation when there are no price changes and savings are more than 6 months' worth of pay. Statements 340–350 perform the same function for increasing prices, and statements 360–370 do the same for decreasing prices. All these statements lead to statement 380 which compares the unemployment of the present month with that of the proceding month and adds twice the difference to the savings rate.

Both bad times and good times end up at statement 500. Statements 500–555 are the noise-generating statements. Removing ''Y=0'' in statement 500 introduces the random factor, or creates the noise. The final version of the program determining savings rates will depend more on controlling the variability of the savings rate than on establishing detailed mechanical rules.

Appendix 4.1

```
10 REM NAME OF PROGRAM IS CH4
15 OPEN "O",#1,"CH4F"
20 DIM D(100,10):DIM P(5,5)
30 FOR I=1 TO 60
40 FOR J=1 TO 4
50 READ D(I,J)
52 DATA 550,1000,6.5,4,560,1000,6.5,4,570,1000,6.5,4
58 DATA 580,1000,6.5,4,600,1000,6.5,4,620,1000,6.5,4
64 DATA 640,1000,6.5,4,660,1000,6.5,4,680,1000,6.5,4
70 DATA 700,1000,6.5,4,720,1000,6.5,4,740,1000,6.5,4
76 DATA 760,1000,6.5,4,780,1000,6.5,4,800,1000,6.5,4
82 DATA 820,1000,6.5,4,840,1000,6.5,4,860,1000,6.5,4
88 DATA 880,1000,6.5,4,900,1000,6.6,4,920,1000,6.8,4.25
94 DATA 930,1010,7,4.5,940,1020,7.2,4.75,950,1040,7.4,5
100 DATA 960,1060,7.8,5.5,970,1080,8,6,980,1100,8.5,6.5
106 DATA 990,1120,9,7,992,1140,9.5,7.5,994,1160,10,8
112 DATA 996,1180,10.5,8.5,998,1200,11,9,1000,1230,11.5,9.5
120 DATA 1000,1240,12,10,1000,1270,12.5,10.5
126 DATA 1000,1300,14.5,11,1000,1330,16.5,12
132 DATA 1000,1370,18.5,13,1000,1410,20.5,14,1000,1440,20,14.5
138 DATA 1000,1470,18,14,1000,1500,16,13.5,1000,1500,14,13
144 DATA 995,1500,13,12.5,990,1450,12,12,985,1400,11,11.5
150 DATA 980,1300,10,11,975,1200,9,10,960,1100,8,9
156 DATA 945,1000,7.5,8,930,900,7.2,7,910,875,7,6
162 DATA 880,850,6.8,5.5,850,825,6.6,5,820,815,6.5,5
168 DATA 790,805,6.5,5,770,800,6.5,5,765,800,6.5,5
174 DATA 760,795,6.3,4.5,755,795,6.2,4
180 NEXT:NEXT
200 PRINT:PRINT "THE LOWER THIRD PERCENTILE OF MATERIAL POSSESSIONS"
202 PRINT "IS CONSIDERED TO BE LESS THAN 3000 POUNDS OF THINGS":PRINT
204 PRINT "FOR EACH OF THREE INDIVIDUALS, ENTER POSSESSION OF THINGS IN"
206 PRINT "POUNDS, ENTER SAVINGS WHERE EACH $1000 REPRESENTS ONE MONTH'S"
208 PRINT "SAVINGS":PRINT:FOR I=1 TO 3:PRINT "INDIVIDUAL: ";I
212 INPUT "SAVINGS IN DOLLARS: ";P(I,1)
214 INPUT "POSSESSIONS IN POUNDS: ";P(I,2):PRINT:NEXT
250 FOR T=2 TO 60
260 FOR I=1 TO 3
270 IF D(T,1)>=950 THEN 400
280 IF D(T,1)-D(T-1,1)>0 THEN 400
305 IF D(T,3)>D(T-1,3) THEN 340
310 IF D(T,3)<D(T-1,3) THEN 360
320 IF P(I,1)>6*D(T,2) THEN 330
325 S=.2:GOTO 380
330 S=.1:GOTO 380
340 IF P(I,1)>6*D(T,2) THEN 350
345 S=.15:GOTO 380
350 S=.05:GOTO 380
360 IF P(I,1)>6*D(T,2) THEN 370
365 S=.25:GOTO 380
370 S=.15
380 D=0:U1=(1000-D(T,1))/1000:U2=(1000-D(T-1,1))/1000
385 S=S+2*(U1-U2):GOTO 500
```

```
400 D=0:IF P(I,2)<3000 THEN 410 ELSE 420
410 S=0:GOTO 500
420 IF P(I,1)>6*D(T,2) THEN 445
425 IF P(I,1)>4*D(T,2) THEN 450
430 IF P(I,1)>2*D(T,2) THEN 455
440 S=.1:GOTO 460
445 S=.02:GOTO 460
450 S=.04:GOTO 460
455 S=.06
460 V1=(D(T,3)-D(T-1,3))/D(T-1,3):V2=(D(T,2)-D(T-1,2))/D(T-1,2)
465 IF V1>V2 THEN 470 ELSE 475
470 S=S/2
475 IF P(I,1)<6*D(T,2) THEN 500
480 V1=12*V1
485 IF V1>D(T,4)/100 THEN 490 ELSE 500
490 S=0:D=.05*(P(I,1)-6*D(T,2)):P(I,1)=P(I,1)-D
500 X=RND(X):Y=RND(Y):Y=0
505 IF X<.5 THEN 510 ELSE 515
510 Z=-1:GOTO 520
515 Z=1
520 IF S>=.2 THEN 540
530 S=S+Z*.25*Y*S:GOTO 550
540 S=S+Z*.15*Y*S
550 IF S<0 THEN 555 ELSE 560
555 S=0
560 P(I,1)=P(I,1)+S*D(T,2)+D(T,4)*P(I,1)/1200
570 Q=((1-S)*D(T,2)+D)/(D(T,3)):P(I,2)=.99*P(I,2)+Q
580 S1=D(T,1):S2=D(T,2):S3=D(T,3):S4=D(T,4)
585 S(I)=100*S:E(I)=D:M(I)=P(I,1)/1000:N(I)=P(I,2)/1000
590 NEXT
600 WRITE#1,T,S1,S2,S3,S4,S(1),E(1),M(1),N(1),S(2),

E(2),M(2),N(2),S(3),E(3),M(3),N(3)
610 NEXT
620 FOR T=61 TO 80
625 FOR I=1 TO 3
630 S=0:X=RND(X):X=0:D=.05+X*.05:Q=D*P(I,1)/(D(60,3))
635 P(I,1)=P(I,1)+P(I,1)*(D(60,4)/1200)-D*P(I,1)
640 P(I,2)=.99*P(I,2)+Q:S(I)=S:E(I)=D*P(I,1):M(I)=P(I,1)/1000:N(I)=P(I,2)/1000
645 NEXT
650 WRITE#1,T,S,S,S,S,S(1),E(1),M(1),N(1),S(2),

E(2),M(2),N(2),S(3),E(3),M(3),N(3)
660 NEXT
670 CLOSE#1:END
```

5

Man as Producer

Forecasting what man does as consumer is one facet of human behavior. The alter ego of man needs to be examined: man as producer. Man as consumer and man as producer do not exhibit the same characteristics of behavior. In fact, it is amazing, in viewing man as producer, that he is also the same person clothed as man as consumer.

Man is a highly complex organism with an innate capacity for extreme emotions, such as love and hate. Dramatizing, or exploiting, love-hate emotions is daily fare on soap operas and a common theme in more serious literature. No one claims that man is any less of a man because he can feel such a dichotomy of emotional response toward people in his life. Some maintain that experiencing emotions is what life is all about—one hasn't lived until he has ridden the roller coaster of being wined, dined, wooed, and rejected. Others argue that a perfectly logical, cool, collected, unemotional, detached-from-life individual can be quite boring as a personality, and potentially dangerous as a leader.

A similar dichotomy of behavior exhibits itself when man as consumer becomes man as producer. Everyone must have experienced, or observed, the metamorphosis of character when man as consumer becomes man as producer, or buyer becomes seller, or tenant becomes landlord. In one case, the economic chameleon is seeking the lowest cost for whatever he is trying to purchase. A split second later, the color changes, and the economic chameleon is seeking the highest price for whatever he is trying to sell.

An example is a person looking for a place to rent. The economic chameleon finds himself playing the role of a consumer. As a tenant, he is buying a place to rest his head. Day and night he prowls the apartment complexes, reads the ads, and does all that he can to obtain the lowest rent and the best terms for the type of apartment he has in mind. He signs a two-year lease. A few months later, he is transferred to another city and needs to sublet his apartment. The economic chameleon now finds himself playing the role of a producer. As a landlord, he is selling a place for someone else to rest his head. His empathy toward those knocking on his door seeking the lowest possible rent will be much like what he experienced from landlords when he was knocking on their doors. As much as he disliked the attitude of landlords during his quest for the lowest rent, he will exhibit the same behavior characteristics when potential tenants knock on his door.

Before, a low rental was in his best interests; now, it is not. The economic chamelon known as man has no problems with this dual role, no inner conflict, no sleepless nights. The economic man relentlessly pursues his best interests with far less difficulty than he, as a human, has when grappling with the inordinate swings of his emotions.

MAXIMIZATION OF PROFITS

Man as producer is viewed from the perspective of owner or manager of an enterprise organized supposedly for the objective of maximizing profits. An owner of a factory attempts to maximize profits to aggrandize his personal worth. From time to time, he measures the value of his worth by totaling up the balance of his bank accounts.

The motivating force behind a manager's decisions is more complex. A manager attempts to maximize profits to the extent necessary for his self-preservation. From time to time, he must pass muster with the board of directors, which, presumably, totals up the corporate bank accounts and judges the performance of the manager accordingly. Both the owner and the manager behave in a fashion that best serves their interests, which means that they are serving their self-interests.

However, complexities abound when one attempts to characterize the behavior of people, even in such simple terms as maximizing profits. Profit is the multiplication of unit gross margin by volume where gross margin is the difference between the selling price of a product and its variable cost of production. There are two principal ways to maximize profits. One owner may price his goods high to achieve maximum profits on unit gross margin, while another may price his goods low to achieve maximum profits on volume. The same profit results whether one has a high gross margin and a low volume or a low gross margin and a high volume. Obviously, the simple objective of maximizing profits can result in far different decisions with regard to pricing.

Similarly, one businessman may think of maximizing profits in the short term, while another may take a long-term view that may extend decades into the future. If the owner is thinking of passing his business on to his heirs, he may even think in terms of generations. Two owners may have the same simple objective of maximizing profits, but their investment decisions can be far different. One may attempt to maximize profits by investing in hula hoops and other items that appeal to the whims of a fickle public. The other may plant trees that will not be harvested for decades. Both are maximizing profits in their eyes—but their investment decisions are hardly comparable.

Maximizing profits even in the same business can yield a fruitful harvest of vastly different decisions. From the point of view of maximizing profits, one can adopt measures that tend to minimize labor costs by hiring and firing as needed. Alternatively, one can do all he can to maximize the contribution of labor to the productivity of the company by fostering worker loyalty to the company. Fostering worker loyalty implies an obligation not to dismiss workers unless conditions are *in extremis*. There is also an underlying assumption that the workers are receiving a fair day's pay for, hopefully, a fair day's work. The simple objective of maximizing profits can lead a manager to take a position on either end of the labor policy spectrum—in terms of pay, working conditions, and the participation of labor in the operations of a company—with equal ease.

Likewise, from the point of view of maximizing profits, one can end up with a decision to minimize material costs by sacrificing product quality and repeat business, or by fostering customer loyalty by building a quality product. In the latter case, the product will have a higher cost of production because of its superior material standards and a lower gross margin if its price were the same as the price of the lower-quality product. Profit maximization is achieved by repeat business from satisfied consumers. In the former case, the manager is attempting to maximize profits by sacrificing product quality in order to gain a higher unit gross margin. His hope to maximize profits depends on consumers' having a short memory span. The other manager has the same objective with regard to profit, but he is depending on a longer memory span.

It should be clear from all this that the simple objective of maximizing profits can yield a wide range of decisions on investment, marketing, and operational strategies. One can end up with an infinite variety of businesses for investment possibilities. A similar diversity of decisions can result in marketing with regard to pricing, product quality, and customer loyalty and in operating a company with regard to labor policies, material standards, and quality control—all in the name of maximizing profits.

OWNERSHIP VERSUS MANAGEMENT

Nevertheless, regardless of the nature of the decisions on where to invest and how to manage the investment, man as producer is motivated, to some small extent, by the desire to maximize profits. In this regard, an owner of a company should be a less complex personality to understand than a manager of a company. There is a closer link between an owner and the profitability of a company because the personal and company bank accounts are virtually one and the same. Therefore, one would expect that an owner's decisions should have some tenuous association with the objective of maximizing profits.

A manager, on the other hand, presents a more complex case in terms of the analysis of human behavior because he usually does not stand to gain as much as an owner from the generation of profits. A manager may receive a bonus that is tied to profits, but the bonus may be a pittance in comparison with the gross profitability of the company. More often than not, a manager is a salaried individual representing the interests of the actual owners of the company. For most large companies, the actual ownership is in the hands of the owners of the shares of stock. The shareholders are interested that a company does what it can to maximize profits. The interests of the shareholders are represented by the board of directors.

If there are individuals with major shareholdings in the company, and if these individuals take an active interest in the operation of the company, then the board of directors may act in the interests of the shareholders. Because the board of directors faces re-election from time to time, major and actively involved shareholders have the opportunity to examine the board members' performance as overseers of a company and cast their votes based on their pleasure, or displeasure, with the results of their review.

Usually, however, the shareholdings of the company are widely diffused, with the myriad of small shareholders taking no real interest in the management of the company. Institutional investors, such as mutual funds and pension funds, are usually passive shareholders. If they do not like how a company is being managed, they tend to liquidate their positions rather than voice their concern to pressure the board of directors to take action. With shareholders in general taking a passive role in expressing their dissatisfaction, other than by selling their holdings, the board of directors may be inclined to represent its own interests rather than the interests of the shareholders.

This may be particularly true if the board room is packed by members of management. Then the interests of the shareholders are served as long as the interests of the shareholders, the desires of management, and the wishes of the outside members of the board are in accord. Like the eclipse of the sun, which occurs when the sun, moon, and earth are lined up just right, there have been recorded instances in corporate history when the interests of the shareholders, management, and outside board members were in agreement—and some will argue that this occurs with about the same frequency as a solar eclipse.

In the operation of a firm with widely diffused shareholdings, the board of directors is not answerable to calls from major shareholders. There are, in fact, no major shareholders to blast the board for not acting in the shareholders' best interest—which, presumably, is the maximization of profits. The shareholders do vote for the proposed slate of members of the board of directors. They may even have the right to vote against a slate of proposed members. However, there is no effective way for a diffuse population of small shareholders to propose an alternative listing of candidates that would give any real meaning to an election of the board of directors. To demonstrate this point, all one has to do is buy one hundred shares in any company and request a listing of shareholders from the company for the purpose of proposing an alternative slate for the next election of members to the board. Even if one is successful in obtaining such a listing, the real effort is yet to begin. Usually the expense and pain necessary to unseat an entrenched board of directors are reserved for proxy fights associated with unfriendly takeovers and mergers.

Many boards of directors are heavily peppered with members of management. The members of the board and management may own virtually no stock in the company other than a token number of shares for a little window dressing on the annual report. Unhappiness with the low price of the stock on the part of disgruntled shareholders is not of vital concern to the members of the board, and to management, from the point of view of personal wealth. One might argue that, under these circumstances, the board of directors is not accountable directly to shareholders and that the interests of shareholders in maximizing profits are not being served.

TOP MANAGEMENT AND PROFIT MAXIMIZATION

In addressing this issue of what motivates the upper echelons of corporate power, it should be noted that boards of directors are not expected to run a company. Their purpose is to review the performance of top management and jostle the seating arrangement around the corporate table. Even here, it may be difficult for the board to take action against management if the board is stuffed with members who also hold top managerial positions. If management is heavily represented on the board of directors, then the outside directors (those members of the board not on the management team) may be beholden to management for their selection as board members. If the selection of outside board members is based on a recommendation from management, and if the board is partially made up of members of management, it may be asking too much for the board of directors to carry out its responsibility to review management performance with impartiality.

Furthermore, it is virtually impossible for a diverse number of shareholders to meet for the purpose of selecting an alternate slate of candidates to unseat the current or proposed board of directors. The end result of all this is that there is no real mechanism for shareholders to ensure that their interests in profit maximization are being pursued. This being the case, which it is for many companies, then top management may begin to focus on things that are not apt to be described as serving the best interests of the shareholders. For instance, top-level managers may be more interested in maintaining their position, their perks, their plush carpeted offices, their company-supplied top-of-the-line automobiles, and their ego-massaging bevy of sycophants than in maximizing profits. After all, maximizing profits can be real work, a real challenge to their competence to manage.

With disinterested shareholders and a friendly board of directors, maximizing profits may become of tangential importance to top management. The appearance of taking action to maximize profits and the making of some amount of profits may simply be requisites for maintaining one's position. After this hurdle has been overcome, then top management can turn to the things that really matter:

position grabbing, protecting turf, covering one's rear, protecting one's flank, watching for frontal assaults, and maintaining six-figure incomes.

Life is short. Relatively few make it to the top of the corporate pyramid, and many more want to reach the top than there are seats available. In the great game of corporate Musical Chairs, one aspiring manager after another is left out in the cold, with only one winner emerging at the end. Another managerial game is King of the Hill. Only one person wins in the game of King of the Hill. And it is much more fun being the single king on the top of the hill than being part of the multitude of struggling aspirants at the bottom of the hill. The prestige of being on top, the exercise of the prerogatives of power and position, may be what the management game is really all about.

MIDDLE MANAGEMENT AND PROFIT MAXIMIZATION

In the game of Musical Chairs, the winner lasts as long as it takes to set up the chairs, turn the record over, and play a new round. And in the game of King of the Hill, one remains king for as long as he can fend off new attacks. There is a transient aspect to positions of power that is true in children's games of fun and in adults' games of life. Nevertheless, whether a king is attempting to maximize the profits of his company or trying to maximize his longevity in power, somewhere in the king's organization, there are middle-level managers. These aspirants to power have not yet risen in position to dream of toppling the king. They are still in the Musical Chairs stage of development. While biding their time until they are in a high enough position to try and topple the king, which may never come about for some, they have to think about something else to justify their jobs. And there is no better justification for a job than thinking about the profitability of the company. What this means is that, while top management and the members of the board may be taking a more tangential view of profitability, there is someone in the organization looking at the price of goods in the marketplace, the cost of making goods on the factory floor, and the inventory of finished goods in the warehouse. That person is making, or recommending, some important decisions:

1. Expanding or contracting production
2. Raising or lowering prices
3. Building a new plant or closing an existing one

These are certainly important decisions if one is a worker employed by this company. These are also important decisions that the king must approve or disapprove—even if he is rubber stamping a henchman's recommendation. These decisions become even more important for the king if he turns out to be wrong. In the game of King of the Hill, as played in the corporate world, wrong decisions can be likened to a concerted and coordinated shove by all to unseat the king. His chances of withstanding the onslaught are nil. Right decisions can be likened to shoving the king from two opposite directions. He might be toppled, but his chances of survival are far greater. Right decisions may or may not preserve the tenure of a king, but one wrong decision can bring about a quick change of reign. Maybe this is the connection between top management and profitability. Maybe we ought to abandon top management as a font of meaningful decisions on the matter of profitability and get down to the nitty-gritty level of middle managers who run the factories.

The question is, How do middle-level managers make their decisions? Perhaps these decisions can be better appreciated by setting up a scenario and observing the behavior patterns of a manager of a factory. Let us suppose that the factory is part of a corporate empire in which top management is ensconced in a big city office and middle management runs the factories located somewhere in the hinterlands, far from the lights, fun, and frolic of the big city. In large firms, members of top management do not run factories in an operational sense. They review the results of those who do run the factories, and approve, or disapprove, major expenditures such as building a new factory. Other than that, the factory manager is pretty much on his own if for no other reason than that the hinterlands are not high on the list of desirable watering holes for those who have made it to the top.

Suppose that we are watching a middle-level manager of a factory that makes widgets along with an assortment of other products. This middle-level manager has both production and marketing responsibilities and reports to a president who is held accountable for the overall operation of the factory by those in the corporate headquarters. Let us also suppose that widgets are widgets. Widgets made by this factory and widgets made by competitive firms are essentially identical. There is a market price for widgets: $10 each. Experience has shown that the production/marketing manager can comfortably handle fluctuations of demand for widgets by having one month's supply in the factory's warehouse.

Each day, the production/marketing manager peers into the warehouse as he walks to his office. He cannot help but notice that the pile of widgets is getting smaller day by day. Sitting at his desk, computer printouts of the daily production of widgets and the daily orders from customers for widgets tell him the same story. The factory manager doesn't have to be a genius to decide that maybe it is time to expand production.

This does not mean that he can necessarily raise the price of widgets. One of the benefits of competition to consumers is that competing firms will expand production to meet growing demand without raising their prices as long as there is spare production capacity and sufficient levels of finished goods in inventory. One reason for this is that production managers have a predilection to run their locomotives full blast and are not always concerned about the price they are receiving as long as the price is above costs. Their satisfaction in life is watching the plant belch huge plumes of smoke while truckloads of widgets pass through the portals of the warehouse on their way to market.

The other, and probably more important, reason why it is difficult to raise prices under these conditions is that the marketing people love to see a competitor increase his price for widgets when there is spare capacity in their factories. There is no better, and easier, way to increase the market share of their product than by advertising their lower (unchanged) price for widgets. Actually, advertising is hardly necessary. The consumer can be depended on to do what is best for his self-interest. He will not pay $11 for the Brand X widget while the essentially identical Brand Y widget is right next to it on the shelf for $10. Nothing pleases marketing more than to grab a nice slice of the widget market pie at the expense of an erstwhile competitor.

The only time the managers in the widget making industry can get away with raising the price of widgets is when all the widget factories are operating at full blast and the inventories of widgets in the warehouses are still continuing to shrink. The smaller the inventories and the faster the rate at which they are shrinking, the greater the price increase. Demand for widgets is exceeding the supply of widgets, and every price hike sticks. The consumer is left with the choice of either paying a higher price or going without. The producer couldn't care less—every widget being manufactured is being gobbled up by a hungry horde of consumers. These are the golden times of the business cycle. These are the times that make golden memories. This is what the game is all about.

"Mr. Metchum, Acme Widget Distributors is on the phone. So is Tantrum Widget Distributors. They want to speak to you."

"Tell them both to go to the devil!"

"You have already done that—several times, as a matter of fact. They want quotes."

"Yeah, well, have them look at all these orders in my hand. Everybody wants widgets. We couldn't produce any more widgets if we wanted to. The warehouse is empty. We make and ship out immediately. I don't need Acme. And Tantrum doesn't even deal with us. Why do you think they are calling me?"

"Obviously, sir, Acme needs more widgets and Tantrum's normal channels have dried up."

"You're telling me? Don't you think I know the situation? Tell Acme that I am not even going to speak with them until they pay off all their past receivables. Then tell them it is cash on the barrel head. When they pay off their receivables and agree to cash terms, then, and only then, will I give them a quote. Then tell Tantrum it's fifty cents above the market, cash on the barrel head. If they don't like it—hang up on them. If they do, ship them the widgets that are going to Lollydorf's. Then call Lollydorf and tell him that the truck loaded with his widgets just fell off a bridge. I'm just not going to waste my breath speaking to Acme with its six-months-to-pay attitude, or to Tantrum, which doesn't deal with us unless they have big problems. Got that? And that memo to the president on building a new factory . . . what's the status on that?"

"The president has already sent it to the head office. I heard through the grapevine that he has personally called the people at the head office and already has their verbal approval."

"At the volume and price that we are selling widgets—I mean, look at these orders— we can pay that baby off in two years, I bet. We can't afford to lose a second getting the new factory on the line."

For anyone who has experienced the business cycle, there comes a day of reckoning.

"Mr. Metchum, I can't get anyone at Acme and Tantrum to take your call. The president wants to know what you are going to do with the inventory that is spilling over into the parking lot. The floor supervisor wants to know what he is supposed to do with the excess workers now that you have cut the production schedule. The personnel director is on the line, and the union representatives are in the outer office waiting to see you."

"Tell the president that I would know what to do with the inventory if I had some orders. Tell him that giving 90 days of credit to Acme has not stirred up a single order and that I would like his permission to extend them 120 days of credit. Tell him that Tantrum won't speak to me, even when I am quoting fifty cents below the market. Ask him if I have his approval to drop the price to Tantrum by another twenty-five cents. Tell the floor supervisor to cut production by another 15 percent, and tell the personnel director to lay off all excess workers. Make sure the union reps listen in to your conversation with the floor supervisor and the personnel director. Then tell them that I don't want to see them. There is nothing I can do. If they want to do something to protect the workers' jobs, let them hit the pavement and dredge up some orders. Just tell them I have no orders—just tell them there is nothing I can do under the circumstances, so there is no use in talking to them about anything. By the way, what have you heard from the grapevine?"

"The bankers financing the new plant are coming here next week to go over our books. I also heard that we are splashing in red ink. Gladys is typing a memo to you from the president asking you for a forecast of sales . . . ."

"With no orders in my hand . . . he is going to ask me for a forecast?"

"Gladys also told me that the head office wants an accounting from the president on what is going on. She also heard heads are going to roll . . . ."

"Enough . . . enough! How much do you think I can take at one sitting?"

ON THE DECEPTION OF ORDERS IN HAND

One aspect of the business cycle that may confuse managers is the nature of the orders in hand. Here the manager with a fistful of orders presumes that they are all real orders. And they *are* all real orders in that when he ships the goods, he can bill the customers. The deception is that the orders may not represent sales to widget consumers.

Companies that produce manufactured goods for the national market seldom sell their products direct to consumers. One usually does not stroll downtown and see five widget stores, each representing a single manufacturer. One sees department stores that sell all sorts of products, including an assortment of competing products. Brand X widgets are sold right next to Brand Y and Brand Z. Thus, the relationship between a manufacturer and a consumer is not direct. Usually anywhere from three to five levels of distributors separate a manufacturer from a consumer.

A manufacturing company may sell its products to regional distributors that, in turn may sell to another level of distributors serving one or two states. These state distributors may serve another level of distributors, who, in turn, cover all the retailers in a county or in several counties.

Suppose that a retailer has been selling ten widgets per week and likes to keep about a two-week supply of widgets on hand. That means that he starts each week with twenty widgets in his inventory and that he orders, on average, ten widgets per week from his local distributor. Suppose that business activity in the widget market increases. The retailer sells fifteen widgets in one week. If the retailer feels that this new level of activity is going to be around for a while, and is not a normal fluctuation in sales, how many widgets does he order? Fifteen? Not quite.

He will eventually be ordering fifteen widgets a week to replace those he is selling, but he will place a one-time order for fifteen widgets plus some more widgets to add to inventory to ensure that he has a two-week supply of widgets on hand. He normally carries twenty in inventory and wants to increase his inventory to thirty, as well as replacing the fifteen widgets that he sold. The retailer will place an order for twenty-five widgets—fifteen to replace what he sold and ten to add to his inventory.

The local distributor does not ask the retailer how many of the twenty-five widgets actually represent heightened demand by consumers and how many represent inventory stocking. The local distributor looks at an order that is 250 percent larger than the usual order for ten widgets. It's a real order. Ship out twenty-five widgets to the retailer, and bill him. He'll pay with real money.

If widget sales are up for other retailers, as one would expect as the business cycle gains strength, others will be submitting orders that reflect both heightened sales activity and heightened inventory stocking. No one asks the dumb question of how many widgets are being sold and how many are being stocked on the shelves. It's an order, a real order, so the smart thing to do is honor it and bill the customer.

After a while, the local distributor gets a little anxious about his inventory levels. Like the retailer, he likes to keep a few weeks' worth of sales on his shelves to handle fluctuations in orders. A given inventory stocking level was satisfactory last week, but that is not true this week. The former level of inventory stocking is no longer satisfactory when individual stores are coming in with single orders 50, 100, 200, 300 percent higher than their customary orders. Thus, the local distributor makes a single large order to replace all that has been drawn down from his inventory by retailers stocking their inventories, plus another large slug of widgets to increase his inventory to a commensurately higher level than before.

This process of ordering to replenish widgets that have been actually sold to consumers and to increase the number of widgets piled in the back room to support enhanced sales works its way through each level of distributor until all that the factory sees, at the end of the daisy chain, is a deluge of orders. A nice portion of the fistful of orders held by the middle-level manager represents nothing more than the stocking of shelves through the three to five levels of distributors separating the factory from the consumer. Are the orders real in the sense that, when the goods are shipped out, the distributors can be billed and the factory can expect to collect the proceeds from the billings? Yes. Are the orders real in the sense that the spare productive capacity of widget making factories may have been exhausted, permitting the managers to hike the price of widgets? Yes. Are the orders real in the sense that they can be used to judge the volume of widgets being sold to consumers in order to rationalize the building of a new factory? No.

The orders are not real in the sense that they accurately reflect actual consumer demand. A goodly portion of the heightened volume of orders does represent consumer demand. The remainder is being stocked in inventory because inventory levels are a function of the volume of sales. If a retailer is selling ten widgets per week, and he feels comfortable with a two-week supply of widgets on his shelves, he wants twenty widgets in stock. Ten are too few, and thirty are too many. Twenty is the magic number.

When sales increase to fifteen widgets per week, then the retailer wants thirty widgets on his shelves. Thirty widgets were too many the week before. Now they are the right number. This is the normal behavior pattern of retailers. This is also normal behavior for wholesalers and factory operators. The greater the volume of business, the greater the desired level of inventories. There is nothing wrong with this behavior pattern except that it sometimes gives a wrong signal as to what actual demand is for a product. The fistful of orders grasped by the middle-level manager exaggerates actual demand. His reaction to the situation reflects the fistful of orders and not necessarily what the fistful of orders means in terms of actual consumer demand.

To provide another illustration of the wrong signal that may sometimes be given by orders in hand from a slightly different perspective, suppose that sales for the retailer under scrutiny fall from fifteen widgets per week back to the original ten widgets per week. If the retailer believes that ten widgets per week will be his future volume of sales, does his order fall from the previous fifteen per week to ten per week? Yes, but after he has made his inventory adjustment. He had thirty widgets in stock last week and was happy with that level of inventory. Now sales are down to ten per week and he is unhappy with thirty in inventory because thirty widgets now represent three weeks' worth of sales. He desires an inventory equivalent to two weeks' worth of sales. He finds himself in a position of having to liquidate his excess inventory.

The retailer would normally be expected to order ten widgets to replace those that have been sold from his local distributor. He also wants to reduce his inventory by ten. There is no easier way to do this than by not ordering any widgets for one week. He can reduce his inventory quite effectively this way. So instead of his order declining by one-third to reflect reduced sales, his order falls by a mere 100 percent on a one-time basis.

The local distributor does not call up the retailer and ask why he has stopped ordering, even for just one week. All he sees is a sharp drop-off in ordering activity from many of his retailers. He looks at his inventory level for the new ordering activity and concludes, rightly so, that his inventory is too large. Again, what easier way is there to reduce excessive inventory levels than by sharply reducing orders to his area distributor. This process of inventory liquidation for the lower volume of sales to consumers works its way up through the three to five levels of distributors. At the end of the daisy chain, the factory manager is left with a dearth of orders. The president of the company wants him to do a forecast of sales at a time when he has very few orders.

This does not mean that there is no demand for widgets. Widgets are still being sold to consumers at the retail stores, although at a reduced volume. But this demand is being satisfied through liquidation of what are now considered to be excess inventories, not by orders to the factories. Both the deluge of orders during peaks in the business cycle and the dearth of orders during troughs in the business cycle are sending false signals to the factory managers. In one case, the volume of orders is higher than actual demand as various levels of distributors expand their inventories. In the other case, the volume of orders is lower than actual demand as the distributors liquidate their inventories.

Businessmen are cognizant of the impact of inventory adjustments on sales. But it is also in their self-interest to plead for a new factory when they are deluged by orders. A manager of a factory knows that some of the orders represent inventory accumulation, and not actual demand. And he also knows that no one in top management is going to review the orders and pontificate on which portion of an order is for inventory stocking and which portion represents actual consumer demand. No one in management is in a position to do so because this analysis cannot be easily done. Even if it could be easily accomplished, it is not in the interest of a manager pushing for a new factory to be built to pursue this point very far.

In a free market environment, the consequence of not building a new factory is loss of standing among one's competitors. If everyone is building a new factory, and if a manager finds himself as the only kid on the block without a new toy factory to play with, how can he preserve his dignity? How can he hold his head up high when all the boys gather around the soda fountain boasting about their new toy factories? Unless a manager is willing to consign his productive plant to the dustbin of industrial history, he will build a new factory when times are booming.

Naturally, one can well guess the consequences of building 101 new factories, but that is not the point. The point is that most companies competing in the same market when times are booming will not exercise restraint when it comes to ordering more productive capacity. This also holds true for the situation in which relatively few companies are competing in the same market. It is not reasonable to expect that Firm A is not going to build a new factory simply because it has concluded that the factories being built by Firms B, C, and D are more than adequate to meet future demand. Firm A will most likely build its own new factory and slug it out with the other firms—or suffer along with them when all four factories come on-line and flood the market with widgets. The fact that the signal for building a new factory—the enhanced volume of orders for widgets—was partially a false signal that exaggerated heightened consumer demand, is, well, just part of the game.

THE MOTIVATION TO CONSOLIDATE

This is the primary reason why mature industries are marked by relatively few competing firms. Take any mature industry—steel, chemicals, oil, copper, textiles—and count the firms that make up most of the total market share in the industry. The number is relatively few—a dozen or less. Yet these industries started out with many fledging companies. In the United States, there were sixty or so independent automobile manufacturers at the turn of the century. Now there are the Big Three. There were a hundred or so fledging companies in the cereal industry when it first started in the late nineteenth century. Most brand name cereals are now produced by a small handful of companies. Why is this so?

The primary reason for consolidation of companies in an industry is to bring the rate of capacity expansion under some semblance of control. As previously discussed, in its first annual report, U.S. Steel prided itself in scrapping a number of steel expansion projects that would have been built had the independent companies, which were amalgamated into U.S. Steel, maintained their independence. And as business is conducted on a more global basis, consolidation of companies on an international scale is sure to follow. If industry is to be plagued with overcapacity from time to time, it is far easier to deal with five too many factories than fifty.

There may be a company or two that does not participate in the craze to build new capacity. They realize that building factories during the good times is the only window, so to speak, for launching new capacity. They also see others building new factories and are keenly aware that, by not participating, they are going to be living with older, less efficient, and eventually obsolete plants.

These companies are planning to acquire new facilities like the others. Their method, however, is a little different. During the good times, they dedicate the profitability of their operations to getting their houses in good financial order before the deluge of new capacity hits the market. When this occurs, they will be in a position to capitalize on the distress of others. Their game is to expand their capacity, not by building new factories, but by acquiring existing new facilities at a fraction of their cost, or by acquiring these assets by merging with firms in financial distress.

Some firms do have the sagacity to refrain from going on a building spree and place themselves in a position to take advantage of the hangover that is going to be suffered by others the morning after the new factory ordering binge. That has little bearing on the conclusion that there is no real restraint being practiced by management in ordering new capacity when factories are booming with activity, inventories are exhausted, and prices are skyrocketing. There may be a physical constraint on the ability of the system to actually deliver new factories, but there is no real restraint on the desire of management, in a collective sense, to order new factories in a free market economy.

ON CUTTING PRICES VERSUS CUTTING PRODUCTION

During the transition from good times to bad times, our manager who peeks into the warehouse on his way to the office will see the gradual buildup of inventory. In his office, he will experience the general inability to make further price increases stick. The widget making industry is now making slightly more widgets than there is demand. Warehouse inventory levels are beginning to climb. Price increases posted by one manufacturer are not being copied by the others. What is the manager to do?

The manager has two throttles to play with on his locomotive—he can adjust the price of widgets, or he can adjust the volume of production of widgets. He has no other control mechanism. Either one will take care of the excess inventory buildup in his warehouse.

If he pulls back on his pricing throttle, and he is among the first to do so, he can get rid of his excess inventory by stealing market share from someone else. He can get away with this as long as his competitors do not match his "sale" price. If the industry as a whole is producing too many widgets for the market, it won't take very long for everyone to lower his price and the inventory buildup to resume. Actually, it might not have ever stopped. It might have been simply shifted from the manufacturer with the lower price to the one with the higher price.

THE LIMITS ON CONSOLIDATION

The manager might pull back on the production throttle and restore the inventory level in what really should be a more effective manner of dealing with the problem than cutting prices. And if there were real coordination among all widget manufacturers, then the price level could be maintained if all widget makers cut back on production. But this means that everybody has to follow orders from the widget king on how many widgets to produce.

The basis of the free market does not allow for the existence of a widget king.

In the United States, the meeting of the heads of competing firms to discuss flower bouquets may be sufficient to accuse them of conspiracy. Leaving aside legal ramifications, it is not easy for competing firms to sit around a table and agree on who will be the widget king. Even if they did agree on who will be the widget king, it would be difficult for them to agree on the procedure to be followed in dividing up the market. In other words, there would be great difficulty in establishing the set of rules or guidelines the widget king should follow in order to tell one manufacturer that he can make 7,641 widgets this month and another one that he can make 12,334 widgets.

Even if such a procedure could be agreed on, every manufacturer would find an excuse as to why the procedure was misapplied in his particular circumstance. Everybody would become an expert on the allocation rules for the expediency of breaking them. Furthermore, without on-site inspection, many, if not most—or perhaps all—would cheat and make a few more widgets than allotted. With the widget king trying to deal with a myriad of whining complaints, someone would sneak in some more capacity and request that his share be increased according to whatever procedure had been put in place for allocating market share among the competing firms. Even if all of this could be administered—which it can't be in a free market setting—there would certainly be at least one manufacturer who would tell the others where to go and produce to his heart's content. And if this were not enough, another manufacturer would actually make an improved version of the widget and upset the whole applecart. With the exception of the improved version of a widget, this drama is being acted out, and reported on, in the daily newspapers . . . the headlines contain the word "OPEC."

The widget king can be effective only as the head of a state-controlled monopoly on the making of widgets. This destroys the entire basis of the free market in which competition keeps the game honest and keeps managers on their managerial toes. While monopolies generally have proved to be inefficient and nonresponsive to the demands of the marketplace, there have been some rare, and notable, exceptions. AT&T maintained its monopolistic control over telephone communication in the United States for about a century by improving the level of service at ever lower costs in terms of real dollars. AT&T was able to maintain its monopoly by demonstrating that the company was not acting as a monopolist. The Nobel brothers also maintained a monopoly on the manufacture of dynamite by not behaving as a monopolist. They made a quality product with a low profit margin. They left little room in terms of quality of product and price (profit) for competitors to make their debut. By and large, however, guaranteeing a protected market for an industry or a firm has proved deleterious to the interests of consumers and taxpayers alike.

If a society wants the manufacturers of consumer products to be efficient and responsive to the demands of the marketplace, then competition has to be present to ensure that the dictates of the marketplace have an impact on the decisions made by managers. For competition to exist, there have to be several companies, and not many at that, that can make independent decisions on production and pricing. In this type of environment, there is no room for a widget king. Those who are considering having a widget king to coordinate production and pricing among supposedly independent firms must first deal with the procedure to be followed for enforcing the widget king's decisions prior to dealing with the procedure by which the widget king will apportion the market among the existing firms. By definition, then, the existence of a widget king means that there is no such thing as an independent firm in Adam Smith's sense of the word.

There are examples of government-sponsored, coordinated decision making among leading manufacturers of a given product. The best example is that of the Japanese government which plays a role in coordinating key decisions among supposedly independent companies in a given industry. However, because Japan, Inc., is a major participant in world trade, the competition faced by Japanese automobile manufacturers, as an example, is located offshore. In other words, no matter how coordinated the production and expansion plans of the Japanese automobile manufacturers are in Japan, these manufacturers still must face competition in their foreign markets, which make up a large portion of their total market.

For those who believe that the world would be better run if matters of this sort were left in the hands of a widget king, one element has not yet been discussed. The sensitive subject that presumably the king will only make right decisions has not been broached. It does not necessarily follow that the concentration of all power into the hands of one man means that all his decisions will be the right ones. Perhaps it is better to have a number of widget manufacturers making their own decisions rather than one making decisions for the industry as a whole. After all, an assortment of right and wrong decisions by several manufacturers should be less damaging than one wrong decision by the widget king.

ADJUSTING PRICE VERSUS PRODUCTION

So we are back to the widget manufacturer making decisions on pricing and production for his specific domain. He probably should cut production and hope his competitors follow. But it is easier at this point to cut price. Cutting production means laying off workers. Regardless of the heartlessness that management may feel toward the workers' plight, there is a good, sound economic reason for not laying off workers willy-nilly at the very first opportunity to do so.

Laying off workers is an expense. The expense may not be so much in severance pay and increased contributions to the state's unemployment benefit program as in replacing these workers when added production is needed and in dealing with the economic consequences of poor worker morale. Looking at the latter issue first, it is a known fact that employee morale affects productivity. A happy work force produces more than does an unhappy one. A happy work force is one in which the workers feel that they are counted in the great scheme of things. Translated into employment, happiness is working for a company that does not lay off its work force at the first whiff of a slowdown in business activity.

Replacing workers who had been previously laid off is an expensive undertaking. The primary reason for this is that if the workers had any sense, and they do, they would find employment in greener pastures. Greener pastures may be interpreted to mean any firm other than the one that laid them off. Greener pastures may be any firm that is willing to pay them a wage. Any job is a greener pasture compared to waiting for better times to rescue the jobless from the unemployment lines. Usually worker replacement requires training and other expenses associated with transforming a greenhorn into a productive and efficient worker. With these points in mind, management may be very reluctant to lay off workers at the first sign of a business slowdown. It is far easier to get rid of a little excess inventory by offering a special discount to a special customer than to deal with the pain and expense associated with laying off workers. Price adjustments require far less effort than that which will eventually be expended in hiring greenhorns and transforming them into an experienced work force.

The situation is quite different once economic activity has plummeted into the trough of the business cycle. Falling prices are probably nearing the variable cost of production. At this point, one would expect management to rely to a far greater extent on cutting production than on cutting price to restore inventories to normal levels.

Under these circumstances, the choice is really out of the hands of management. The nature of the decision has nothing to do with the self-interests of the managers. If the market price of widgets is $6 and it costs $7 to make a widget, a manager no longer has the option to cut his price further to get a larger slice of the widget market pie to sustain his volume of production. He has no real choice but to slash production from one week to the next until inventory levels have been restored. Such slashing of production has to occur before the price has fallen below the breakeven point. This is not a maneuver by a manager to serve his self-interests but a maneuver by a company for its self-preservation.

Thus, it seems reasonable that a manager facing growing inventories during the good times would prefer to fiddle with the pricing throttle before he touches the production throttle as he guides his locomotive through the peaks of the mountainous terrain known as the business cycle. During the bad times, when price erosion has already whittled the profit margins down to next to nothing, he will be using his production throttle to guide his locomotive through the valleys of this mountainous terrain. And between the two extremes, he will be using both throttles in some proportional degree.

PRODUCER BEHAVIOR SIMULATION

If man as producer is basically motivated by profit maximization, with some elements of greed and fear mixed into his decision making process, then his behavior will be determined to some extent by the degree of profitability and the size of his inventories. One might note that a modeling of his behavior should incorporate the volume of sales, and the level of production, and, perhaps, price and variable cost of production.

Profitability is based on price and cost of production. There is no need to be concerned with price and cost of production as independent variables. What matters is the difference between the two figures. Managers are motivated to behave in certain ways by the existence of profits or losses—and the degree of these profits or losses. The two components of profit or loss are not themselves of particular concern beyond the fact that cost is subtracted from price to determine profitability, or lack thereof.

The same holds true with regard to inventory. Inventory includes volume of production and volume of orders. A factory's inventory is the net result of what a factory produces and what it ships out to its customers. A manager can make decisions based on the size of his inventory without regard to the volume of production and the volume of orders per se. This is essentially the same process used to determine profitability. Referring to the island economy located somewhere in the middle of a vast sea, the behavior of managers, or man as producer, might be described in a few succinct statements:

1. The good times mentality prevails whenever there are profitable operations with reasonably sized inventories. Reasonably sized inventories, from the point of view of the factory manager, are arbitrarily set at about five to ten weeks' worth of orders in his warehouse.

2. If operations are unprofitable, and if inventories are reasonably sized, there will be a very strong incentive to increase prices until operations are in the black. Moreover, these price increases will stick. Managers cannot remain in business if they operate indefinitely at a loss. More to the point, managers will not be able to keep their jobs if they do not raise their prices when they have their inventories under control and are operating in the red. They are in a position to arbitrarily keep on increasing the price of their goods until their costs are covered and they are operating in the black.

3. Once operations are profitable, there will be difficulty in increasing the price further until shortages of inventory develop in the factory warehouse. As long as a manager has spare production capacity, he will attempt to maximize profits by increasing his volume of production and capturing as much market share as he can.

4. As factory inventories fall below a comfortable level, and as spare productive capacity is exhausted, the industry as a whole can increase prices and enjoy the enhanced profitability to its heart's content.

5. As spare capacity is exhausted, and as prices are being pushed up, labor can win some favorable wage concessions as long as the supply of unemployed workers is also dwindling away. When more workers are needed to further expand production, and, at the same time, there is a limited supply of workers available, a manager will try to bid workers away from other firms in order to keep his facilities working at full tilt. The existence of labor unions may quicken the process of workers' gaining pay raises by their coordinated threats to strike if wage concessions are not made. Managers

are much more apt to settle the matter quickly because a strike under booming business conditions can be very costly in terms of lost profits. Regardless of the effectiveness of unions in accelerating the process of wage hikes, increases in wages will tend to lag increases in prices. In other words, a manager can more easily—and quickly—raise the price of his product than a work force can negotiate a pay hike.

6. As spare productive capacity diminishes, and if operations are profitable, management will order the building of new factories. This enthusiasm for ordering more productive capacity will be conditioned both by the state of utilization of existing capacity and by the magnitude of the profitability of new facility operations.

Bad times are the antithesis of good times. The transition from good to bad times is initially marked by factory inventories that exceed the "comfort range"—what management considers to be reasonably sized inventories. As excess inventories begin to accumulate, managers will desire to cut price first before cutting production levels. If price cutting does not restore an equilibrium condition between the production of goods entering a factory warehouse and the shipment of goods to customers, then production cuts will inexorably follow until there is a redress in the imbalance of factory inventories. Production cutbacks become more extensive as gross margins begin to disappear. When operations become unprofitable, management will have the intestinal fortitude to cut wages. Strikes are no threat to management when the red ink is flowing. Management might well welcome a strike under these conditions as a more rapid means to liquidate excess factory inventories. Finally, one can expect that factory building will cease once utilization of existing plants can amply cover demand, regardless of the magnitude of the gross margin. If current plant capacity is operating at 50 percent, it does not make a great deal of sense to build more capacity, even if the profitability of new factories can financially support such an investment.

A STEP CLOSER TO A SIMULATION

The appendix accompanying this chapter contains a simulation of the behavior of man as producer under varying conditions of consumer demand for a manufacturer's product. All the following exhibits are derived from the running of the simulation programs in the appendix.

The good and bad times behavior patterns of managers toward pricing and production in relation to the size of factory inventories are shown in the following two exhibits. In both exhibits, the manager feels most comfortable with five to ten weeks' worth of inventory in his warehouse. Of course, the good times are when inventory levels are on the low side of the comfort range, or below it. By default, the bad times are when inventory levels are on the high side of the comfort range, or above it. A manager has two throttles to control the situation: he can change the price, and he can change the volume of production. Exhibit 5.1 shows the pricing sensitivity to the ratio of factory inventories to orders for profitable and unprofitable operations.

Exhibit 5.1
Price Sensitivity

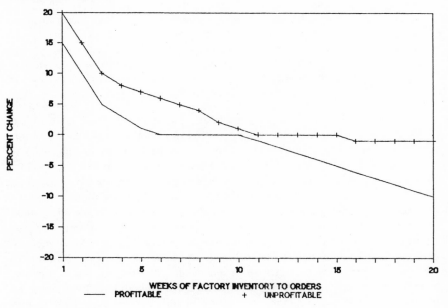

WEEKS OF FACTORY INVENTORY TO ORDERS
—— PROFITABLE   +   UNPROFITABLE

Factory orders are not sales to consumers. Factory managers do not see consumer sales. Their world operates around orders from distributors whose ordering
might distort actual consumer demand to some degree, depending on the extent
of their inventory accumulation or liquidation. The managers operate their factories to the extent that their inventories cover a certain range of weekly orders.
Their signal to change prices, and production, is a floating marker. It is a ratio
of two variables: the size of inventory in the factory warehouse and the number
of orders in hand. Therefore, an inventory that had been in the "comfort range"
last week might be below the comfort range or above the comfort range this
week, even though there has been no change in its physical size. A declining
number of orders or a rising number of orders will have a significant impact on
how comfortable a manager feels about the size of an inventory today, even
though he felt very comfortable about its size yesterday.

When operations are profitable, price increases can be made to stick if there
is less than six weeks' worth of factory inventory. As will be seen, productive
capacity is being expanded as rapidly as possible to the extent that there is spare
capacity available. Price hikes are not possible when factory inventories climb
above six weeks' worth. The marketing people are too eager to increase their
market share as consumers shop around from one producer to another trying to
get the best deal for their money. There is simply a bit too much inventory in
the warehouses to permit price hikes.

It is only when inventories are near the lower end of the comfort range, or below it, that managers develop the intestinal fortitude to make price increases stick. Not too much intestinal fortitude is necessary because customer demand cannot be satisfied. Managers are not raising the price so much as customers are aggressively bidding up the price in order to satisfy their needs. When inventories are adequate, customers will run from competitor to competitor seeking a better deal. And a better deal can always be had as long as a competitor has sufficient inventory to honor the order. The efforts of marketing to maximize sales prohibit price hikes unless there is a more or less universal shortage of goods. When goods are in short supply, price hikes are merely a response of man as producer to the demands of man as consumer.

Above ten weeks' worth of inventory, price discounting begins as managers begin to scramble to reduce inventory levels. The greater the ratio of inventory to orders, the more severe the price cutting. As seen in Exhibit 5.1, when there are twenty weeks' worth of inventory in relation to factory orders, prices are being cut at a rate of 10 percent per operating period. The operating period is one month long. As long as inventories are at a very high level in relation to orders, price reductions of 10 percent per month will rapidly turn a profitable operation into a losing proposition.

Referring to Exhibit 5.1 for unprofitable operations—which occur, naturally, when price no longer covers the cost of production—managers are able to start increasing prices when factory inventory levels are less than eleven weeks' worth of orders. These price increases become more significant as the ratio of inventory to orders falls from that level. Again, these price increases are unilateral, and managers are adamant about making them stick. The market is there for their product, and no manager worth his salt is going to ship out goods at a price that does not cover his costs when his inventories are under control. If he insists on selling his product below cost with reasonably sized inventories, he will find himself justifiably locked out of the game of Musical Chairs. Consequently, he is no longer in contention to play King of the Hill.

When he has between eleven and fifteen weeks' of inventory, the manager cannot increase the sales price, even though he is not covering his costs. If inventory levels exceed fifteen weeks' worth of orders, price erosion continues at a slow pace, even when variable costs are not being satisfied from revenues. These losses are shared by labor because labor has no defense against unilateral cuts in pay. Times are rough enough for labor in that continued production cuts are extending unemployment lines from one end of the island to the other. Their resistence to pay cuts is nil. Under these conditions, management would welcome a good, long strike. The strike would be costly—but not to management.

The factory manager has another throttle to play with—production volume. Exhibit 5.2 shows the sensitivity of production to the ratio of factory inventory to orders.

When times are unprofitable (that is, when the sales price does not cover the variable cost of production), production is being cut at the rate of 10 percent

Exhibit 5.2
Production Sensitivity

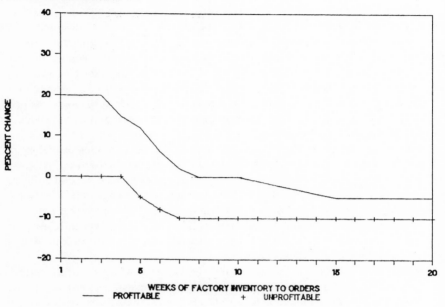

WEEKS OF FACTORY INVENTORY TO ORDERS
——— PROFITABLE　　　　　　　+　UNPROFITABLE

per month, unless there is less than seven weeks' worth of orders in inventory. Production is not cut back at all if there is less than five weeks' worth of inventory on hand. There is little use in cutting production at this point because, referring to Exhibit 5.1, price hikes should soon restore profitability.

Once conditions are profitable for the manager, he will increase production as the factory inventory falls below eight weeks' worth of orders. These increases in production are, of course, constrained by the total productive capacity of the factory. As inventories begin to exceed ten weeks' worth of orders, small production cuts begin. These production cutbacks are less than the corresponding price cutting and remain that way as long as operations remain profitable. When that standard is violated, production cutbacks increase to 10 percent per month if the size of the inventory is equivalent to seven or more weeks' worth of current orders. Any change in production, up or down, has a direct and immediate impact on the number of employed workers.

Consumer demand has to be assumed in order to examine the behavior of man as producer. Suppose that, for purposes of illustration, demand for goods is as shown in Exhibit 5.3.

Consumer demand in the island economy starts at 20,000 pounds per month and grows at a rate of 1,000 pounds per month until month 30. Then its incremental monthly rate increases to 2,000 pounds per month until it levels off at

Exhibit 5.3
Consumer Demand

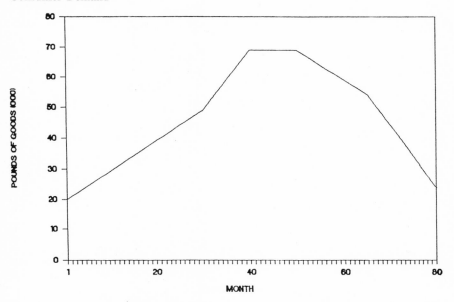

month 40. Demand starts declining at a rate of 1,000 pounds per month at month 51. Beginning at month 66, the rate of decline is 2,000 pounds per month.

The manager of a factory does not see consumer demand directly. He receives orders from distributors who, serving their best interests, are accumulating or liquidating inventory as consumer demand changes. Orders to the factory include consumer demand plus or minus the distributors' inventory adjustments. It is assumed that distributors desire their inventory to be equivalent to eight weeks' worth of current sales. The distributors' orders to the factory are compared to consumer demand in Exhibit 5.4.

As illustrated in Exhibit 5.4, factory orders are initially higher than actual consumer demand because distributors are accumulating inventory to maintain an inventory level equivalent to eight weeks' worth of consumer demand. Factory orders and consumer demand match when consumer demand is flat. When consumer demand declines, factory orders fall even further as distributors liquidate their inventories in order to maintain no more than eight weeks' worth of sales on their shelves.

The factory manager does not sense consumer demand directly, nor does he know the extent of the inventories held by the distributors. All he sees are the resulting orders. The factory inventory for a particular month is the previous month's inventory plus production minus shipments made in response to orders. The factory owner is always a bit slow in adjusting his production to consumer demand because he realizes that the signals of actual consumer consumption are

Exhibit 5.4
Factory Orders Versus Consumer Demand

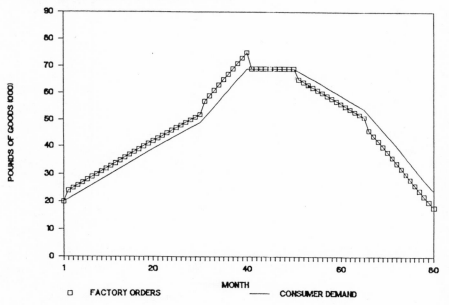

a little distorted. The factory owner is slow to increase production and does not do so until he is at the short end of his comfort range. Then he increases production slowly. Large-scale increases in production are ordered only when it becomes apparent that he may run out of factory inventory.

The factory owner is also slow in cutting production. He does nothing until the factory's inventory reaches the high end of his comfort range. Then he decreases production modestly and does not take more drastic action until he is swimming in inventory. His relative slowness in reacting to shifting demand for his product reflects both uncertainties with regard to actual consumer demand and his reluctance to adjust production. Adjusting production requires laying off workers or hiring new workers. This is an effort that an owner is willing to make once he is convinced that it is necessary for him to take such action. Otherwise, his natural inclination is not to touch the production throttle because he is reluctant to fire or hire workers. It is far easier to order this week's production at the same level as last week's and fool around with the pricing throttle if the situation requires a little adjustment.

The factory manager is sensitive to the fact that factory orders are an unreliable barometer of actual demand. His natural course of action is to do nothing with the production throttle until the evidence is quite convincing that he should take some remedial course of action. With the factory manager changing the production level only when he feels compelled to do so, it should not be too much

Exhibit 5.5
Distributor and Factory Inventories

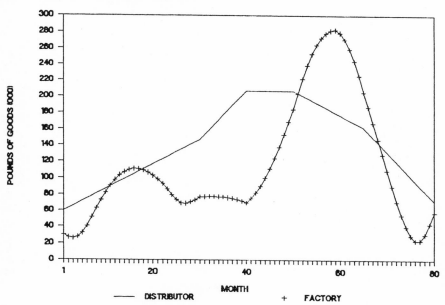

of a surprise to discover that factory inventories are more volatile than distributor inventories, as is illustrated in Exhibit 5.5.

Factory inventories start out at 30,000 pounds. With initial orders of a little over 20,000 pounds per month, this is equivalent to one-and-a-half months' or six weeks' worth of orders. This is a bit on the low side of the comfort range. Factory managers increase production, but not fast enough to compensate for heightened consumer demand and the accumulation of inventory by distributors. Soon a real shortage of factory inventories results. Factory managers increase production at the maximum permissible rate for profitable operation, which from Exhibit 5.2 is 20 percent per month. This is done by hiring machine operators. Each machine operator can produce 200 pounds of goods per month. The owners continue to hire until the number of machine operators doubles to 200 by month 5. The total work force can now produce 40,000 pounds of goods per month at a time when factory orders are still less than 30,000 pounds per month.

With production now exceeding factory orders, factory inventories increase rapidly. This induces the factory owners to stop hiring machine operators. As shown in Exhibit 5.6, employment for machine operators levels out when factory inventories are brought back into the comfort range. Production, however, is still too high with relation to consumer demand. Production is cut back, as seen by the small declines in the number of machine operators, after inventories exceed the comfort range.

Exhibit 5.6
Number of Machine Operators

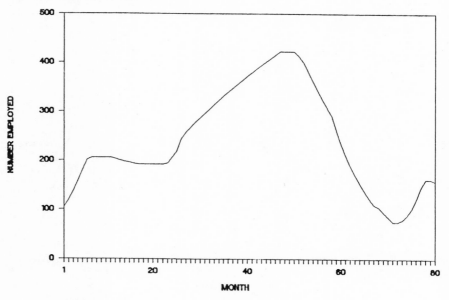

In other words, the factory owners are cutting production at a time when consumer demand for their product is still growing. The factory owners don't know this. All they know is that their inventory levels are a little too high in relation to the magnitude of orders. Once factory inventory levels are back in the comfort range, the factory owners keep production constant. However, consumer demand is still growing and, eventually, is outstripping production. The ratio of inventories to orders continues to fall. However, factory owners do not react to the situation by hiring machine operators until factory inventories have fallen to the lower end of the comfort range, which occurs around month 25.

One may well ask why the factory owners hired too quickly to begin with, why they cut production while consumers were buying more products, and why they delayed in increasing production again. The answer to this is that they do not know actual consumer demand, and in their rush to restore their inventory levels to a more comfortable range, they initially hired too many workers. Once factory inventories became too burdensome, there had to be some cutbacks in production. When inventories were restored to a comfort range, production was stabilized and was not increased, as it should have been, until inventories fell to the lower end of the comfort range.

Factory owners are dealing not with the actual situation but with the situation as they see it. There is a difference between the two. One would expect, therefore, that the factory owners will not see demand flattening out at the moment that it actually occurs. Exhibit 5.6 shows that they continue to hire workers after demand has leveled out. This causes factory inventories to get totally out of hand, as seen in Exhibit 5.5. Production is then cut back by laying off machine operators. Layoff piles on top of layoff until the inventory situation is squared away. By this time, too many workers have been laid off, and the factory owners are forced to hire some back around month 72, even while consumer demand is still dropping.

There are elements of too little too soon and too much too late in the decisions of factory owners in the face of shifting consumer demand. This variability in decisions would not be so bad if factory owners had a better handle on actual consumer demand. If they had a direct tie-in to department store cash registers and did not have to judge actual demand from orders in hand from distributors, then they could be more responsive to the situation, and factory inventories would not be so volatile.

A constraint on production is the number of machines. Each machine operator needs one machine. Obviously, the number of machine operators cannot exceed the number of machines. The number of machines was initially set at 300 with a natural decay rate of 2 percent per month. This reflects machinery slowly transforming itself back to dust and ashes. This decay could also include product obsolescence. As consumer preference for goods changes, machines of a different type come into demand. Machines dedicated to build products no longer desired by consumers have to be scrapped and new ones built to handle the shifting patterns of consumer preference for different types of goods. The natural decay of productive capacity, or number of machines, is shown in Exhibit 5.7 prior to month 20.

The upward sweep of the number of machines after month 20 indicates that the machine builders were busy adding machine capacity. Before that time, they were unemployed. The resumption of the relentless downward trend in machine capacity around month 55 means that their livelihoods came to an end. The employment of the machine builders is not linked directly to the employment of machine operators, but rather to the utilization rate of the existing plant capacity.

The machine operator population started out at one hundred and expanded to two hundred before the factory managers put a hold on further hiring to get their factory inventories under control. The initial machine population was set at three hundred. This meant that initial utilization was a little over 30 percent. Machine utilization, as shown in Exhibit 5.8, initially rose rapidly as a net result of the natural decay of machine capacity and the employment of an increasing number of machine operators. It continued to rise, albeit at a slower rate after machine operators' employment leveled off, and then declined somewhat because the number of machines continued to decline.

Machine utilization then reached 100 percent and remained there until month 50 or so. A comparison of Exhibits 5.6 and 5.8 shows that the constraint on hiring new machine operators was the building rate on new machines. One new machine, which can make 200 pounds of goods per month and which requires

Exhibit 5.7
Number of Machines

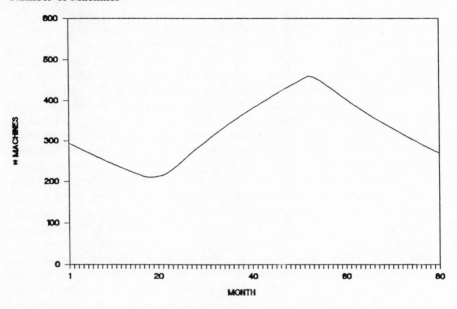

Exhibit 5.8
Machine Utilization

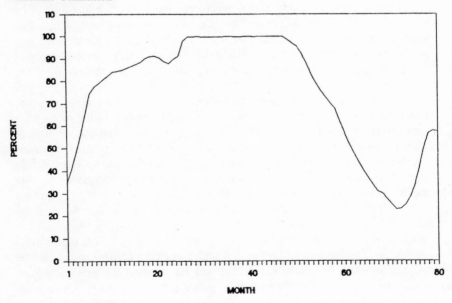

Exhibit 5.9
Number of Machine Builders

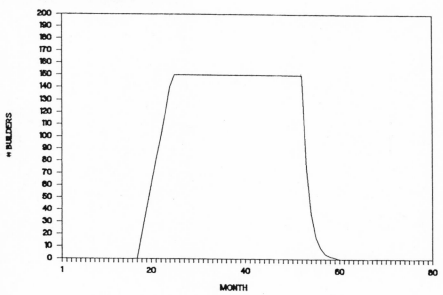

the services of one machine operator, takes ten man-months to complete. In other words, ten machine builders have to be hired to build one new machine per month. Exhibit 5.9 shows the number of machine builders with gainful employment.

For purposes of illustration, it was arbitrarily assumed that a maximum of 150 machine builders could be hired. That means that no more than 15 machines could be built in any given month. No construction of new machine capacity could take place until utilization of existing capacity exceeded 85 percent. This models the behavior of managers in using present resources to the fullest before spending the funds necessary to expand production. Moreover, expansion of machine capacity was prohibited unless new plant capacity could be operated profitably. In other words, utilization had to be above 85 percent, and new machine capacity had to pass a profitability test before machine builders could be hired. Profitability was judged in terms of the payback period for new machine capacity.

The rate of hiring machine builders was limited to 40 per month. This was done to model the fact that there is a time delay between deciding to build more capacity and corraling the resources that are necessary to get construction underway. A lesser degree of profitability slowed down the rate of hiring machine builders, as detailed in the appendix. Exhibit 5.10 combines Exhibits 5.8 and 5.9 to demonstrate the relationship between the rate of hiring of machine builders and the utilization rate of existing machine capacity.

Exhibit 5.10
Number of Machine Builders and Percentage of Utilization

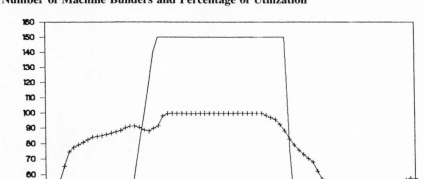

Employment in the construction industry, or in the manufacture of machinery for new plants, is not terribly secure. Machine operators have a greater degree of security than do machine builders. One would expect that construction workers, or machine builders, would receive premium pay compared to that of factory workers, or machine operators, to compensate for their greater risk of being unemployed.

Exhibit 5.11 shows the price of goods in dollars per pound during this eighty-month period of time. To understand the ups and downs of prices, one needs to refer to Exhibit 5.4 for factory orders, to Exhibit 5.5 for factory inventories, and to Exhibit 5.1, which shows the sensitivity of price changes to the ratio of factory inventories to orders.

Factory production initially lags the influx of orders, causing factory inventories to decline. As factory inventories fall below the comfort range, managers can raise prices, and these price hikes stick as long as inventories remain low. This is consumer (distributor) demand bidding up the price of goods when the suppliers have little to offer. The managers are responding to a situation of short supplies. This is the time that they can seemingly initiate what appears to be unilateral price hikes. They appear to be unilateral and arbitrary, but managers can get away with this behavior because the distributors, as consumers, have no choice but to pay or go without.

As factory inventories increase into the comfort range, further price rises are

Exhibit 5.11
Price of Goods

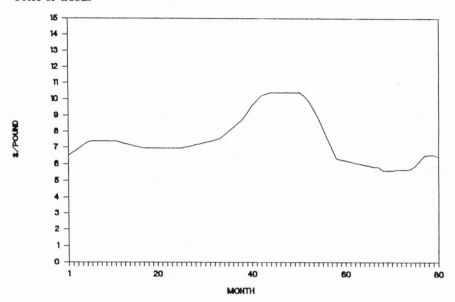

not possible because competitive firms have sufficient inventory to honor orders and, if necessary, to take orders away from firms that are trying to increase prices. This demonstrates the weak position producers find themselves in when inventories are at sufficient levels to satisfy market demand. Consumers can defeat producers' desires to push up prices by doing a little comparison shopping. As previously discussed, marketeers are more than eager to slice another piece of the pie for themselves. That eagerness of man as producer to increase his market share works in the interest of man as consumer to buy at the lowest prices.

Slight price declines ensue as factory inventories temporarily climb above the comfort range and then even out in the comfort range around month 20. During the period from month 25 to month 30, factory inventories are about 60,000 to 70,000 pounds (Exhibit 5.5), and factory orders are averaging a little over 40,000 pounds per week (Exhibit 5.4). This results in an inventory-to-orders ratio of about one-and-a-half months, or six weeks. This is near the low range of constant prices (Exhibit 5.1). However, escalating factory orders after this period cause sharp increases in prices as the inventory-to-orders ratio declines sharply. Increasing factory production does not build up sufficient inventories to bring further price escalation to a halt until shortly before month 45. Between then and month 50 or 51, prices stabilize as the inventory-to-orders ratio remains in the comfort range.

Then burgeoning factory inventories, coupled with declining factory orders, cause prices to take a sharp dive as factory managers do all they can to get rid of their excess inventories. The price decline suddenly ends shortly before month 60. This can occur for either of two reasons. One, factory inventories have been restored to the comfort range; two, the sales price no longer covers the cost of production. The second condition is the one that is true. Managers suddenly shift from the pricing throttle to the production throttle because further price cuts only exacerbate the degree of losses. Near the end of the eighty-month period, there are some price increases because factory inventories have been reduced too much in relation to orders.

When times become unprofitable, managers abandon the pricing throttle and grab the production throttle in a panic to redress the imbalance between their inventories and the level of orders. This can be seen in Exhibit 5.6 in which the declining employment of machine operators is a direct result of production cutbacks by factory managers. The acceleration of the pace of layoffs just before month 60 reflects the turning point from profitable to unprofitable operations.

Exhibit 5.12 shows the wage levels of workers. Workers start out at $1,000 per month and begin to win wage concessions from the managers as machine utilization reaches 100 percent. These wage gains could occur only if there were also a shortage of available workers during the time of full utilization of productive capacity. It would not be possible for labor to win pay raises if there were still a ready force of available workers to fully utilize machine capacity. Wage hikes depend on the availability of workers to operate the machines, and

Exhibit 5.12
Monthly Wages

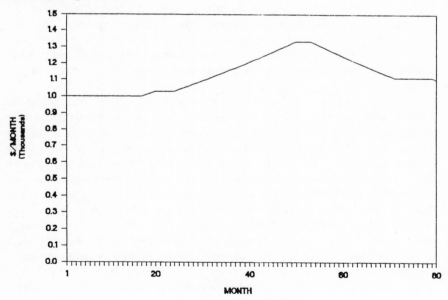

this is independent of the degree of machine utilization. For demonstration purposes only, it has been presumed that full utilization of machine capacity more or less coincides with the exhaustion of the available manpower pool of machine operators. A shortage of manpower is presumed to exist between months 25 and 50.

Prices start falling around month 50 as inventory levels start to become burdensome. Employment also starts declining at that time (see Exhibit 5.6). The model contained the condition that management can start cutting wages once utilization had fallen below 80 percent. Wage cuts are achieved by laying off more workers than necessary and then hiring in workers who had been previously laid off but are willing, more than willing, to work for less pay. Later on, as price declines decimate profitability, labor rates continue to fall. The reason now is that management is able to reduce the labor pay unilaterally because a threat of a strike, the ultimate weapon of a dissatisfied work force, has no impact on management thinking. In fact, it is quite the reverse. Management would welcome a long strike as a means of hastening the liquidation of excess inventory.

One criticism—among many, perhaps—of the model is that it is static. This is particularly true in Exhibit 5.3. Consumer demand simply does not follow such a neat straight-line pattern. Exhibit 5.13 is the same as Exhibit 5.3, except that noise has been introduced. The random factor is a random number (which can vary between zero and one) multiplied by plus or minus 10 percent of the consumer demand shown in Exhibit 5.3. The average consumer demand for

Exhibit 5.13
Consumer Demand with Random Factor

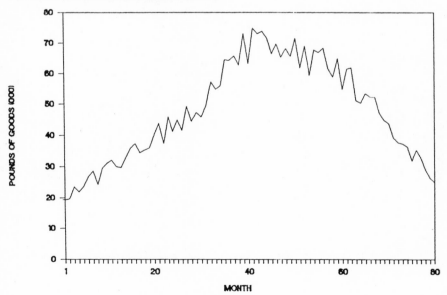

Exhibits 5.3 and 5.13 is the same, but the latter exhibit introduces noise of anywhere between − 10 to + 10 percent of the values indicated in Exhibit 5.3.

One would hardly suspect that Exhibits 5.3 and 5.13 represent essentially the same consumer demand. Yet they do. Exhibit 5.14 shows the dramatic impact the noise has on factory orders. In fact, the variability in factory orders was introducing too much noise in the simulation of the decision making process of managers. Alterations had to be made to the simulation program to make the system work more smoothly. The signal to managers with regard to adjusting pricing and production was the running average of the present and previous months' levels of factory orders. This smoothed out the extreme fluctuations in factory orders but still was insufficient to avoid stockouts in factory inventories. These stockouts led to skyhigh pricing and enormous profitability for the factory owners. To reduce the extreme price levels, the pricing throttle was cut back a little when factory inventories were in short supply and operations were running profitably. A comparison of Exhibit 5.15 with Exhibit 5.1 shows somewhat less sensitivity to price hikes when factory inventories are in short supply and gross margins are positive.

Of greater importance in stabilizing the simulation was changing the settings on the production throttle. A comparison of Exhibit 5.16 with Exhibit 5.2 shows a greater ability to push the production throttle forward when factory inventories are nearing the exhaustion point with regard to orders. It was also necessary to

Exhibit 5.14
Factory Orders Versus Consumer Demand with Random Factor

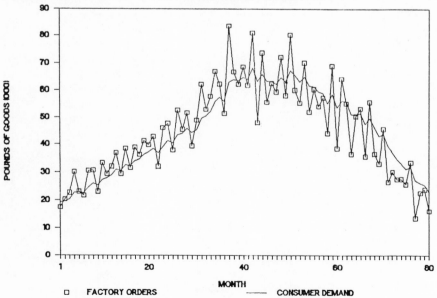

Exhibit 5.15
Price Sensitivity with Random Factor

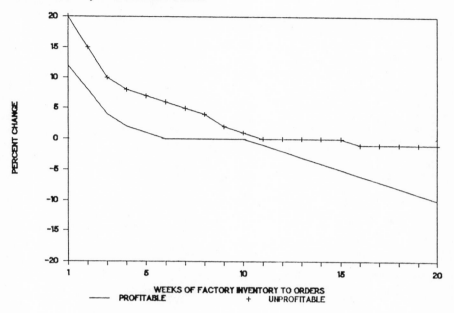

increase production cuts when factory inventories were far too high in relation to orders.

The final modification to the simulation was the incorporation of overtime, which was not present in the simulation without the noise, or random factor. When factory inventory was less than six weeks' worth of orders, production was increased by 25 percent, reflecting the fact that machine operators were working a ten-hour rather than an eight-hour day. This was in addition to any production gain caused by hiring new machine operators, as indicated in Exhibit 5.16. The incorporation of overtime made factory owners much more responsive to falling inventories. The resulting distributor and factory inventories with the random factor, or noise, to simulate variability in consumer demand are shown in Exhibit 5.17.

A comparison of Exhibits 5.5 and 5.17 shows somewhat less volatility in factory inventories with the random factor. Actually, there was originally more volatility, necessitating programming modifications to change the settings on the pricing and production throttles and to incorporate overtime in order to reduce the extreme swings in factory inventories. Adjustments of this sort are necessary in simulating the workings of an island society to make the model reflect a greater degree of reality. It would be entirely presumptuous of the model builder to stipulate that the initial, and quite arbitrary, settings of the various control mech-

Exhibit 5.16
Production Sensitivity with Random Factor

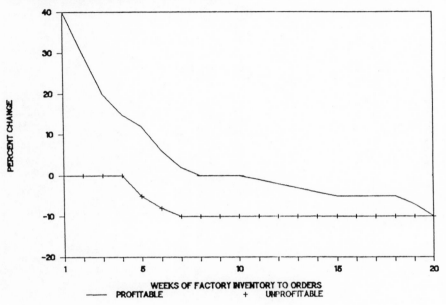

WEEKS OF FACTORY INVENTORY TO ORDERS
——— PROFITABLE   +   UNPROFITABLE

anisms and the rules modeling the behavior of man as consumer or producer are also the final settings and rules.

Exhibit 5.18 tracks the employment of machine operators. A direct comparison with Exhibit 5.6 is not really possible because Exhibit 5.18 incorporates overtime on the part of the machine operators, whereas overtime did not exist in the earlier model.

Employment increased the first one or two months and then settled out until month 10. Then a large number of machine operators were hired in response to falling factory inventories and rising orders. Utilization reached a high level, inducing owners to hire machine builders. However, the number of new machine operators hired was sufficient to restore the ratio of factory inventories to orders to the comfortable range. Meanwhile, the horde of machine builders was adding to machine capacity, and machine utilization began to fall because machine operators were not being hired to man the newly built machines. This is the reason why utilization started falling around month 18 and kept falling until around month 22, as seen in Exhibit 5.19.

Falling utilization and a test of profitability, as described in the appendix, fulfilled the conditions necessary for factory owners to start laying off machine builders. This condition for laying off machine builders persisted long enough for all the machine builders to be laid off before falling factory inventories (Exhibit 5.17) induced managers to hire more machine operators. As more

Exhibit 5.17
Distributor and Factory Inventories with Random Factor

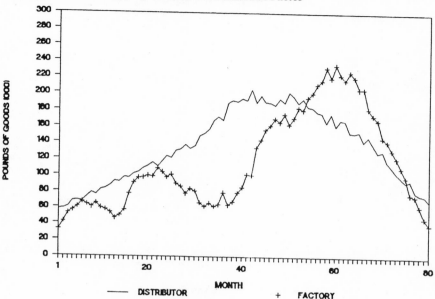

machine operators were hired around month 25 (Exhibit 5.18), utilization increased sufficiently for factory managers to begin rehiring machine builders to enhance their productive capacity. The interplay between machine utilization and machine builder employment is seen in Exhibit 5.20. The number of machines in Exhibit 5.21 shows the impact of the two waves of hiring machine builders.

The changing slope of the second hiring wave of machine builders in Exhibit 5.20 from months 25 through 35 is caused by varying degrees of profitability. The profitability test was the payback period for new machine capacity. Payback is a function of both the labor costs to construct new machines and the price of goods produced by the new machines. Exhibit 5.22 shows that prices were constant during this time period. However, as illustrated in Exhibit 5.23, labor costs were going up during this period of time.

As discussed in the accompanying appendix, the rate of hiring new machine builders is influenced by the degree of profitability, as measured by the payback period. The payback period is the period of time, in months, needed to recoup the investment in a new machine. The interplay between the price of goods to be produced by the new machine and the cost of labor to construct the new machine was sufficient to cause the employment rate for machine builders to be slowed down, and speeded up, as the degree of profitability for new plant capacity changed.

Exhibit 5.18
Number of Machine Operators with Random Factor

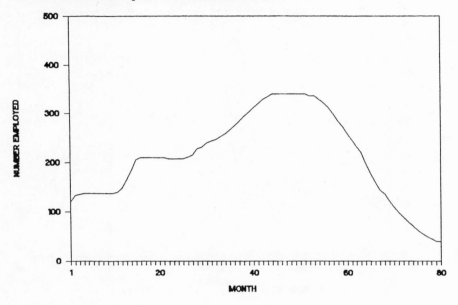

Exhibit 5.19
Machine Utilization with Random Factor

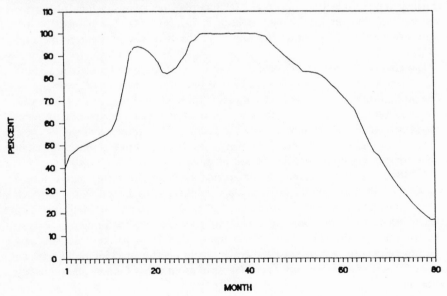

Exhibit 5.20
Number of Machine Builders and Percentage of Utilization with Random Factor

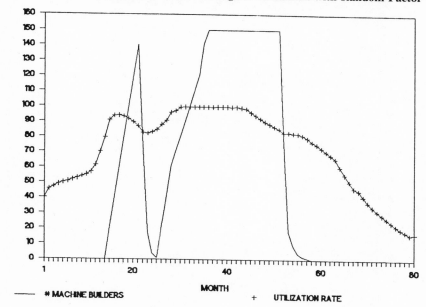

Exhibit 5.21
Number of Machines with Random Factor

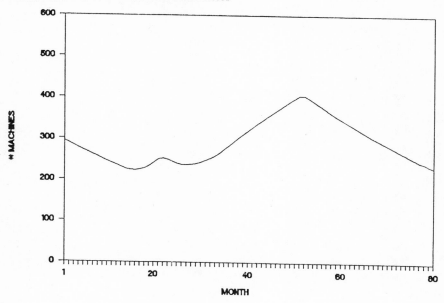

Exhibit 5.22
Price of Goods with Random Factor

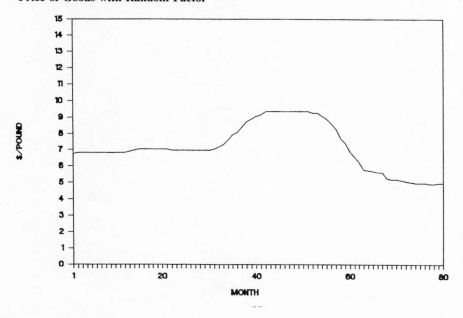

Exhibit 5.23
Monthly Wages with Random Factor

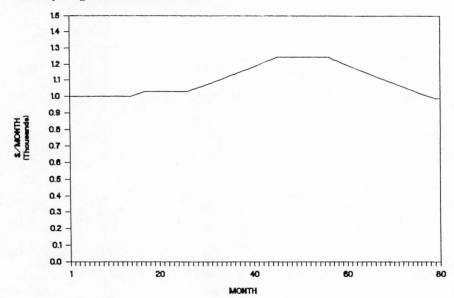

APPENDIX

There are two programs in this appendix. The first one is the simulation used for the first set of exhibits without the random factor. Statements 50–96 are the internal data base for price and production sensitivities to the ratio of weeks of factory inventories to orders. The first two figures in each row represent price sensitivies and the last two figures in each row are the production sensitivies, as illustrated in Exhibits 5.1 and 5.2. The internal data for consumer demand, as shown in Exhibit 5.3, is generated in statements 100–108. The file for storing the data from running the simulation is opened in statement 130.

Variable V is the distributors' inventory, and V1 is the factories' inventory. The distributors' inventory is initially set at 60,000 pounds, and the factories' inventory is initially set at 30,000 pounds. The initial number of machines (variable M) is set at 300, and the initial number of employed workers (variable N) is set at 100. The initial price (variable P) is set at $6.50 per pound, and the initial wage (variable L) is set at $1,000 per month. All this is done in statement 140. Statement 145 sets the previous month's price of goods and wage rates at the initial values. For an eighty-month period starting in statement 150, the distributors' inventory is reduced by consumer demand (statement 155), and factory orders reflect both consumer demand and any adjustments necessary to maintain an eight-week (two-month) supply of goods in the distributors' warehouses (statement 160).

All factories are treated as one single entity. Variable V1 in statement 165 is the factory output being added to its inventory. The output of the factory is the number of machine operators multiplied by 200 pounds of goods per manned machine. In statements 170–180, orders to distributors are honored to the extent that there is available inventory at the factory to do so. Care has to be exercised to ensure that no negative inventories arise.

In statement 185, calculations are performed to determine the profitability of operation. The variable Q is the monthly output of 200 pounds of goods multiplied by the price of goods per pound less the cost of labor to operate the machine. The variable B is the payback period in months. It is assumed that construction workers receive a 20 percent premium in pay as compensation for their additional risk of being laid off in comparison to machine operators. The total cost of construction of one machine is the ten months' worth of premium pay. This divided by the gross margin of one month's operation (Q) yields the payback period in months.

The key variable—the ratio of weeks of inventory to orders—is derived in statement 189 with provisos in statements 190–197 to keep the variable W within the range of 1 to 20. Price is changed according to its sensitivity to the ratio of weeks of inventory to orders: statement 203 covers profitable operations, and statement 204 covers operations that are not profitable. Production is adjusted in statements 210–225 according to the production sensitively to the weeks-of-inventory-to-orders ratios for profitable and unprofitable operation. Statements 225–230 calculate the utilization rate with the proviso that the number of workers cannot exceed the number of machines.

Statement 232 checks to see if operations are profitable. If so, and if utilization is above 95 percent, or if utilization is above 90 percent and increasing, then labor rates increase by 1 percent (statements 233–240). If operations are profitable, but utilization is below 80 percent and decreasing, then labor rates fall by 1 percent (statements 245–250). When times are unprofitable, labor rates also fall by 1 percent per month (statements

232 and 250). Otherwise, labor rates remain unchanged. The program assumed that high utilization rates meant exhaustion of available manpower. This might not be necessarily true but was incorporated in the model for demonstration purposes.

The hiring of machine builders is performed starting in statement 255. If utilization is above 85 percent, and if there are more machine operators working this month as compared to last month (statement 257), then machine builders are hired according to the following table (statements 264–274):

PAYBACK PERIOD IN MONTHS	NUMBER OF MACHINE BUILDERS HIRED
>48	0
37–48	10
25–36	20
<25	40

The number of machine builders hired is sensitive to the degree of payback. Machines decay at a rate of 2 percent per month. Over a period of four years, there would not be much left of the initial supply of machine capacity. Therefore, factory owners would not be too keen on adding capacity when the profitability of new capacity, as measured by the payback period, exceeds the normal operational life of a machine. They would require a quicker recoupment of investment than that. At the other extreme, a payback period of less than two years for a machine that has a useful life of something over four years would represent an extremely attractive investment. Factory owners would add capacity at the maximum possible rate under those conditions. The rate of addition of machine capacity with payback periods of between two and four years would be a blend of the two extremes.

If operations turn unprofitable, all the machine builders are laid off in one fell swoop (statements 260, 262, 280, and 282). This is a rather draconian move. In the simulation, all the machine builders were already laid off by the time operations turned the corner from profitable to unprofitable. For the times when machine operator employment is falling, with utilization still above 85 percent, the number of machine builders laid off is as follows (statements 284–296):

PAYBACK PERIOD IN MONTHS	NUMBER OF MACHINE BUILDERS LAID OFF
>48	−20
37–48	−10
<37	0

This reflects nervousness on the part of managers about continuing to add machine capacity during times when they are cutting back on production, even though production is still at a high level of utilization. If production falls below 85 percent, and if employment of machine operators continues to fall, then half of the machine builders are laid off (statement 305). If production is below 85 percent, but the employment of the machine operators has stabilized or is expanding, then one-fourth of the machine builders are laid off (statement 310). The total population of machine builders cannot exceed 150 (statements 350 and 355). The total number of machines in any month is 98 percent of the previous month's machine capacity plus any new machines, taking into account that it requires ten man-months of effort to build one machine (statement 360). The values of the variables used in constructing the exhibits are written to a file named CH5F in statement 370, and the procedure repeats itself over the eighty-month period (statement 380).

The language used in writing the programs in Chapters 4 and 5 is the version of BASIC found on IBM compatible personal computers. After the program was run, the file CH5F was renamed CH5F.PRN in order to import the data file into the LOTUS spreadsheet environment with the command File Import Numbers. All the exhibits were created using conventional LOTUS graph commands.

Appendix 5.1

```
10 REM NAME OF PROGRAM IS CH5
20 DIM U(30,5):DIM D(100)
50 FOR I=1 TO 20
52 FOR J=1 TO 4
54 READ U(I,J)
56 DATA 1.15,1.20,1.2,1.0
58 DATA 1.10,1.15,1.2,1.0
60 DATA 1.05,1.10,1.2,1.0
62 DATA 1.03,1.08,1.15,1.0
64 DATA 1.01,1.07,1.12,0.95
66 DATA 1.00,1.06,1.06,0.92
68 DATA 1.00,1.05,1.02,0.9
70 DATA 1.00,1.04,1.0,0.9
72 DATA 1.00,1.02,1.0,0.9
74 DATA 1.00,1.01,1.0,0.9
76 DATA 0.99,1.00,0.99,0.9
78 DATA 0.98,1.00,0.98,0.9
80 DATA 0.97,1.00,0.97,0.9
82 DATA 0.96,1.00,0.96,0.9
84 DATA 0.95,1.00,0.95,0.9
86 DATA 0.94,0.99,0.95,0.9
88 DATA 0.93,0.99,0.95,0.9
90 DATA 0.92,0.99,0.95,0.9
92 DATA 0.91,0.99,0.95,0.9
94 DATA 0.90,0.99,0.95,0.9
96 NEXT:NEXT
100 D(1)=20:FOR I=2 TO 30:D(I)=D(I-1)+1:NEXT
102 FOR I=31 TO 40:D(I)=D(I-1)+2:NEXT
104 FOR I=41 TO 50:D(I)=D(I-1):NEXT
106 FOR I=51 TO 65:D(I)=D(I-1)-1:NEXT
108 FOR I=66 TO 80:D(I)=D(I-1)-2:NEXT
130 OPEN "O",#1,"CH5F"
140 V=60:V1=30:M=300:N=100:P=6.5:L=1000
145 P1=6.5:L1=1000
150 FOR I=1 TO 80
155 V=V-D(I):IF V<0 THEN 157 ELSE 160
157 V=0
160 R=D(I)+(8*D(I)/4-V):IF R<0 THEN 163 ELSE 165
163 R=0
165 V1=V1+200*N/1000
170 A=V1-R:IF A<0 THEN 175 ELSE 180
175 V=V+V1:V1=0:GOTO 185
180 V=V+R:V1=V1-R
185 Q=200*P-L:B=1.2*L*10/Q:IF R=0 THEN 187 ELSE 189
187 IF V1=0 THEN 193 ELSE 197
189 W=INT(4*V1/R)
```

```
190 IF W<1 THEN 193 ELSE 195
193 W=1:GOTO 200
195 IF W>20 THEN 197 ELSE 200
197 W=20
200 IF Q>0 THEN 203 ELSE 205
203 P1=P:P=P*U(W,1):GOTO 210
205 P1=P:P=P*U(W,2)
210 IF B>0 THEN 215 ELSE 220
215 J=3:GOTO 225
220 J=4
225 N1=N:N=INT(N*U(W,J)):IF N>M THEN 227 ELSE 230
227 N=INT(M)
230 U1=U:U=N/M
232 IF Q<0 THEN 250 ELSE 233
233 IF U>.95 THEN 240 ELSE 235
235 IF U>.9 THEN 237 ELSE 245
237 IF U>U1 THEN 240 ELSE 245
240 L=L*1.01
245 IF U<.8 THEN 247 ELSE 255
247 IF U<U1 THEN 250 ELSE 255
250 L=L*.99
255 IF U>.85 THEN 257 ELSE 300
257 IF N>=N1 THEN 260 ELSE 280
260 IF B<0 THEN 262 ELSE 264
262 C=0:GOTO 350
264 IF B>48 THEN 350 ELSE 266
266 IF B>36 THEN 268 ELSE 270
268 C=C+10:GOTO 350
270 IF B>24 THEN 272 ELSE 274
272 C=C+20:GOTO 350
274 C=C+40:GOTO 350
280 IF B<0 THEN 282 ELSE 284
282 C=0:GOTO 350
284 IF B>48 THEN 286 ELSE 290
286 C=C-20:IF C<0 THEN 288 ELSE 350
288 C=0:GOTO 350
290 IF B>36 THEN 292 ELSE 296
292 C=C-10:IF C<0 THEN 294 ELSE 350
294 C=0:GOTO 350
296 C=C:GOTO 350
300 IF N<N1 THEN 305 ELSE 310
305 C=INT(C/2):GOTO 350
310 C=INT(C/4):GOTO 350
350 IF C>150 THEN 355 ELSE 360
355 C=150
360 M=.98*M+C/10
370 WRITE#1,I,D(I),R,V,V1,M,U,P,L,N,C
380 NEXT
390 CLOSE#1:END
```

The second program contains additions to the first to introduce noise. The data base in statements 50–96 was changed, as illustrated in Exhibits 5.15 and 5.16. Statements 150–155 generate the noise—a variation of anywhere between − 10 and + 10 percent—in the consumer demand, as seen in Exhibit 5.13. In addition, if the previous month's ratio of inventory to orders is less than six weeks, overtime is initiated which increases production by 25 percent above normal rates (statements 165–169). Statement 200 was changed to include a running two-week average for the variable W in determining production and pricing changes with respect to the ratio of inventory to orders. This was necessary to smooth out factory owners' reactions to large swings in factory orders generated by the random factor. Otherwise, the program is the same as the one described previously.

Appendix 5.2

```
10 REM NAME OF PROGRAM IS CH5R
20 DIM U(30,5):DIM D(100)
50 FOR I=1 TO 20
52 FOR J=1 TO 4
54 READ U(I,J)
56 DATA 1.12,1.20,1.4,1.0
58 DATA 1.08,1.15,1.3,1.0
60 DATA 1.04,1.10,1.2,1.0
62 DATA 1.02,1.08,1.15,1.0
64 DATA 1.01,1.07,1.12,0.95
66 DATA 1.00,1.06,1.06,0.92
68 DATA 1.00,1.05,1.02,0.9
70 DATA 1.00,1.04,1.0,0.9
72 DATA 1.00,1.02,1.0,0.9
74 DATA 1.00,1.01,1.0,0.9
76 DATA 0.99,1.00,0.99,0.9
78 DATA 0.98,1.00,0.98,0.9
80 DATA 0.97,1.00,0.97,0.9
82 DATA 0.96,1.00,0.96,0.9
84 DATA 0.95,1.00,0.95,0.9
86 DATA 0.94,0.99,0.95,0.9
88 DATA 0.93,0.99,0.95,0.9
90 DATA 0.92,0.99,0.95,0.9
92 DATA 0.91,0.99,0.93,0.9
94 DATA 0.90,0.99,0.90,0.9
96 NEXT:NEXT
100 D(1)=20:FOR I=2 TO 30:D(I)=D(I-1)+1:NEXT
102 FOR I=31 TO 40:D(I)=D(I-1)+2:NEXT
104 FOR I=41 TO 50:D(I)=D(I-1):NEXT
106 FOR I=51 TO 65:D(I)=D(I-1)-1:NEXT
108 FOR I=66 TO 80:D(I)=D(I-1)-2:NEXT
130 OPEN "O",#1,"CH5RF"
140 V=60:V1=30:M=300:N=100:P=6.5:L=1000:W1=6
145 P1=6.5:L1=1000
150 FOR I=1 TO 80:X=RND(X):Y=RND(Y):Z=1:IF X<.5 THEN 152
152 Z=-1
155 D(I)=D(I)+Z*Y*.1*D(I):V=V-D(I):IF V<0 THEN 157 ELSE 160
157 V=0
160 R=D(I)+(8*D(I)/4-V):IF R<0 THEN 163 ELSE 165
163 R=0
165 Z=1:IF W1<6 THEN 167 ELSE 169
167 Z=1.25
169 V1=V1+200*Z*N/1000
170 A=V1-R:IF A<0 THEN 175 ELSE 180
175 V=V+V1:V1=0:GOTO 185
180 V=V+R:V1=V1-R
185 Q=200*P-L:B=1.2*L*10/Q:IF R=0 THEN 187 ELSE 189
186 Q=200*P-L:B=1.2*L*10/Q:IF R=0 THEN 187 ELSE 189
187 IF V1=0 THEN 193 ELSE 197
189 W1=W:W=INT(4*V1/R)
```

```
190 IF W<1 THEN 193 ELSE 195
193 W=1:GOTO 200
195 IF W>20 THEN 197 ELSE 200
197 W=20
200 W=INT((W1+W)/2):IF Q>0 THEN 203 ELSE 205
203 P1=P:P=P*U(W,1):GOTO 210
205 P1=P:P=P*U(W,2)
210 IF B>0 THEN 215 ELSE 220
215 J=3:GOTO 225
220 J=4
225 N1=N:N=INT(N*U(W,J)):IF N>M THEN 227 ELSE 230
227 N=INT(M)
230 U1=U:U=N/M
232 IF Q<0 THEN 250 ELSE 233
233 IF U>.95 THEN 240 ELSE 235
235 IF U>.9 THEN 237 ELSE 245
237 IF U>U1 THEN 240 ELSE 245
240 L=L*1.01
245 IF U<.8 THEN 247 ELSE 255
247 IF U<U1 THEN 250 ELSE 255
250 L=L*.99
255 IF U>.85 THEN 257 ELSE 300
257 IF N>=N1 THEN 260 ELSE 280
260 IF B<0 THEN 262 ELSE 264
262 C=0:GOTO 350
264 IF B>48 THEN 350 ELSE 266
266 IF B>36 THEN 268 ELSE 270
268 C=C+10:GOTO 350
270 IF B>24 THEN 272 ELSE 274
272 C=C+20:GOTO 350
274 C=C+40:GOTO 350
280 IF B<0 THEN 282 ELSE 284
282 C=0:GOTO 350
284 IF B>48 THEN 286 ELSE 290
286 C=C-20:IF C<0 THEN 288 ELSE 350
288 C=0:GOTO 350
290 IF B>36 THEN 292 ELSE 296
292 C=C-10:IF C<0 THEN 294 ELSE 350
294 C=0:GOTO 350
296 C=C:GOTO 350
300 IF N<N1 THEN 305 ELSE 310
305 C=INT(C/2):GOTO 350
310 C=INT(C/4):GOTO 350
350 IF C>150 THEN 355 ELSE 360
355 C=150
360 M=.98*M+C/10
370 WRITE#1,I,D(I),R,V,V1,M,U,P,L,N,C
380 NEXT
390 CLOSE#1:END
```

6

Man as Consumer Meets Man as Producer

Man as consumer and man as producer were dealt with in isolation in Chapters 4 and 5, respectively. It is time for the two of them to meet. Man as consumer meets man as producer in two places. They stand on opposite sides of a table in the marketplace, and they stand in the same line at the teller's window in the bank. Both meeting places have to be meshed together in order to provide a mechanism for forecasting business conditions. The meshing of the two aspects of man requires that certain matters be dealt with prior to constructing a simulator of man's behavior as both consumer and producer.

The purpose of the simulation is to investigate the possibility of identifying the conditions surrounding turning points in the business cycle. In making business predictions, it is customary to assume that business activity as it now exists will continue more or less intact over the forecast period. The nature of things forces man to make this assumption because forecasting turning points in the business cycle is a tough proposition. Moreover, it has to be recognized that man has not been given the gift of peering into the future. Thus, it is impossible for a forecast of business conditions to take the form of "continued growth in economic conditions at an annual rate of 3 percent for the next four months with a sharp turndown thereafter."

That is too ambitious as a goal. It is also too presumptuous of anyone to think that this can be accomplished. Man cannot peer into the dark clouds of the future with precision or with confidence. Therefore, the best that can be hoped for is some sort of indication that basic business conditions may change during the forecast period. The purpose of the simulation of the meeting of man as consumer and man as producer is to glean what sort of signs, or warning posts, a forecaster can identify that would indicate that a turn in business conditions is a distinct possibility during the forecast period.

Simple simulations of basic free market economies with differing degrees of government interventionist policies can be constructed. Then each can be examined during the transition periods from good to bad times and from bad to good times. The results of the examination are not analyzed in an attempt to forecast the turning points of the business cycle with precision. Rather, the purpose is to aid the forecaster in identifying the signs that indicate that a turning point in the business cycle may occur during the forecast period. A sensitivity to the possibility of a turning point in the business cycle during the forecast period would certainly strengthen the utility of a forecast as part of the corporate planning function.

In the Western world, there still remains a strong tradition of free enterprise in which individuals can organize their resources to supply goods and services in competition with others. This is the essence of a free market. The free market exists when consumers have choices because a given product is manufactured by a number of competing firms. These competing firms are, in turn, free to make decisions on what products they will make at what level of quality, the price they will charge, and the level of service they will provide. The marketplace provides the opportunity for consumers and producers to interact, with both parties making independent decisions on what wares to buy and to sell. The environment of buying and selling is under the guidance of democratic government institutions with a tradition of limited control over the actions of individuals. The essence of Adam Smith remains, despite the growth of state intervention in the conduct of business.

Yet, in spite of the increase in government intervention in the Western world during the twentieth century, there has been, in recent years, a growing global trend away from centrally planned economies and the welfare state. There is also a trend away from protected and regulated industries within a country. This falls under the umbrella of "privatization." More firms are going private through government sales of shares than are joining the ranks of those being propped up by massive government subsidies. Government experience with propping up industries has been not much more than a continual hemorrhaging of public funds without any correction of the underlying problems within the industry. Privatization places the responsibility on management and labor to take corrective actions or be liquidated in the course of events.

Globalization of the world marketplace is coming about as trade barriers are dismantled and removed, thus promoting the entry of foreign-made products into domestic markets. Removal of trade barriers, low cost transportation in relation to the value of goods, easy communications between various parts of the world, and the ready means of processing huge mounds of data have encouraged the globalization of world industry. The world has moved closer to Adam Smith in that the number of competitors in each domestic market has increased markedly with the influx of foreign imports. Despite the polemics of political leaders to the contrary, there is a worldwide shifting away from Karl Marx and toward Adam Smith.

The peoples of today's world seem less apt to judge economic systems by their political underpinnings than by their performance. Maybe the world is becoming bored with the rhetoric of politicians. Maybe the people simply want more goods and less striving for utopian societies. Perhaps the world is moving toward the utilitarianism of John Stuart Mill as the final arbiter in selecting the optimal economic system. Take the economic system that seems to work best, and adapt that to the culture of the people—and forget about the political ramifications of selecting such a system. For whatever reason, and probably for the reason of demonstrated failure, the world is moving away from central planning to a more market-oriented mechanism for setting prices and allocating resources.

No one really cares that the world is drifting away from Karl Marx and moving closer to Adam Smith. Neither individual enters into the discussion as nations modify their way of producing goods and supplying services. The choice is based on the demonstrated efficacy of the system and not on the political writings expounding the virtues of that system. As a result of this tendency away from central planning toward market allocation of prices and resources, the art of forecasting business conditions, and particularly the timing of its turning points, is in its ascendancy.

Man as consumer and man as producer meet in the marketplace and in the bank. The meeting in the marketplace is a face-to-face meeting where there is a more or less even exchange of money. Both man as consumer and man as producer are standing in the same line when they meet in the bank. Neither one knows what the other is going to do when he reaches the teller's window. Thus, there is a marked difference between the meetings at the marketplace and those at the bank.

THE MEETING IN THE MARKETPLACE

In the marketplace, man as consumer is the buyer, and man as producer is the seller. Man as consumer is on one side of a commercial transaction, and man as producer is on the other side. What man as consumer spends on the purchase of goods becomes the revenue received by man as producer. A producer's revenue is generated by consumers buying his wares. To have wares to sell, workers have to be hired and paid to manufacture the goods. The marketplace is the exchange site at which the expense of having to hire a labor force to make goods is transformed into revenue when the workers spend the money they have been paid to buy the goods they have produced.

This is a perpetual round robin. Money flows from producers to consumers back to producers. Workers fulfill the twin roles of being both an expense to the producers and a source of income. Producers need consumers to purchase their goods. Producers need workers to manufacture the goods. Workers become consumers by spending their paychecks to purchase goods. Man as consumer and man as producer are one and the same. Both are intertwined and cannot be separated. More to the point, a consumer is one side of a coin, while the producer is the other: neither one can exist without the other.

THE MEETING IN THE BANK

The meeting in the bank is not as clear cut as the meeting in the marketplace. In a commercial transaction, money passes between man as producer and man as consumer. Leaving out savings for the moment, $1 paid to a worker to make goods becomes $1 of revenue when the worker acquires goods. When producer and consumer meet in the bank, it is not necessarily an even exchange. They are both standing in the same line, either to deposit or withdraw savings or to borrow. It is not necessarily complimentary action where one is borrowing what the other is saving. Both could be depositing funds; both could be withdrawing funds. One could be depositing, while the other is withdrawing. Their actions are independent of one another, which is quite unlike what occurs in the marketplace.

Before any integration of man as producer and man as consumer can be achieved, some thought has to be given to the banking system so it can handle withdrawals by consumers and producers that exceed the cash reserves stored in the banks' vaults. This has a higher order of priority than deciding on the nature of the role of government in the great scheme of things. Of the two, the banking system is more critical because history has shown that a financial crisis, in the form of a collapse of the banking system, can do more damage to an economy than any hands-on or hands-off, even or heavy-handed, approach of the government in tinkering with the delicate mechanism known as an economy.

In the Western world, for the most part, the scope of government mismanagement, or nonmanagement, in tinkering with the machinery of commerce has not been sufficiently detrimental to cause the conduct of business to cease overnight. Indiscriminate tinkering with the machinery of commerce by various government agencies may have long-term adverse effects on productivity. Nothing, however, can cause the commercial engine of business activity to grind to a halt in as short a period of time as a good old-fashioned banking crisis. Banking crises have occurred repeatedly during the nineteenth and early twentieth centuries. Some observers feel that the banking crisis of the early 1930s contributed more to the prolongation of the Great Depression than any other single factor, including the 1929 stock market crash. The unparalleled intervention by Roosevelt's New Deal could not really undo the damage inflicted on the economy by the banking crisis in the early 1930s. That was taken care of by World War II.

When man as consumer meets man as producer in the marketplace, the worst that can happen is that there is leakage in the continual cycling of money between man as consumer and man as producer. Man as consumer may not be spending all his income. He may be saving a portion of it. If the work force as a whole is saving money, the revenue stream will shrink with each cycle of wages paid to workers and sales revenue received from consumers. A metaphor may be pouring water between two buckets where one bucket has a hole in it. Eventually, one will run out of water.

The metaphor holds only for as long as there is a hole in the bottom of one of the buckets. The hole is sealed when savings reach a level at which workers feel confident that their nest eggs can tide them over the bad times. The hole is sealed when workers stop saving or when the savings from one group of workers is balanced by withdrawals by another group. The metaphor of the leaky bucket does not cover the situation when there are net withdrawals from the bank. This can happen during the best of the good times when workers, confident of their security and the size of their nest eggs, draw down a portion of their savings to add to the spending stream. This, coupled with the normal pay for the workers, adds to the revenue of the producers. The sales revenue of producers expands with each cycle. The revenue stream for man as producer is larger than the pay being earned by man as consumer. Now one of the buckets does not have a hole at its bottom, but a spigot spouting water.

The metaphor that likens savings to a leaky bucket does not hold when the savings of consumers are being borrowed by producers to build more machinery capacity. To enhance productive capacity, the manufacturers must hire machine builders. The money not being spent by the machine operators is being deposited in the bank in the form of savings, and the bank turns around and lends the money to the factory owners. The factory owners take the savings of the machine operators and pay the machine builders to expand the productive capacity of the factories. The amount of savings of one group of consumers, the machine operators, is, in effect, being transferred to another group of consumers, the machine builders. As long as all the savings of machine operators, and builders for that matter, are being transferred to the spending stream of the manufacturers, there is no leaky bucket. The leak is sealed when the banking system takes the savings of one group of workers and lends it to the factory owners to hire another group of workers.

The leaky bucket is back in operation when the savings rate is high and the utilization of existing machinery capacity is low. Now there is no need to hire machine builders to expand capacity during times when there is plenty of unused capacity lying about gathering rust. Under these conditions, a portion of each cycle of money from man as consumer to man as producer is being deposited in the banks and is not being fed back into the system. During each cycle of money exchanged between producer and consumer, some amount dribbles out of the bottom of the leaky bucket because not all the income paid to workers is coming back in sales of goods. Carried to its ultimate conclusion, there will come a time when there is no water left to pour from one bucket to the other.

Even here, there is trouble with the metaphor. Plenty of plant capacity and high savings rates are signs of a depression—or, to cast a brighter light on things, a trough of a business cycle. If prices have plummeted too far, producers may have to borrow the money being deposited by the consumers to keep their corporations solvent. This might not directly help man as consumer because no jobs are being created. However, low prices do provide more purchasing power to those consumers who still hold a job. A rapid liquidation of excess inventories may clear the way for the business cycle to shake off the doldrums and start crawling its way out of the valley of despair.

Unfortunately, though, this might not be the only sequence of events. If prices sink too low, producers may or—to be more realistic—producers *will* be forced to slash wages and jobs unilaterally for their self-preservation. Then the corporations do not need to borrow from the banks to maintain their solvency. Fewer workers at less pay means less gross purchasing power. The continued firing of workers causes those with jobs to save more money. Then it's back to the leaky bucket where purchasing power is being reduced on each cycle of pay and spend. Each time the producers pay their workers $1,000 in wages, they get back $800 in sales of goods. The remaining $200 lie fallow in some bank account. If this keeps up long enough, business activity may fade from view.

Again, the metaphor may collapse under its own internal contradictions. Workers who lose their jobs now start to withdraw from their savings accounts. If the withdrawals exceed the savings rate of those still holding a job, then the producers may see their revenue increasing with each cycle of paying a diminished work force and counting their cash receipts. Their revenues may rise relative to what the producers are paying their work force if there are net withdrawals from the banking system. Again, the hole has been sealed and the spigot turned on.

In addition, during severe downturns in the business cycle, government spending may balloon in the form of compensation to the unemployed or in some sort of pump priming to resuscitate business activity. Meanwhile, government revenues, in the form of taxation of incomes or of sales, may decline sharply because both incomes and sales of goods are headed south. With revenue sources drying up and expenditures climbing, the government must tap savings as a source of funds. Money spent by the government means either employment or some form of compensation for the unemployed. When workers spend their income from either government employment or government benefit programs, they counteract the loss in revenue to the manufacturers in the form of savings by the workers.

SIMULATION RESOLVES COMPLEXITIES

In considering all the choices, it really isn't all that crystal clear how well the two separate entities of man as producer and man as consumer are going to mesh. Qualitative assertions as to exactly what occurs during various phases of the business cycle are not convincing as to the selection of the appropriate policy a government should follow. Integration of man as consumer and man as producer is a complex matter. Simulation of behavior patterns with various forms of government interventionist policies may clear away some of the confusion and permit us to gain a degree of insight into the repercussions of different policies.

ROLES OF GOVERNMENT AND BANKS

The integration of man as consumer and man as producer requires that some thought be given to the roles of government and banking during good and bad times. What started out as a seemingly pure economic model is already contaminated by political considerations. Even laissez faire economics is concerned with political considerations. The hands-off policy of government is a political consideration—and many pages of laissez faire economics are dedicated to this proposition. Regardless of the nature of the role of government in running the economy, from the hands-off policy of laissez faire economics to the hands-on interventionism of the welfare state, it cannot be ignored in the meshing of man as consumer and man as producer.

Financial or, better yet, banking considerations have also entered the picture. One role has already been mentioned that is not part of banking in a commercial sense. Did you notice the comment concerning insolvent firms that borrow from the banks in times of dire trouble? That is not laissez faire banking. In the world of laissez faire, a factory owner who walks into the bank looking for an infusion of cash to save him from an impending insolvency does not face a high probability of success. The banker wants to play it safe with his depositors' savings and will demand assurances of repayment which the factory owner, with his back up against the wall, cannot provide. The banker must then refuse the loan request, and the factory owner, and his workers, then face the consequences.

The question of the role of banking during the tough times of a business cycle cannot be put aside in the meshing of man as consumer and man as producer. In terms of laissez faire economics, when companies cannot satisfy loan terms in the making of interest and principal payments, the proper role of banking is to liquidate the assets of the offending firms. The role of commercial banking, in this context, is to make a bad situation worse. Liquidating firms with their backs up against a wall during tough times is not exactly a prescription for getting well. It is the euthanasia of an economy.

During really bad times, banking, behaving strictly as a commercial enterprise, could end up liquidating the whole economy. And to add a note of consistency with laissez faire economics, the banks themselves ought to be liquidated when they can no longer honor requests for withdrawals from depositors. Loans to companies that cannot honor their obligations mean that the banks, in turn, cannot honor their obligations to depositors when large numbers of them show up to withdraw their savings. The honoring of the terms of a debt instrument that might result in the liquidation of an entire industrial complex of a society and, in turn, the entire banking system itself may be putting too much of a price on the fine print of a debt instrument. Once a society experiences the banking system wiping out the industrial sector, and then having the banking system itself wiped out, the citizens of that society might reconsider having a banking system that runs purely on commercial terms.

If the pain of the bad times is made worse by strictly following the dictates of Adam Smith, then, perhaps, it is time to call on John Stuart Mill. He will permit us, for utilitarian reasons, to admit that the liquidation of industry and banks alike is not in the interests of the people. Adam Smith was dead before the first business contraction. Had he lived through one, he might not have been quite so laissez faire.

What is the role of banks during the various phases of the business cycle? No one argues with the fact that the role of banks is to divert the savings of consumers into the expansion of profitable enterprises. That takes care of the good times of a business cycle. That also takes care of the commercial aspects of banking. The question that really must be addressed concerns the role of the banks during the bad times of a business cycle. If banks operate on purely commercial terms, then their role is unquestionably to make a bad thing worse. Times are tough enough during the trough of a business cycle without banks forcing factory after factory to close its doors and lay off its entire work force because the payments of interest and principal are in arrears.

The role of banking during the bad times is only part of the consideration. Another consideration is who is going to save the banking system during the worst of the bad times. The fact that banks are closing businesses means that loans are going bad. From a banker's point of view, loans are assets created by transferring savings from workers to factory owners. Every time a loan goes belly up, a portion of the savings of depositors (which are liabilities on the bank's books) has just been flushed down the drain in a corporate bankruptcy proceeding.

The banks themselves are going to face difficult times when depositors begin withdrawing money at the same time the banks are liquidating the economy. The next logical step, once banks are permitted to liquidate the industrial base of a society, is the liquidation of the banking system itself. This seems eminently fair considering what bankers have just done to the corporations that were in financial trouble. It is hard to believe that the cleansing process of liquidating both the industrial and the banking enterprises of a society during particularly bad times would aid in any subsequent recovery of the business cycle.

The integration of man as consumer and man as producer requires that the banking system be sufficiently flexible to accommodate those times when man as consumer and man as producer are not meshing well. If man as consumer and man as producer are both net savers, the banking system is, by definition, solvent and liquid. Liquidity means that there is sufficient cash in the vaults to honor withdrawals. Because there are no net withdrawals by the population of consumers and producers, the bank is, by definition, liquid. Solvency means that the banks are able to sell assets to generate the funds necessary to remain liquid. Liquidity is assured as long as a bank can sell assets for cash to satisfy withdrawals. Insolvency results when the bank cannot sell sufficient assets to satisfy the cash demands of its depositors who want out.

If either man as consumer or man as producer is withdrawing funds while the other is saving, and if the savings are in excess of the amount being withdrawn, the banking system is still, by definition, liquid. If one is withdrawing in excess of the savings of the other, there may be a liquidity crisis once the cash in the vault is gone. The only asset a bank has is its loans. If the bank cannot sell assets (that is, loans to factory owners) or cannot raise cash by other means, then the bank becomes insolvent.

This is the making of a banking crisis, which occurred with some degree of regularity during the nineteenth and early twentieth centuries. Banking crises are caused by the divergent financial behavior of man as consumer and man as producer. Both are free to save or withdraw at will, and their free choices may not mesh. Man as consumer and man as producer, standing in the same line before the teller's window, can take actions much to each other's detriment.

It is necessary to deal with this situation before a simulation model is constructed integrating man as consumer and man as producer. This cannot be avoided—not because of its merits but because computer instructions demand that every contingency be covered with, of all things, detailed instructions. In effect, the computer will ask what is to be done when withdrawals exceed the cash reserves of the bank. An instruction is required, even if that instruction is to print the word "TILT" and stop the program—in effect, letting a banking crisis destroy whatever remnants of the economy are still in operation.

A NON–LAISSEZ FAIRE BANKING SYSTEM

The amount that man as consumer saves may or may not neatly match up with the funds that might be required by man as producer. There is no guarantee within the system that the funds needed by factories are going to be forthcoming from the workers. The propensity to save on the part of man as consumer has nothing to do with the need for funds on the part of man as producer. During the good times of a business cycle, this is not a critical matter. If factories cannot produce goods because of a shortage of capacity, and if more capacity cannot be built because there are insufficient savings of workers in the bank to draw on, then, eventually, prices will sharply escalate as shortages begin to develop. The profits generated by higher prices can then fund the expansion of industry. This may not be the optimal way to handle expansion of factory capacity, but it will work.

During the upswing of the business cycle, the workers as a group, are net savers as long as they are in the process of building up their nest eggs. Savings would probably diminish as the good times continue and the nest eggs grow to a comfortable size. Money flows into the banking system throughout the good times and floods into the banking system during the initial phase of a downturn in the business cycle. The more or less fully employed work force sharply increases its savings rate at the first real signs that the business cycle has taken a turn for the worse. As the bad times continue and more workers are laid off, unemployed workers are withdrawing from their savings to feed, clothe, and shelter their families. Depending on the severity of the downturn, workers may begin to become net withdrawers from the banking system.

Man as producer represents a different picture than man as consumer. During the upswing of the business cycle, corporations may be depositing or withdrawing money depending on the relationship between the level of prices, the volume of sales, and the amount being spent on plant expansion. During the business downswing, the corporation may be a depositor or withdrawer depending on the timing and magnitude of its ability to cut expenses by laying off machine builders and operators in relation to the fall in revenue both in price and volume of sales.

The banking system has a third customer in addition to man as consumer and man as producer. That customer is the government, which collects taxes and provides services. The revenue depends on the business cycle in that it usually takes the form of a tax against sales or against income, both of which fall during the downswing of a business cycle. Unless a government desires to increase the tax rates during a business depression, something that rarely occurs in life, the government would most likely be running a deficit, or withdrawing funds from the banking system, during the worst of times.

Thus, during the worst of a prolonged downturn in business activity, it may be possible for consumers, on balance, to be withdrawing money from their savings accounts to get them through the bad times of high unemployment. The corporations might be withdrawing money to keep themselves solvent at a time when prices of goods have fallen below the variable cost of production. The government may be withdrawing money from the banking system because tax revenues are not compensating for government expenditures.

Even in an island economy where presumably all money is locked into the system, it is possible for the banking system to suffer from a liquidity crisis, that is, running out of cash in the vaults. This was the great disadvantage of having business conducted on a gold standard. On a gold standard, withdrawals could rapidly escalate to a rush to withdraw all deposits once there was doubt that the banks did not possess sufficient coin to honor all deposits. This point is usually driven home once it is revealed that there are companies that cannot repay their debts.

Once depositors are disturbed by the thought of losing their savings, the gut reaction is to be first in line as soon as possible. The emotional aspect of a loss of confidence in the banking system rampages through the population. The lemming drive to the sea spreads faster than anyone can imagine. This guarantees the good old-fashioned banking crisis when lines form outside the banks once there is doubt that the coins deposited yesterday cannot be withdrawn today. Banking crises lead to banking holidays and usually bankruptcy for a financial institution or two. As banks begin to close their doors, a solvent corporation may find itself deprived of funds at a critical moment and join the banks, and other companies, already in the mortuary. This escalates the bankruptcies of other corporations that might have been strongly dependent on the bankrupt firm as a major customer. Not too long after this, bankruptcy spreads to individuals who bring up the rear of the march of total liquidation (another example of a positive feedback system).

GOLD HAS NO ELASTICITY

Suppose that there are no banks and that the only money is gold coins. Everyone carries gold around in his pocket. What he doesn't spend is still in his pocket. When tough times come and the individual loses his job, the gold is still in his pocket. He can keep himself going until he has no more gold in his pocket.

Once, however, he deposits his gold in the bank, he can no longer guarantee the liquidity that once was in his pocket, no matter what the bank says about its own liquidity. Suppose that the bank receives ten thousand gold coins from its depositors and stores them in its vaults. The depositors have no immediate need for the gold coins, and factory owners need the gold coins to hire workers to enhance their productive capacity. So the bankers do what is normal behavior for them and lend eight thousand gold coins to the factory owners. There are still two thousand gold coins in the vaults to handle any unusual demand for withdrawals. The bankers are receiving interest in payment of their services. The depositors don't seem to mind getting a small cut of the interest as an inducement to deposit their unneeded gold coins in the bank as long as they feel confident that they can always withdraw their gold coins at a moment's notice.

The bankers make that pledge of total liquidity because they must in order to attract deposits. They also know from experience that only a small portion of the depositors would demand their money back at any moment in time. Therefore, it can be shown to be prudent to keep a portion of the deposits on hand to meet normal withdrawal patterns and lend the rest out to creditworthy borrowers. Nobody is more creditworthy than a factory owner wanting to expand his productive capacity during times of great profitability. It would not be considered normal behavior for a banker to sit idly on a hoard of ten thousand coins without lending any of it out just to be prepared for the highly improbable day when every depositor turns up at his door demanding his money back.

Suppose that the banker feels that the two thousand gold coins in his vaults are more than sufficient to meet normal patterns of withdrawals from his depositors. Given the price of goods and the cost of labor, the factory owners are enjoying very profitable times. They want to expand their capacity faster than their cash flow permits. They ask the banker to borrow some of the gold, with a financing charge, to help them expand their capacity. The banker acquiesces with glee as he envisions the flow of interest income from his financial astuteness. He may actually believe that he is doing a service to society in addition to enriching himself. In fact, he *is* doing society a service, and he *is* also enriching himself by earning interest on the borrowed funds. Some of that he shares with the depositors as an inducement for them to deposit their gold coins in his bank. The factory owners take the coins, spend them on building new factories, and promise to repay the coins, plus financing charges, over the next five years.

There are still two thousand gold coins in the vaults—more than enough to handle normal gold transactions during normal times. In addition, there is a promise on the part of the factory owners to repay the borrowed coins over the next five years with interest, naturally. If they can't, they have agreed, in essence, to turn their factories over to the banker. That's prudent banking.

Everything is just fine until normal times lose their normalcy. The normal gold transactions of yesterday are no longer normal today. People are becoming nervous over the prospects of the bank, given the fact that the borrowers, the factory owners, are having a hard time. How do they know the factory owners are having a hard time? The first hint is that they are losing their jobs. The second hint is that the factories are now owned by the bankers. The depositors rush to the bank, and the first to arrive get their money. Those not at the head of the line, who represent the remaining 80 percent of the deposits, are in deep trouble. They are demanding gold coins from an institution that no longer has any gold coins in its vaults.

The bankers may have freshly signed documents of ownership of a dozen or so new factories, but no gold coins. This is the banking crisis that puts the finishing touches on a sinking economy. The banks cannot avert this crisis by demanding immediate payment from the still solvent factory owners because the banks have agreed to a five-year repayment period. Even if there were such a clause in the loan agreement permitting the lender to demand immediate repayment from the borrower, the borrower has already spent the gold in building a new factory. As any lender knows, you cannot squeeze blood from a stone. Throwing a company or a person into bankruptcy does not mean repayment of the money owed. It may well guarantee that the money will never be repaid.

This is the inherent problem with gold as a medium of exchange. A withdrawal by one person has to be more or less balanced by a deposit by someone else. But we know a priori that there can be times when consumer, producer, and government may have to make simultaneous withdrawals. If one maintains that every withdrawal will be matched by a deposit somewhere else in the system, he ignores the possibility that the depositor can simply keep his withdrawal in his pocket. This is particularly true when money is gold coin. Once depositors lose confidence in the banks' ability to pay them back the gold coins they have deposited, there will be a banking crisis. At one time when gold was money, withholding coins from the banks was called *hoarding*. Excessive hoarding can also destroy a banking system.

There is little virtue in having a banking crisis—no one gains from it. Man as consumer does not benefit when he cannot withdraw his savings to support himself. Man as producer does not benefit when he cannot withdraw funds to keep his firm afloat. And man in his role as government does not benefit by not being able to take corrective action during a business bust because there is no gold in the banks' vaults. From a purely utilitarian point of view, banking crises are to be avoided because society does not gain by having companies and banks close their doors, never to be reopened again.

Gold, the money of feudal times and the days of early capitalism, is not elastic. In fact, it is perfectly inelastic, which explains why it is a perfect storehouse of value. It is also a perfect medium of exchange as long as it is never deposited in a bank. The problem with banking is that it has to assure its depositors that their money is always available on demand. Then the bankers lend the money out to all sorts of worthwhile enterprises, praying that most of the depositors do not simultaneously show up at their doors demanding their money. During good times, the depositors cooperate. When things get tough, they don't. The first ones in line get paid off and the rest get nothing—which goes a long way toward explaining why panics, once started, spread so fast and are virtually impossible to stop.

Bankers, in a way, are running a con game. They always have—and always will. They cannot, with a totally clear conscience, promise to repay all deposits on demand and then lend out a goodly portion of the deposits with a five-year repayment schedule. Gold simply does not lend itself well to such shenanigans. It is the ultimate in inelasticity. What is really needed is elastic money. The banking system would work better if the supply of money could be expanded to satisfy the demand of depositors to withdraw their funds, even when the bank vaults are empty.

ELASTIC MONEY

An elastic money is something that can be easily, and cheaply, reproduced to meet unexpected demand. Paper money is ideal. But modern man can produce money even more cheaply with a magnetic swiggle on a plastic tape covered with iron oxide fed into a computer made up of silicon (the primary ingredient in sand) chips doped up with a speck of rare earth elements.

In effect, something has to be essentially created out of nothing to ensure that there is enough pretend-gold in the vaults to keep the population confident in the banking system. Confidence is the feeling that there is no need to rush down to the bank to withdraw all one's savings. One can achieve a sense of security with a pocketful of gold coins. But the same sense of security cannot be achieved if money is in the form of a magnetic signal on a rust-covered strip of plastic tape. It is hardly comforting to carry it around in one's pockets. One might as well leave it in the bank as long as the depositor is confident that the money can be spent when and as needed.

An elastic money system requires a name for a deposit that is going to be made to keep the banking system liquid, and solvent. Let us call it bank credit. Bank credit is a phony deposit placed in the banking system to ensure that all withdrawals can be satisfied. Bank credit is needed in the daily operation of the banking system. Take, as an example, a savings bank that specializes in home mortgages. It takes deposits from savers and promises every one of them the privilege of instant withdrawal of all of their funds with no advance notice of any kind. To honor this pledge, perhaps 5 or 10 percent of the deposits are set aside for normal withdrawals. The remaining 90 or 95 percent of the funds are plowed into thirty-year mortgages. In theory, the savings bank has assets to cover its liabilities. The assets are the speck of cash in the vault and a mountain of thirty-year mortgages. The liabilities are the savings accounts that can be withdrawn in their entirety without advance notice. Where is the liquidity if depositors start making withdrawals that exceed the cash in the vault?

Under the gold standard, the bank would close its doors overnight. Every other bank in the neighborhood becomes suspect. Lines start forming, and panic spreads because it doesn't take long for everyone to recognize that the con game is over. A full-fledged banking crisis ensues. The closing of banks means that corporations may not have access to the cash they need to keep themselves going. Then firms begin closing their doors. Laid-off workers rush to withdraw what they can, but they are already too late. The economy goes into a tailspin, and nobody comes up a winner, except for a speculator or two who can pick up valuable producing assets for ten cents on the dollar.

Under an elastic money system, such as paper currency, someone, such as a government agency, keeps depositing funds into the bank until the depositors get tired of withdrawing their funds. During the banking crises under the gold standard, bank runs were stopped by timely shipments of gold from other banks or from the government's vaults. To this extent, there is some elasticity in the gold system—but not enough to cover a more general run on the banks.

Where does the government agency obtain the funds to keep the banks liquid when money is a pretty design printed on paper? Let us ask the question another way. Who knows whether the deposit being made by the government agency is real in the sense that the government agency is withdrawing paper money from another account, or whether the deposit has simply been printed for the occasion? Answer: No one. The question could be phrased slightly differently. Who cares whether the deposit being made by the government agency is real or printed for the occasion? Answer: No one.

The beauty of an elastic money system, such as paper currency, is that no one knows if the government has run its printing presses overtime or has made a bona fide withdrawal from one of its accounts within the banking system. What is even better about the system is that no one really cares. As long as depositors are receiving paper currency to cover their paper currency deposits in the banking system, they really do not care whether it has just been freshly printed or withdrawn from a bona fide cash account. As a matter of fact, they probably feel more confident about the system if they know that the government itself would never have any difficulty in raising the cash needed to keep the system liquid.

Bank credit is an essentially phony deposit made by a government monetary agency to ensure that there will never be a run on the banks. It is a deposit made out of nothing, having no intrinsic value other than the value of the paper it is printed on or the value of a small magnetic field on a computer tape or in a silicon chip. It is simply an imaginary accountant's entry on an imaginary ledger. Obviously, such a system is open to abuse—but abuse is not the subject under discussion. Our discussion deals with the ability of a government monetary agency to create money out of nothing to ensure the liquidity of the banking system.

MANAGEMENT OF INTEREST RATES

Bank credit has another use besides guaranteeing the liquidity, and therefore the solvency, of the banking system. The degree to which bank credit is used can control the level of interest rates within certain bounds. In other words, if sufficient bank credit is added to the system, interest rates may fall. If sufficient bank credit is removed from the system, interest rates may rise.

To illustrate this phenomenon, let us first consider the situation in which there is no bank credit. According to the laws of supply and demand, a net withdrawal of funds from the banking system should cause interest rates to rise. The reason for this is that the banking system has to attract more funds in order to prevent a liquidity problem from developing. As funds are withdrawn from the banking system, cash reserves start falling. Bank officers become nervous and increase the interest rate in the desperate hope that higher interest rates may attract more savings. Increasing the interest rate could attract funds in the form of incremental savings to counter the funds being withdrawn from the system. Increasing the interest rate could also attract funds from other banks that pay a lower interest rate on their deposits. This is the only tool bank officers have to attract additional funds, and it is difficult to conceive of the bankers standing idly by with the same old interest rate as their cash reserves are dwindling before their eyes.

On the other hand, a surfeit of funds by depositors, far in excess of what can be lent out, would be an inducement for the bankers to cut their interest rates. It is the old law of supply and demand in action again. Now there is no need to attract more savings. Sooner or later, one bank official is going to suggest cutting the interest rate as a signal to the saving public that their continued pouring of funds into the banking system is not particularly welcomed.

Even if the bankers are a little slow in reducing interest rates, one can count on corporate financial officers to start shopping around from one cash rich bank to another cash rich bank, seeking lower interest rates on their borrowings. If a bank is flush with cash, it might as well try to lend money to a company at a lower interest rate than what the company is paying to another bank in order to increase the amount of funds earning income for itself. The company borrows from one bank and uses the proceeds to pay off a more expensive loan—that is, a loan at a higher interest rate—at another bank.

This form of behavior on the part of financial officers is no different than consumers shopping around for the best price on a sofa. The bankers are acting exactly like a sofa manufacturer whose warehouse is spilling over with excess sofas. This refinancing of high interest debt with low interest debt will eventually result in cuts in interest rates being paid by bankers to depositors.

Suppose that society adopts an elastic money system that permits monetary authorities to place a deposit in a bank credit account, which, in all appearances, is just another account. Suppose, furthermore, that the monetary authorities decide to increase interest rates during the good times of a business cycle. Their decision to increase interest rates may have been arrived at by considering the degree of inflation and the desire to ensure that depositors have sufficient inducement not to withdraw their funds from the banking system and aggravate inflationary pressures by spending the money. Increasing interest rates can be accomplished by the monetary authorities withdrawing funds from the bank credit account. This tends to deplete the cash reserves of the bank. If these withdrawals are of sufficient magnitude, the banks will be forced to start bidding for more deposits to rebuild their cash reserves and interest rates will start to climb.

During a downturn in a business cycle, the government monetary authorities may desire to reduce interest rates as an inducement for industry to expand its plant capacity. This is really a mistaken belief on the part of monetary authorities because factory owners add capacity when their plants are busy and profitable. During downturns in business activity, plants are idle and generally unprofitable—hardly an incentive to add capacity regardless of the level of interest rates. Nevertheless, if interest rates are considered too high, adding funds into the banking system via phony deposits to the bank credit account can reduce interest rates.

Note that two separate issues have been raised. One is the idea of government fiscal policy. The government has revenue based on a tax rate applied against incomes or sales or both, and it has expenditures. Fiscal management has to do with balancing the budget by controlling the expenditures and the tax rates which affect revenues. Fiscal management is the workings of government budgetary operations in the realm of real money. It can result in government surpluses, deficits, or a balanced budget.

The other entirely separate issue is government monetary policy. In the context described herein, monetary policy has to do with the creation of bank credit— an essentially phony, Alice-in-Wonderland entry in the ledgers of the banking system. Its purpose is to ensure that the banks always have sufficient liquid reserves to honor all requests for withdrawals, even when the amount of withdrawals exceeds the cash stored in the vault. By maintaining a positive liquidity for the banking system, bank credit also assures the solvency of the system. Furthermore, by varying the amount of bank credit with regard to the other, and real, sources of deposits (personal, corporate, and governmental), the monetary authorities can control interest rates within reasonable bounds. In the real world, monetary authorities have often times abused the system with huge additions of bank credit. The supposition contained in this discussion is that the monetary authorities are not abusing the system, nor are interest rates grossly out of line with the expectations of depositors.

7

Forecasting in a Laissez Faire Society

The previous chapters have been primarily concerned with laying the foundation for incorporating human behavior into the forecasting process. Chapters 4 and 5 described the two faces of human behavior as consumer and producer of material goods. Chapter 6 discussed the interaction of these two aspects of behavior in the marketplace and in the bank. All this has been a prelude to this chapter in which the behavior characteristics of man as producer and man as consumer are integrated in a dynamic, though simple, simulation of business activity. The groundwork has been laid—it is now time to complete the structure of the simulation.

The simulation under discussion (programming instructions for which are listed in the appendix) illustrates the nature of the process of setting up a society in which business activity is influenced by the attitudes of its inhabitants. No pretense is made that the simulation contained in this chapter is the final product of a national, regional, or global economy. It barely reflects the complexities of an island economy. The purpose of the simulation is to demonstrate the idea that business cycles are, at least in part, the consequences of human behavior. In particular, turning points in the business cycle are a chain of events triggered by human responses to certain aspects of business activity. The objective is to try to identify the conditions that mark the beginnings of the turning points of a business cycle from good times to bad and from bad times to good. These conditions may lead to a shift in behavior on the part of man as consumer and man as producer, which, in turn, contribute to the vagaries of business activity.

The simulation contained herein is intentionally simplistic in structure to demonstrate the feasibility of forecasting business activity on the basis of certain aspects of business activity that could trigger changes in human behavior. Its purpose is to show that the development of certain business conditions over the forecast period might stimulate changes in the attitudes of man as consumer or producer. Such a change of attitude may trigger a series of events which, if of sufficient magnitude, may be termed in hindsight a turning point in the business cycle. If this is the case, then the development of such conditions that are a prelude to a change in attitudes or behavior patterns may signal a turn in the business cycle for the better, or for the worse, over the forecast period.

The protocol underlying the instructions for the simulation program contained in the appendix to this chapter starts with the establishment of the initial conditions.

ESTABLISHMENT OF INITIAL CONDITIONS

The settings of the pricing and production throttles used by a factory manager in guiding his locomotive over the peaks and valleys of the mountainous terrain of the business cycle are shown in the following set of exhibits.

Exhibit 7.1 shows the settings for the pricing throttle when the ratio of factory inventory to orders is increasing. Profitability is defined as price compensating for the variable cost of production. A factory manager behaves in markedly different ways when the sales price of something he is making is meeting the fixed costs of operation, or contributing to the overall profitability of a firm, and when it is not. When the ratio of factory inventories to orders is growing, and when the sales price exceeds the variable cost of production, the factory manager

Exhibit 7.1
Pricing Throttle: Ratio Increasing

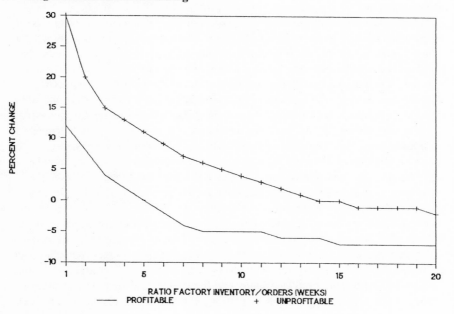

will show little reluctance to cut prices to restore factory inventories to a more satisfactory level in relation to the size of incoming orders. However, he will exhibit great reluctance to cut prices to reduce a growing inventory in relation to orders if the sales price cannot cover the cost of production. Or, in more succinct terms, the factory manager tends to rely on the pricing throttle to keep inventory in line with orders when each manufactured item is covering fixed costs or contributing to the profitability of the company. When the sales price does not cover the cost of manufacture, the factory manager is motivated to abandon the pricing throttle and grab the production throttle as a means of restoring factory inventory to the desired relationship to incoming orders.

It would not be considered normal behavior for the factory manager to pull back on the pricing throttle when a loss is being incurred every time he makes and sells a product. If he is reluctant to cut prices further when the price already does not cover the cost of labor and material in manufacturing the product, then he has no choice but to grab the production throttle to rectify a situation of growing inventory with relation to orders.

Exhibit 7.1 shows two distinct behavior patterns. One is a general willingness to cut prices when the ratio of factory inventory to orders from distributors is growing under conditions of profitability. Thus, the factory manager is more likely to provide a discount to a favorite customer to get rid of excess inventories than to cut production. Under conditions of unprofitability, his behavior is quite different. Then the factory manager has the intestinal fortitude to raise prices, even when the ratio of inventory to orders is growing. There is little satisfaction in producing an item when every item coming off the assembly line is generating a direct operating loss. As will be seen shortly, the factory manager is relying to a much greater extent on the production throttle. However, there is a point at which the ratio between factory inventory and orders is so out of hand that some price erosion takes place, even though the sales price does not compensate for the cost of manufacture.

The factory manager's behavior also changes markedly when the ratio of inventory to orders is decreasing. He is now making decisions in an environment in which he feels he has the upper hand, even with a current excess of inventory with respect to orders. A producer, by definition, has the upper hand when inventories are small in relation to orders. As long as the ratio of inventory to orders is dropping, even with excess inventory, a producer perceives that he will eventually gain the upper hand. All he has to do is wait. And if waiting is all he has to do to gain the upper hand, he is going to show far more reluctance to cut prices when the ratio of inventory to orders is shrinking than when it is growing.

The factory manager's behavior is influenced by his perception that time is either on his side or not on his side. If time is on his side, he merely has to wait for the inventory to reach a point at which he has the upper hand to raise prices willy-nilly for his personal, or his company's, gain. The shift in a producer's attitude toward price adjustments is similar to the shift in a poker player's attitude

Exhibit 7.2
Pricing Throttle: Ratio Decreasing

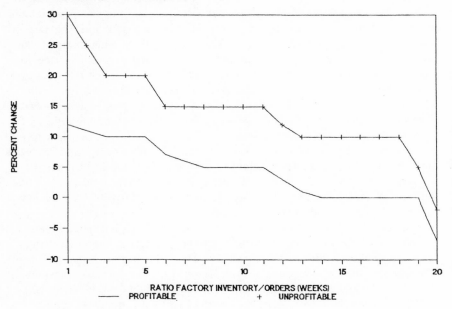

when he is first dealt a pair of deuces and then draws three kings in a hand of five card draw. The player's strategy reflects the nature of the cards in his hand—which, in turn, affects his behavior. His strategy with regard to betting will be influenced by the fact that a pair of deuces has become a full house. The factory manager's pricing policy will be similarly influenced by changes in the direction of the ratio of factory inventory to orders. A growing ratio that shifts direction and starts shrinking is similar to a pair of deuces becoming a full house. The principal difference between a poker player and a factory manager is that one has to keep a straight face and the other doesn't. Exhibit 7.2 shows the settings on the pricing throttle when the ratio of factory inventory to orders is shrinking, strengthening the hand of the factory manager.

A comparison of Exhibits 7.1 and 7.2 shows a much greater inclination to raise prices when the ratio of factory inventory to orders is decreasing than when it is increasing. This simulates the feelings of managers that things are going their way when the ratio is shrinking, while things are not going their way when the ratio is increasing. This could also simulate the betting aggressiveness of a poker player as he views one card at a time being dealt to him in a game of five card stud. A poker player generally bets more aggressively if the ratio of good cards to bad is going his way, and he tends to bet less aggressively if the ratio of good cards to bad is not going his way. Of course, a poker player may shift

Exhibit 7.3
Production Throttle: Ratio Increasing

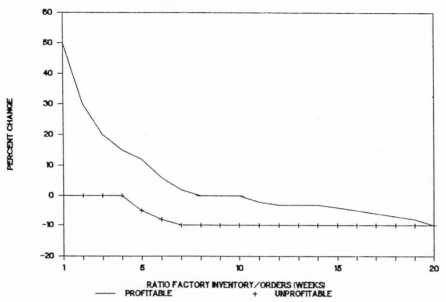

RATIO FACTORY INVENTORY/ORDERS (WEEKS)
PROFITABLE   +   UNPROFITABLE

his betting strategy for the sake of bluffing his opponents. A factory manager has much less reason to bluff.

Exhibit 7.3 contains the settings on the production throttle when factory inventories are increasing with respect to orders from distributors. The throttle settings in the middle range of the ratio are far less dramatic than are the settings on the pricing throttle. This reflects the inclination of the factory manager to rely on the pricing throttle when factory inventories are more or less in line with the volume of incoming orders. A low inventory level in relation to orders from distributors calls for significant increases in production, even with a growing ratio, as long as there is an element of profitability to producing goods. This models the behavior of the factory manager whose responsibility it is to ensure that the factory warehouse has an ample supply of finished goods to meet normal fluctuations in orders. The factory manager would order even greater increases in production when the ratio of inventory to orders is decreasing, as will be seen in Exhibit 7.4. Naturally, production can be enhanced only to the degree that spare productive capacity is available. A desire on the part of the factory manager to increase production when the productive plant is already at maximum output capacity remains a desire. His only course of action is to hire more machine builders, not machine operators.

When each product manufactured generates a direct operating loss, the factory manager will change his behavior with regard to how he handles the production throttle. As seen in Exhibit 7.3, production is never increased unless there is an element of profitability in the manufacture of goods. Even with a relatively modest level of factory inventory to orders, the factory manager is ordering production cutbacks on a continuing basis as long as he is not being compensated for the cost of producing goods. This simulates the behavior of a factory manager to shift control of his locomotive to the production throttle once profitability has been removed from the game.

When the ratio of factory inventory to orders is decreasing, as shown in Exhibit 7.4, there is a corresponding change of behavior with regard to the handling of the production throttle. The inclination of the factory manager is to increase production at a more dramatic pace than when the ratio is rising, as long as there is spare productive capacity available and an element of profitability in the making of goods. A comparison of Exhibits 7.3 and 7.4 illustrates the effects on behavior caused by shifts in the direction of the ratio of inventory to orders. The factory manager's change in behavior is motivated by a fear that he might exhaust his inventory and suffer the consequences of lost sales. An empty warehouse makes for tough sledding in generating profits, no matter how high the price of goods. The normal behavior of the factory manager is to order significant increases in production as he watches the inventory stored in the factory warehouse dwindle away to nothing.

When there is no profitability in the manufacture of an item, the factory man-

Exhibit 7.4
Production Throttle: Ratio Decreasing

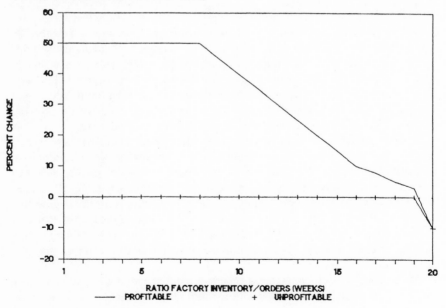

ager does not change the volume of production until price increases have restored profitability. During times when the inventory-to-orders ratio is decreasing and the sales price does not compensate for the cost of production, a factory manager guides his locomotive with the pricing throttle. When the sales price compensates for the cost of production, he shifts over to the production throttle.

The throttle settings illustrated in Exhibits 7.1 through 7.4 are contained in the internal data base in statements 50–96 of the simulation program. In establishing initial conditions, there are many other aspects to deal with besides the throttle settings. The salient features of an island economy have to be established. Among these are the characteristics of the general population. A simplistic description of the population is desirable from the point of view of demonstrating the feasibility of simulating business activity. Six categories have been selected to describe the contribution of the people to the functioning of society: government workers, corporate overhead staff, the unemployables, the unemployed, the machine operators, and the machine builders.

The first population group provides those basic services that society feels should be provided by the government and paid for through some form of taxation. These services may include medical care, education, defense, recreation (parks), police and fire protection, roads, harbor facilities, airports, and anything else deemed the responsibility of government by the populace who is also willing to be taxed in some way to pay for these services.

Those who work for the government have a greater degree of employment security than do those who work for corporations as machine operators or builders. Government employees receive less pay than do workers who face a far higher degree of employment insecurity. This is not by government fiat but by the free workings of the marketplace. The security of government employment is such that workers would willingly sacrifice some pay to obtain a government job. When the government advertises a job opening, the response is sufficient for the job to be filled at a lesser salary level than that of a machine operator. The fact that government remuneration is below the remuneration of private industry is the result of free choice of people seeking the relative security of government employment.

The second category is the overhead component of corporate activity. This group includes management, sales, service, accounting, transport, engineering, research and development, and other functions involved in operating a company other than the building and manning of machines. These workers have a greater degree of job security than do the workers who build and operate the machines.

The third population group is comprised of those who cannot contribute to the productive output of the society. It includes the mentally and physically disadvantaged and those who do not wish to participate in the workings of a productive society. The members of this latter subgroup could be handicapped from a lack of education and training, or they could be attitude handicapped in that they cannot effectively function in the disciplined environment of an industrial society. Regardless of the reasons, and regardless of whether those in this category can or cannot participate in the workings of society, this group is deemed "unemployable." The unemployable category consists of family units in which no one member is capable of holding, or willing to hold, the type of job deserving of a paycheck. No member of these family units produces any goods or provides any services for which society will pay them. The members of these family units do dedicate their efforts to ensuring their own survival. But building a cabin, cultivating a garden, hunting game or fishing for sustenance, and performing menial tasks for a pittance are not counted in the tabulation of what is called economic activity. Thus, they are outside the mainstream of economic life.

The other categories are made up of family units in which at least one member is capable of and willing to hold a job or position that generates a paycheck on a regular basis. However, there are times when the employed become unemployed. There is a difference between being unemployed and being unemployable. The unemployable are family units in which no member is willing or able to earn a paycheck. The unemployed are those who can get a job during the good times and may lose that job during the bad. In a laissez faire society, those who can't, or won't, make a direct contribution to the functioning of society—be they unemployable or unemployed—are left to their own devices, or to the charity of others.

The fourth category is made up of machine builders and machine operators who have lost their positions. These are the unemployed who will, under more auspicious times, fill the ranks of the machine builders and operators. The fifth category includes those who man the machines. This group produces all the goods purchased by the entire population on the island. The sixth category is made up of those who build the machines.

These six categories comprise the entire population of the island and provide the island society with the totality of its manufactured goods and required services. The population of the island economy is 300 households, of which 40 provide basic services, 20 are assigned to corporate overhead, and another 20 are unemployable for any number of reasons. The remaining 220 households are machine builders, machine operators, or the unemployed. In setting up the initial conditions, 69 are presumed to be unemployed, and the remaining 151 are presumed to be employed as machine operators; there are no machine builders. Other pertinent factors initially assigned to the population are as follows:

POPULATION GROUP	GROUP CODE	SOURCE OF PAY	SAVINGS		POSSESSIONS (POUNDS OF GOODS)	
			MIN	MAX	MIN	MAX
Basic Services	1	Government	$2,000	$ 8,000	3,000	12,000
Corporate Overhead	2	Corporate	4,000	8,000	5,000	17,000
Unemployable	3	None	0	0	0	0
Unemployed	4	None	3,000	15,000	3,000	15,000
Machine Operators	5	Corporate	4,000	14,000	4,000	14,000
Machine Builders	6	Corporate	4,000	14,000	4,000	14,000

The initial conditions with regard to savings, possessions, and other pertinent matters are arbitrarily assigned to start the simulation process. The savings of machine builders and operators have been initially assigned higher values because these population groups can lose their jobs. Their idea of a satisfactory nest egg in the form of savings is higher than for population categories 1 and 2 which are in far less danger of being laid off (none to be exact in this simulation). Nevertheless, it is presumed that there is some risk and, therefore, some need for savings among these two population categories.

The relative scaling of pay among the groups varies according to their category assignments. The general principle is that people are able to earn something close to what is earned by machine operators. A teacher, a government administrator, or a person providing medical care receives remuneration in relation to what a factory worker earns. This principle holds even though the factory worker is the only one actually producing goods. Well-being is measured by the ability to purchase goods, and those who provide services to the society are able to maintain their well-being at a level fairly comparable to that of machine operators, with some differential reflecting the relative degree of risk of being laid off. This can be seen in modern society. There is no meaningful difference in pay among school teachers, firemen, policemen, and factory workers. Whereas the school teachers, firemen, and policemen provide vital services, only the factory workers produce material goods.

Government workers receive 80 percent of what is earned by machine operators. Those seeking government employment are willing to accept less remuneration in return for the guaranteed security of not being laid off every time business activity takes a turn for the worse. Personnel assigned to corporate overhead receive 100 percent of what is earned by machine operators. These individuals are the most well off members of society because their employment is guaranteed, for purposes of the simulation; they receive remuneration comparable to the factory workers without the risk of being laid off. The model could permit layoffs of government employees and those assigned to corporate overhead during the bad times, but, for the sake of simplicity, layoffs are restricted to machine builders and operators. Nevertheless, the saving habits of government workers and those assigned to corporate overhead reflect the possibility of layoffs, through to some lesser degree than for the workers.

Members of the unemployable group receive no benefits from society in the form of government support. Their ability to stay alive is dependent on charity and on what they can do for themselves to provide food, clothing, and shelter. This is consistent with the philosophy of laissez faire economics in which there are no free rides. The unemployed also receive no benefits from society, and they sustain themselves by drawing down on savings. Because society does not provide any income support for those who lose their jobs, accumulating a nest egg during the good times is a necessity.

The base pay of the machine builders is 120 percent of the base pay of the machine operators, reflecting the fact that they are on the front lines of layoffs when the bad times start. Construction workers generally are the highest paid workers because they are the last to be hired when bad times turn to good and the first to be fired when good times turn to bad.

The initial base pay for machine operators is set at $1,000 per month, the initial price of goods is set at $7.50 per pound, the distributors' inventory is initially set at 70,000 pounds and the factory inventory at 60,000 pounds, the ratio of factory inventory to distributors' orders is 10 weeks of orders, the population has a bad times mentality, and there are 170 machines and, as already mentioned, no machine builders, 151 machine operators, and 69 unemployed workers. The initial interest rate is 4 percent, and the tax rate on sales is 16 percent. All these settings are arbitrary to start the simulation process.

Overtime pay is a 50 percent premium over normal pay. Factory managers resort to overtime according to the following table:

DEGREE OF OVERTIME	RATIO OF WEEKS OF FACTORY INVENTORY TO ORDERS
40%	1
30	2
20	3
15	4
10	5
5	6

The total savings of the workers have been lent out to the corporations and to the government, with corporate debt amounting to 75 percent of all savings and government debt amounting to 25 percent of all savings. There is no bank credit in the system—another characteristic of a laissez faire society. In a laissez faire economy, there are no frivolous uses of debt, such as the acquisition of consumer goods. Savings are used only to finance new factories and cover temporary government shortfalls in meeting expenses. These initial conditions are established in statements 100–140 of the simulation program contained in the appendix.

PROTOCOL OF THE SIMULATION

The protocol, or the general set of instructions for running the simulation, is as follows:

1. At the start of each month, reduce the amount of possessions to reflect the conversion of material things to dust and ashes.

2. Pay each individual for work or services provided, and determine the portion to be spent and the portion to be saved.

3. Divide the amount of money to be spent by the price of goods to determine the amount of goods purchased by the population.

4. Subtract the amount of goods purchased by the population from the distributors' inventory.

5. Determine orders from the distributors to the factory on the basis of maintaining the distributors' inventory within a desired range of weeks of current sales.

6. Adjust factory inventory to reflect production of goods by machine operators and orders from distributors.

7. Calculate the ratio of weeks of factory inventory to orders, and adjust production and pricing accordingly.

8. Hire or fire machine operators as necessary to achieve production adjustments.

9. Change the productive capacity by taking into account the number of machines being phased out as a result of age and obsolescence and the number of new machines delivered by the machine builders.

10. Hire or fire machine builders as dictated by utilization of existing machine capacity and degree of profitability.

11. Adjust the base wage scale as necessary.

12. Determine state of mind of the population from overall employment rates and changes thereto.

13. Calculate the cash flow and bank balance for the government, and adjust the tax rate, if necessary.

14. Adjust interest rates with regard to changes in prices for goods and the state of the economy.

15. Debit and credit bank accounts to reflect the payment of debtors' interest to savers.

16. Record the data, and repeat the process for the next month.

A more detailed description of the protocol incorporated in the simulation program follows. Not every aspect of the simulation is contained in this description because a simulation can be set up with a great deal of variance in how the protocol is accomplished. For instance, the simulation will operate whether the maximum number of builders that can be hired in any given month is 10, 20, 30, or any other number. The simulation will operate whether the maximum savings rate is 1, 5, or 10 percent. The results of the simulation will differ in detail, but the overall operation of the simulation in creating peaks and valleys in business activity will not be affected. The purpose herein is to demonstrate the ability to create peaks and valleys, and not to perform a detailed topological survey of the heights and depths of a particular business terrain generated by various sets of assumptions.

Aging of Possessions

With the exclusion of the unemployables who possess little in the way of goods, the population's possessions are measured and aged at a rate of 1 percent per month. This simulates the conversion of all material goods to dust and ashes. Aging is accomplished in statements 205–207.

Saving, Dissaving and Spending Patterns

Dissaving occurs under two conditions. One is when the person is unemployed, in which case dissavings can vary between 5 and 10 percent per month of the amount of savings in the bank during the period of unemployment. The other condition is when savings are at a level that satisfies the minimum size of a nest egg and when times are good with a high level of employment. The minimum nest egg is considered to be an average of six to seven months' pay for those whose employment is considered safe (government and corporate overhead) and nine to ten months' pay for the workers. Although the simulation does not permit government employees and those assigned to corporate overhead to be laid off, their saving patterns do reflect some risk of unemployment.

The attitude toward saving varies with the three states of mind: the good times, the cautionary times, and the bad times. Voluntary dissaving occurs only during the good times when the nest eggs have grown beyond the size desired by the particular category. When nest eggs have not reached the size required to provide a feeling of comfort among employed workers, their savings rate varies between 5 and 10 percent. During the times of caution, the savings rate ranges from a minimum of 7.5 percent to a maximum of 15 percent of the paycheck. During the bad times, the savings rate jumps to something between 10 and 30 percent of the paycheck if a worker has above average savings in the bank and between 20 and 40 percent if he has below average savings in the bank. In addition, the element of fear is reflected in a savings rate kicker that varies from zero to two times the rate of increase in unemployment from the previous month, with an overall maximum savings rate of between 60 and 80 percent. The savings rate for government employees and those assigned to corporate overhead is much less sensitive to changing business conditions, although definite changes in saving patterns reflect changes in the state of mind.

The exact values assigned to these variables, which should be descriptive of what people actually do save in a society, are not critical for the functioning of the simulation. The simulation will create the ups and downs of the business cycle with a wide range of savings rates. However, the timing and the magnitude of the swings of the business cycle will be affected by the nature of the selected savings rates. Generally speaking, the greater the swings in savings patterns with changing conditions of business activity, the greater the volatility of the business cycle. The converse is also true. The smaller the swings in savings patterns, the greater the stability. A small downdraft in business activity can be transformed into a bust by a dramatic swing in the rate of saving. The nature of the cycles is also affected by the degree of savings in addition to the swing in savings. Lower savings rates contribute to greater price volatility on the upswing of the business cycle. The time to recover from the downswing of the business cycle takes longer because the cut in spending is more pronounced in a society with a low degree of savings. Statements 208–395 contain some degree of noise to reflect variability in individual decisions. Statements 400–405 keep track of money to be spent for goods, including dissavings, and money to be deposited in the bank as savings.

Distributor and Factory Inventories

The total amount of spending is translated into sales of goods by dividing the amount spent by the price of goods. The distributors' inventory is reduced by the amount of goods purchased by the entire population. Orders from distributors to the factory reflect both the amount of goods purchased by the consuming population and the amount of goods desired as inventory. This, in turn, is influenced by changes in price and in the general mood of the times.

If prices are increasing, the distributors will expand their inventory to something between seven and ten weeks' worth of current sales in order to enjoy the gain from inventory profits. Times are good for a distributor when he can make a profit by not selling off part of the inventory. Time is on the side of the distributor as long as prices are rising; failure to complete a sale today means that his worth will be enhanced tomorrow. And the more goods packed in the warehouse, the larger the inventory profits. These profits cannot be realized until the inventory is sold, but this salient point seems to escape the notice of the owner of the inventory as long as prices are rising. However, when prices stabilize and begin to fall, the point that an inventory has to be sold to realize inventory profits is driven home with vengence.

When prices are steady, the distributors' desired level of inventory is between six and eight weeks' worth of sales. This amount of inventory makes distributors sufficiently comfortable because they know they can satisfy the vagaries of consumer demand. When prices are declining, the distributors' desired inventory shrinks to four to seven weeks' worth of sales in order to avoid—or, more accurately, minimize—inventory losses. Yet they must keep some inventory on hand in order to justify their being in the business of distribution. This level of inventory is a balance between customer dissatisfaction when an item is not in stock and inventory losses during times of declining prices. This same level of four to seven weeks' worth of sales also holds during the bad times, regardless of price changes. This represents the cautious frame of mind of distributors who generally do not expand their inventories during a recession. During bad times, distributors cut their inventories to the minimum practical level to protect themselves from the possibility of further price declines. In addition, they are motivated to add to their cash positions to ensure their survival—which, by definition, requires the liquidation of a portion of their inventories.

Factory inventory adjustments take into account production on the basis that each machine operator can manufacture 200 pounds of goods per month, adjusted for overtime, and that distributor orders are honored. All these points concerning distributor and factory inventories are contained in statements 415–465.

Adjusting Pricing and Production

A factory manager does not see final sales to consumers; he sees only orders from distributors. The factory manager compares what he holds in his inventory to the orders received from the distributors. This ratio, expressed in terms of weeks of inventory to orders from distributors, determines changes in the price of goods and the volume of production. As already discussed, this adjustment is made according to whether the selling price compensates for the variable cost of production and whether the ratio of inventory to orders is increasing or decreasing. Adjusting the pricing and production throttles is accomplished in statements 470–529.

Hiring and Firing Machine Operators

If the production throttle adjustment calls for greater output, more machine operators have to be hired. The number to be hired cannot exceed the spare productive capacity of the plant (the number of unused machines). Unemployed machine operators are hired first. When this source of employment is exhausted, then machine builders are hired to fill the ranks of machine operators. The conversion of employment from builders to operators is necessary to prevent the situation in which builders are producing more machines than there are operators to man the machines. Completed factories do not stand idle during good times for lack of workers. It is presumed that some builders would be willing to join the ranks of operators, sacrificing their premium pay for the comfort of a relatively greater degree of security.

If the adjustment to the production throttle calls for layoffs, the requisite number of machine operators are simply reassigned from category 5 to category 4, thereby joining the ranks of the unemployed. Statements 535–705 handle the hiring and firing of machine builders.

Adjusting Productive Capacity

The conversion of machines to dust and ashes proceeds at a pace of anywhere between 0 and 6 percent of total machine capacity per month. This reflects normal aging and deterioration of plant and equipment. In addition, there is a 10 percent chance that the rate of deterioration may be increased up to a maximum of a doubling. This means that there is a small chance that a maximum of 12 percent of all machine capacity can be stripped from the books in a single month. This simulates obsolescence caused by shifting consumer product preferences, which results in scrapping perfectly workable machines and building new ones to satisfy changes in consumer demand. Machine capacity is expanded on the basis that ten man-months of machine builders' time are required to build one unit of machine capacity. Adjustment to the number of machines, which can be interpreted to mean the productive capacity of the society, is performed in statements 530–534.

Hiring and Firing Machine Builders

The number of machine builders to be hired is determined by the utilization of existing plant capacity (the number of machine operators compared to the number of machines). The rate at which machine builders are added is determined by both the extent of utilization and the degree of profitability of adding new machine capacity. The maximum rate of hiring new machine builders is 20 per month. This limit takes into consideration the planning necessary to add more capacity. The measure of profitability is the payback period adjusted to reflect the level of interest rates. The payback period is calculated in statements 500–510, and the hiring of machine builders is handled in statements 710–785. Alternatively, if utilization declines sufficiently, machine builders are laid off at a rate that reflects both the degree of unused capacity and the degree of profitability. Statements 790–865 take care of firing machine builders.

Adjustments to Labor Wages

During times of high rates of employment, labor is able to raise the general level of pay primarily because factory managers bid up the labor wage in an effort to keep their factories fully manned. The presence of labor unions can accelerate this process. During times of high unemployment, factory managers can reduce labor costs by laying off higher-cost labor and rehiring others who are unemployed and willing to work for less pay. The presence of labor unions can decelerate the rate of pay loss through this process.

However, during times of general unprofitability, when the sales price does not recoup the cost of manufacture, management has the motivational and in-testinal wherewithal to take direct action to cut labor wages in its effort to restore profitability. This is the time when management welcomes the threat of a strike by the labor unions. A strike would aid in management's efforts to cut production and restore inventory to a better balance with incoming orders. Labor is not in a strong negotiating position when the chief weapon in its arsenal has been disarmed. Labor wage adjustments are performed in statements 870–886.

Determining the State of Mind

The state of mind reflects the feelings one has during good and bad times and the times in between. The good time mentality, which induces dissaving if the nest eggs are too large and a lesser savings rate if they are not, and larger distributor inventories if prices are rising, is determined by the state of employment and changes thereto. The good times occur whenever unemployment is less then 5 percent of the work force, the workforce being categories 4, 5, and 6, or 220 family units. The bad times mentality ensues when unemployment exceeds 10 percent of the labor force and is steady or increasing. Cautionary times occur whenever unemployment is between 5 and 10 percent and whenever unemployment is between 10 and 40 percent and is decreasing. Increasing employment, even in the midst of hard times, is sufficient to move one from the mentality of bad times to that of cautionary times. This has a significant impact on spending patterns because the savings rate, as already described, is substantially reduced as one moves from the mentality of bad times to that of cautionary times. The state of mind is determined in statements 890–924.

Government Fiscal Matters

Government expenditures are the wages of those on the government payroll who provide basic services (category 1). In a laissez faire economy, the government does not provide any benefits to the unemployable, who are left to the tender mercies of charity and to their own resources. Nor does the philosophy of laissez faire economics permit the government to provide any compensation to the unemployed. Those who lose their jobs must rely on their savings—and then on charity when their savings are exhausted.

The source of government funds is a sales tax. The sales tax is cut by 1 percentage point when the government balance in the banking system is positive and growing. Conversely, the sales tax is increased by 1 percentage point when the government balance in the bank is negative and becoming more so. Tax increases can only occur during the good times. The government generates a deficit during bad times because of falling revenue. Revenue drops because its source is a sales tax on spending, and spending declines during bad times. Because government expenditures (funding the payroll of those providing basic services) are essentially constant, deficits begin to mount. However, no tax increases can be approved during the bad times. Government fiscal matters are taken care of in statements 925–945.

Corporate Cash Flow and Bank Balance

The corporation receives, as revenue, all of the money spent for material goods by the population. The corporate account thus is the totality of spending received by the factory and the distributors. Its expenses are the wages for personnel assigned to corporate overhead, machine builders, and machine operators. The distributors are counted among those in the corporate overhead, although, in reality, they usually are independent businessmen. Accumulating inventory adds to the expense side of the corporate ledger because machine operators are being paid to manufacture goods that are not being sold. Similarly, inventory liquidation adds to the income side of the ledger because there is no need to pay machine operators to manufacture the goods being liquidated from inventory. The machine operators have already been paid for the manufacture of these goods during times of inventory accumulation. These points are summed up in statement 950.

Interest Rate

The rate of interest rises at one-quarter of a percent per month during the good times when prices are also increasing with a maximum of 10 percent. The rate of interest remains unchanged if prices are stable as long as the rate of interest is above 4 percent. The rate of interest falls one-quarter of a percent per month whenever prices are declining with a minimum rate of 2 percent.

Although these rates may sound low, the model has been intentionally constrained to limit the ability of labor to raise its wages during the good times and the ability of management to reduce wages during the bad times. A review of the results shows that prices remain within certain bounds if labor wages exhibit little in the way of variability. The simulation automatically adjusts prices in relation to costs. If labor can crush capital during the upswing of a business cycle by winning higher wages without commensurate gains in productivity, prices increase to compensate capital for the higher costs of production. Similarly, if capital can crush labor during the downswing of a business cycle by arbitrarily reducing the wage level, prices fall to ensure that all goods produced can be purchased by the consumers, who are largely the workers. The interest rate range of variability was arbitrarily selected knowing in advance that there would be more or less a constant average price for goods throughout the simulation. More programming steps are necessary to model interest rates for long-term inflationary and deflationary trends if there is a marked disparity of strength between labor and capital.

The model did not contain bank credit as a separate entity, but it was assumed to exist from the point of view of guaranteeing liquidity during the bad times and in providing the monetary authorities a tool to manage the level of interest rates, if necessary.

Those in debt pay interest on their indebtedness to savers in proportion to the amount of their savings. Statements 960–1100 take care of adjusting the interest rate and debiting and crediting interest to the various bank accounts. The bankers are included in category 1—essential services provided by the government. The model could be modified to establish an interest rate differential such that the difference supports the bankers. This was not done for the sake of simplicity.

Recording Data

The following is recorded at the end of each month of the simulation.

- Average possessions (pounds of goods)
- Total savings, dissavings, and spending
- Price of goods
- Pounds of goods made and bought
- Distributors' inventory and factory inventory
- Orders from distributors to factory
- Weeks of distributors' inventory to sales
- Weeks of factory inventory to distributors' orders
- Payback period
- General wage level
- Number of unemployed and number of machine operators and builders
- Number of machines and utilization rate
- State of mind of population
- Interest and tax rates
- Government, corporate, and population bank balances
- Government, corporate, and population cash flow

RUNNING THE SIMULATION

Perhaps the most instructional aspect in running the simulation is that business activity in a laissez faire economy need not be cyclical. It is possible for the simulation to settle out at a maximum level of employment with just the right balance between machine operators and builders so that the builders are replacing machine capacity more or less at the rate at which it is aging or becoming obsolescent. The price varies within a fairly narrow range, reflecting the actions of factory managers who adjust the pricing throttle to prevent inventories from becoming too large or too small for comfort in relation to the size of orders from the distributors. The price is the right price for the population to buy all the goods that are produced by the machine operators. The price is also the right price to ensure that the corporation can pay its overhead staff and the machine operators and builders, and maintain a balance between revenue and expenditures to earn about a 4 percent return on its investments in productive assets.

Adjustments to production are more narrow in scope than are adjustments to pricing, with any layoffs affecting small numbers of workers for short periods of time. Workers do not make any rapid departures from their normal rate of saving because the good times continue indefinitely, with slight interruptions for a cautionary frame of mind. No matter how arbitrary the initial settings, the "invisible hand" of laissez faire economics makes itself plainly visible as it guides the economy to the right combination of price for a given labor wage and employment pattern for maximum production and efficiency of operation. And it does not take long for the "invisible hand" to transform the initial instability of starting the simulation into stability at the highest level of productivity.

Thus, in a world of slow change with regard to technology and consumer preferences for products, in a world of little greed among distributors to expand their inventory holdings when prices are increasing, in a world in which workers don't panic and dramatically alter their savings rate in response to lengthening unemployment lines, there is little in the way of a business cycle. Or what pass for the troughs of business cycles are recessions that are both shallow in depth in terms of the unemployment rate and short in duration. In a world of this sort, society functions close to its maximum productive output, and prosperity reigns in the sense that it is not possible to produce more goods, given the constraints of machine productivity and the portion of the population dedicated to the production of consumer goods and capital goods to support the consumer goods industry. It is a world that clearly does not exist. But it is a world that could exist if change came slowly and if the emotions of greed and fear were subdued.

MEASURES OF CYCLICALITY

Exhibit 7.5 shows the cyclicality of business activity over a 500-month period, using the production of goods as a measure of cyclicality. It reflects a world in which there is sufficient change—that is, sufficient greed and fear—to set off the chain of events called a business cycle.

In viewing Exhibit 7.5, there appears to be a tantalizing hint of a background "long wave" upon which is imposed the obvious ups and downs of the choppy waters of the "short waves" of business activity. The background wave may be just in the eye of the observer—or merely coincidence. Running the simulation over several thousand months would address the possibility of a long-term cycle underlying the short-term cyclical swings of business activity. However, maneuvering the ship of business through the choppy waters of the short-term cycle is the subject at hand. Exhibit 7.6 views an arbitrarily selected portion of Exhibit 7.5 between months 300 and 400.

Other aspects of the cyclical nature of business activity over this one-hundred-month period of time can be seen in the price of goods which, naturally, tends to go up when times are good and down when times are bad, as illustrated in Exhibit 7.7.

The base labor wage shows the same cyclical pattern in Exhibit 7.8. Labor can push its rates up when times are good, and management can push them down when times are bad.

Exhibit 7.8 reveals a downward bias in labor rates during this period of time. The labor wage started at $1,000 per month and was about $1,050 at the end

Exhibit 7.5
Cyclicality of Business Activity: Production of Goods

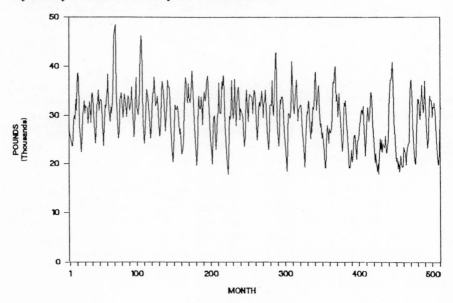

Exhibition 7.6
Cyclicality of Business Activity: Production of Goods

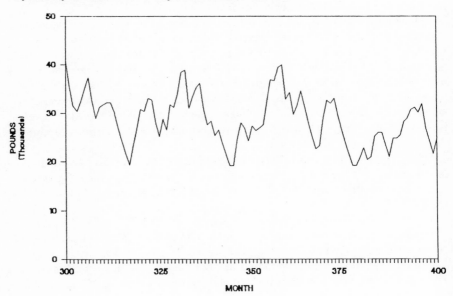

Exhibit 7.7
Price

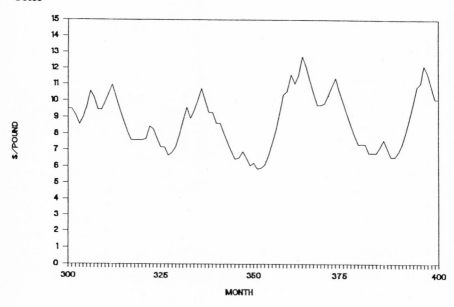

Exhibit 7.8
Base Labor Wage

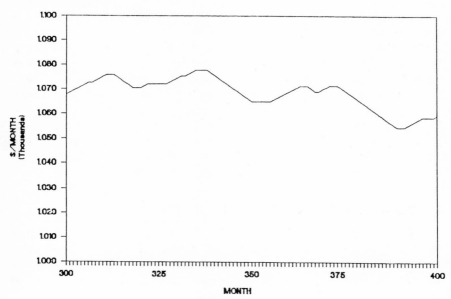

of the five hundred-month simulation. Labor wage adjustments were set at values that minimized overall labor rate changes over the course of the simulation in order to maintain a somewhat constant average price throughout the simulation.

PRICES RESPOND TO WAGES

If wages were permitted to escalate, or deescalate with time, then the overall price level would rise or fall accordingly. In a laissez faire society, price finds its proper level with respect to labor costs to ensure that all goods made are eventually sold. If the price is too high in relation to wages, goods would pile up from one end of the island to the other. If the price is too low in relation to wages, the warehouses would be empty. By running the simulation with labor having the upper hand (the ability to raise wages) over a series of business cycles and with management having the upper hand (the ability to lower wages) over a series of cycles, the price of goods always settles out at a level that ensures that, ultimately, the goods made can be purchased by the population.

Prices are set by the cost of labor and not vice versa. There is no real advantage for management to "crush" labor because stability in a laissez faire society depends on the price of goods being at a level at which the total output of goods can be purchased by the population. In fact, there may be less profitability when management has the power to "crush" labor because machines are built at relatively higher labor costs in relation to the subsequent revenue received for goods produced. Prices for goods decline subsequent to the building of a machine because labor costs are going down as management wins in its crusade to lower labor costs.

Thus, it appears that between the two sins of a little inflation and a little deflation, business might appear to be better off in an inflationary climate in which labor wages are increasing. Old investments in machines would appear more attractive as the cost for new ones goes up with labor costs. Distributors might be less apt to reduce their inventory holdings from fear of inventory losses when there is an upward bias in price trends. On the other hand, workers have to save more to ensure the constancy of the purchasing power of their nest eggs. This reduces spending and, therefore, business revenue. But inflation and deflation are both sins. The best overall performance in a laissez faire economy can be achieved when average prices and labor wages change little from cycle to cycle. There appears to be no inherent advantage in either inflation or deflation.

OTHER MEASURES OF ECONOMIC ACTIVITY

This one hundred-month segment of time was not the best of all times during the five-hundred-month simulation. Besides a decline in wages, there was also an overall decline in the amount of goods possessed by the population, as illustrated in Exhibit 7.9, another hint of the existence of a long background wave.

Exhibit 7.9
Possession of Goods

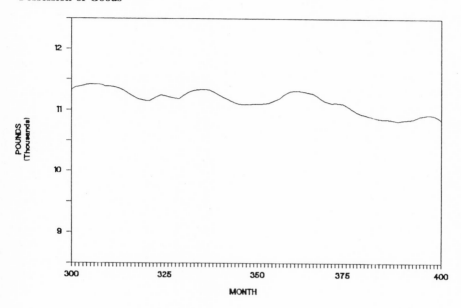

The volatility of the ratio of factory inventory to incoming orders from distributors is obvious when viewing Exhibit 7.10. The primary cause of this
volatility is the changing number of desired weeks of current sales to be kept
on hand by the distributors. Distributor orders to the factory vary within a range
of weeks of consumer sales desired to be stored on their shelves. The shifting
of distributor orders to consumer sales within this range, and the shifting of the
range itself in response to changing prices and business conditions, generates
"noise" which makes the factory manager's job of assessing actual consumer
demand much more difficult.

During downturns in the business cycle, the ratio reached high levels, which
means that factory inventory was high in relation to the size of incoming orders
from distributors. During upturns in the business cycle, the ratio had low values,
reflecting a relative shortage of factory inventory with regard to the size of
incoming orders from distributors. This, of course, had a direct effect on whether
the factory manager was pushing or pulling on his pricing and production throttles. A weighted average of the ratio of factory inventory to orders was used to
simulate the reluctance of managers to jerk the pricing and production throttles
from one month to the next.

The payback period is a measure of the profitability in investing in new machine
capacity. Machinery depreciated—that is, wasted away—at an average rate of
approximately 3 percent per month. This would imply that the period of time

Exhibit 7.10
Factory Inventory/Orders

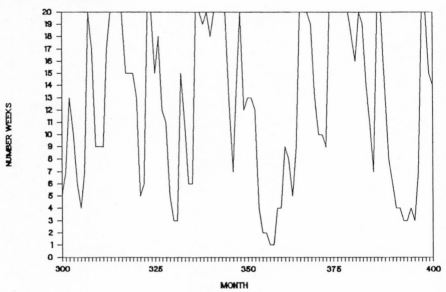

in which the machine could generate sufficient income to pay back its investment would be on the order of thirty to forty months. A payback period that is longer than this means that a machine has operated its entire life without generating enough funds to recoup the initial investment to build the machine.

Using a payback period of forty months or less as the necessary justification for investing in new machines, including some provision for the payment of interest, one can see from Exhibit 7.11 that bad times are not the best of times for adding new machines from an investment viewpoint. The government policy of reducing interest rates during bad times in the business cycle in hopes of spurring economic activity is understandable. Cheap money is an inducement for plant managers to expand their productive capacity. This creates jobs and may help to drag an economy out of the doldrums. However, the policy shows a remarkable lack of understanding of what motivates a plant manager to build a new factory. Regardless if money is expensive or cheap, a manager will not build a new plant if his existing plant is half idle and prices have declined to a point where there is no hope of recovering the invested capital. Nevertheless, the "invisible hand" was able to select a price that ensured a new factory would recoup its investment, and a return on that investment, over the life of the asset, which might include several business cycles.

The cyclicality associated with interest rates is illustrated in Exhibit 7.12. Interest rates rose when the price of goods was going up and fell when the price of goods was going down in response to the instructions built into the simulation

Exhibit 7.11
Payback Period

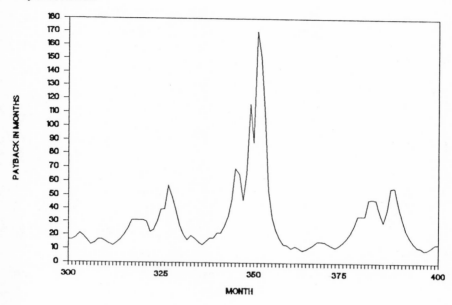

Exhibit 7.12
Interest Rate

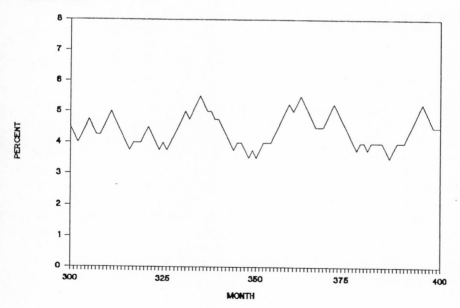

Exhibit 7.13
Tax Rate

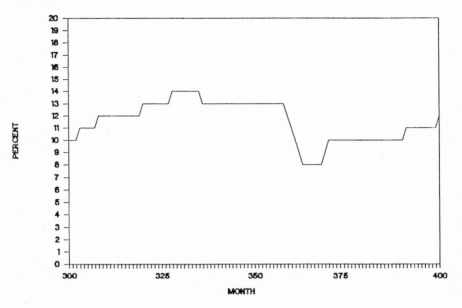

program. The simulation presumed that interest rates were being managed by the government monetary authority through the use of bank credit, although no bank credit was incorporated in the program.

Tax rate adjustments during this period are shown in Exhibit 7.13. Tax hikes could be enacted only during good times when there was a growing deficit in the government account in the bank. Tax cuts could be enacted any time there was a growing surplus of government funds in the banking system.

One violation of a pure laissez faire economy was the impossibility of a corporate bankruptcy. Another was that hoarding (cash withdrawals from the banking system that were not spent) was also impossible. The surplus in one account was balanced by the deficit in another. The total credit in the system was zero, meaning that the savings of the population and the government surplus, if any, were equal to the money owed to the bank by the corporation and the amount of the government deficit, if any. In other words, a dollar in the system was locked in the system and had to be found in an individual, company, or government account. Exhibit 7.14 shows something rarely seen in the twentieth century—a more or less balanced government budget over a sustained period of time. Prior to and during the early part of the twentieth century, balanced budgets were normal in the course of government fiscal management, except during periods of war.

Exhibit 7.14
Account Balances

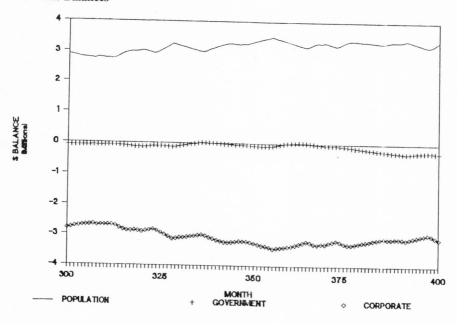

—— POPULATION   + GOVERNMENT   ◇ CORPORATE

MICROEXAMINATION OF A BUSINESS CYCLE

It is now appropriate to take more of a microlook at the workings of the business cycle. The period from month 320 to month 340 was arbitrarily selected for the analysis of good times turning bad and bad times turning good. Other periods could have been selected, and the theme of the story would have been the same.

Rather than looking at an exploded view of the cyclicality of the production of goods during this period of time, one can better sense the cyclicality by viewing the state of mind of the populace, as shown in Exhibit 7.15. Exhibit 7.16 shows why there was a change of sentiment—changes in the unemployment pattern mirror changes in the state of mind.

The number unemployed is a direct result of layoffs of operators (Exhibit 7.17), which result in idle plant capacity (Exhibit 7.18) which, in turn, leads to declining employment for machine builders (Exhibit 7.19).

Exhibits 7.15 and 7.16 are one and the same: increasing and decreasing unemployment rates change the state of mind of the workers. However, changes in worker attitude follow after the fact. That is, something else happened before the attitude changed from good to bad or from bad to good. Something happened during months 320–322 preceding the change from good times to bad, and

Exhibit 7.15
State of Mind: 1–Good, 2–Cautious, 3–Bad

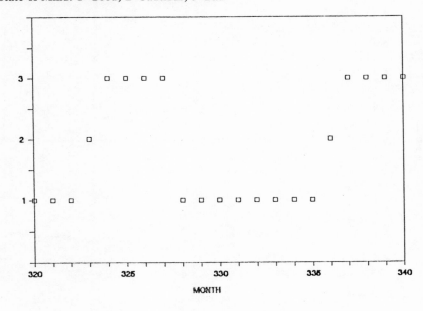

Exhibit 7.16
Number Unemployed

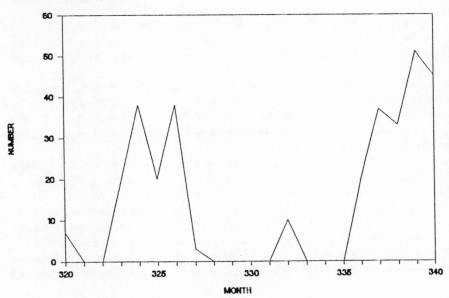

Exhibit 7.17
Number of Operators

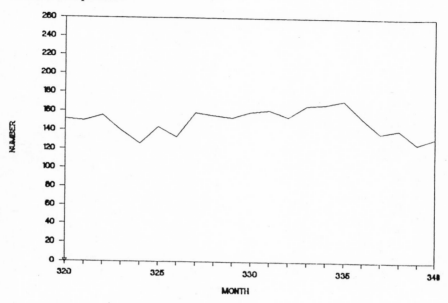

Exhibit 7.18
Utilization

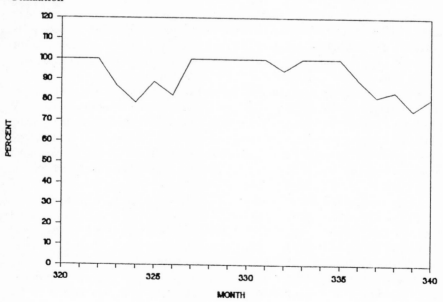

Exhibit 7.19
Number of Builders

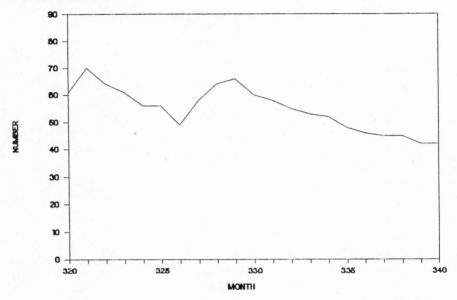

something happened during months 324–327 preceding the change from bad times to good, and something happened during the latter part of the period of months 328–335 preceding the change from good times to bad.

Exhibit 7.20 shows that a shift in the price of goods actually presages a shift in attitude. The price peaks shortly before good times turn to bad, and the price hits its nadir just before bad times turn to good. Thus, a general change in the direction of prices may be a warning of a possible change in the direction of a business cycle.

But price is merely a reaction on the part of a factory manager to a change in the number of weeks of inventory in his warehouse compared to orders from distributors and dealers. Price is a result of pushing or pulling on the pricing throttle to keep inventory in line with orders. Thus, it is necessary to take one more layer off the onion and peer deeper inside. Exhibit 7.21 reveals what appears to be an almost inverse relationship between distributor and factory inventory.

A comparison of Exhibits 7.15 and 7.21 shows that distributor inventory is falling and factory inventory is rising for some period of time before the roof caves in on business activity. Conversely, distributor inventory is rising and factory inventory is falling for some time before there is a recovery in business activity, as signaled by a change of worker attitude.

What is happening? During the early stages of the good times, distributors are expanding their inventories at a faster pace than consumers are buying the

Exhibit 7.20
Price

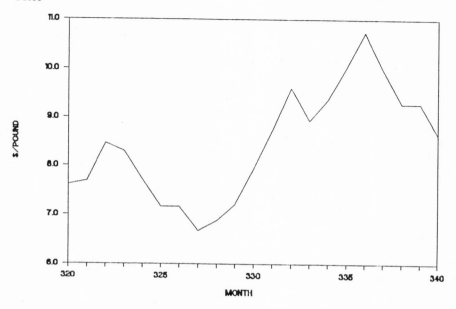

wares coming out of the factories. This gives a false signal to the factory managers as to the actual magnitude of demand for goods. The orders from the distributors represent both consumer demand and inventory accumulation on the distributors' shelves. This means that the workers are not buying all the wares they are making. Factory orders are exceeding actual consumer demand, and the excess manufactured goods are filling up the shelves in the distributors' warehouses. Generally speaking, factory orders exceed consumer demand during the first portion of the good times, as seen in Exhibit 7.22.

And, generally speaking, Exhibit 7.22 shows that factory orders lag consumer demand during the bad times. However, Exhibit 7.22 is a consequence of Exhibit 7.21. One would expect factory orders to exceed consumer demand during times when the distributors are accumulating inventory, and one would expect factory orders to lag consumer demand during times when the distributors are liquidating inventory. Dealing with factory orders in Exhibit 7.22 is "after the fact" in terms of examining turning points in business activity. Therefore, Exhibit 7.21 has to be the key exhibit from the point of view of being able to predict turning points in the business cycle.

TURNING POINTS IN A BUSINESS CYCLE

During the initial phases of a business recovery, more people are joining the actively employed work force, and total take-home pay is increasing. This

Exhibit 7.21
Distributor and Factory Inventory

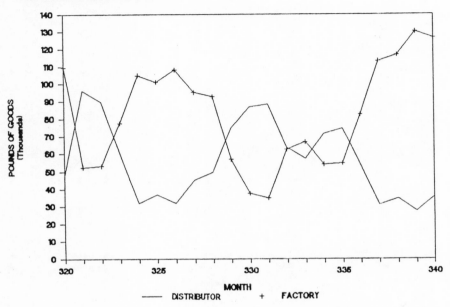

increases spending. As unemployment lines dwindle, consumer confidence increases, and saving decreases. This also increases spending. These twin sources of increased spending cause distributors' inventory to be drawn down. The distributors send orders to the factory not only to replenish what has been sold but also to accumulate more inventory so that they have sufficient wares on the shelves to cover the increased volume of business. This increases the volume of orders to the factory. As the factory honors a higher volume of orders, its inventory starts dropping. The factory manager pushes forward on both the production and the pricing throttles by hiring more workers and by increasing the price of goods. The more workers he hires, the greater the increment to the spending stream. Once utilization of existing machine capacity begins to tighten up, the factory manager hires machine builders, again adding to the spending stream of consumers.

The increasing price acts as an inducement for the distributors to add even more to their inventory in order to make a fast buck in inventory profits as well as to have enough inventory to service the higher volume of sales. Because this adds to demand, as perceived by the factory manager, he hires more builders and operators, and he raises prices. Thus, the first part of good times can be described in terms of expanding distributor inventory, shrinking factory inventory, rising prices, higher employment rates, and a feeling that things are getting better.

Exhibit 7.22
Factory Orders Versus Consumer Demand

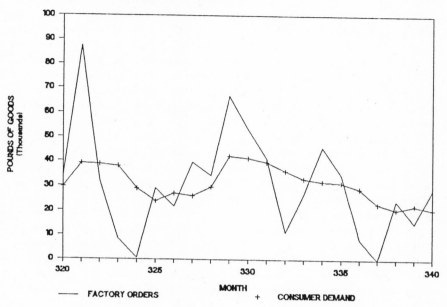

This process continues until all the workers are busy producing goods and building machines. When all the workers have been hired, their aggregate spending flattens out because no more workers are being hired to increase the spending stream. Nor are they buying all the wares they are making. Earlier price increases have occurred as a result of inventory accumulation by the distributors. The wares that cannot be purchased by the population are accumulating dust on the shelves of the distributors, who are enjoying the inventory profits from rising prices.

At some point, however, the distributors are no longer willing to add to their inventory, even with increasing prices. This can happen when they have run out of shelf space. While distributors may desire to add to their inventory, they cannot accumulate an infinitely sized inventory. Hence, they stop at some finite amount of goods on their shelves. When the distributors have built up what they consider to be sufficient inventory, considering changes to prices and the volume of sales, their orders to the factory start to decline.

At this point in the business cycle, prices are actually too high for the population to purchase all the wares being produced by the machine operators. The factory manager does not take any action because he is unaware that the distributors have decided to maintain rather than continue to expand their inventories. The factory manager is too busy ordering new factories and having too much fun enjoying the profits to note that the nature of the game has changed:

he was unwittingly passed over the watershed of the Good Times mountain range.

When distributors cease to accumulate inventory, orders to the factory fall. The factory manager sees his warehouse beginning to fill and nudges his pricing throttle. At the first sign that further price increases are not in the offing, and at the first inkling of price discounting, the distributors become nervous about the pile of goods stocked on their shelves and begin liquidating a part of their inventory as the inventory profit whirlwind romance begins to cool. Their orders to the factory decline at a faster pace. With less being shipped to the distributors, and with factory output remaining unchanged, the factory manager watches the inventory in his warehouse continue to mount.

If the factory manager does not nudge the pricing throttle sufficiently, then the price of goods does not fall to the degree necessary for the population to purchase the goods being produced. Distributors' inventory continues to rise, inducing the distributors to further reduce their orders to the factory. The factory manager nudges his pricing throttle again. If the price change is still inadequate to generate consumer spending that will liquidate the inventory accumulating at the distributor level, the distributors pass the problem on to the factory by sharply cutting back their orders. The precipitous falloff in distributor orders causes the ratio of factory inventory to incoming orders from distributors to skyrocket. The factory manager panics, hits the production throttle, and begins to lay off workers.

What is about to be described need not happen. If the downward adjustment in the amount of inventory distributors want to hold is not too severe, and if the factory manager cuts prices sufficiently, consumer spending power is enhanced to the degree necessary to liquidate the distributors' excess inventory. With their inventory restored to a desirable level, the distributors increase their orders to the factory in time for the factory inventory to be liquidated before the factory manager has pulled back on the production throttle to any meaningful degree.

The factory manager can accommodate normal perturbations caused when distributors change their desired inventory level, as dictated by circumstances, by appropriate changes in prices. However, there is no guarantee that these price adjustments will be sufficient to permit the consuming public to liquidate the pile of goods that the distributors want off their shelves. If this is the case, then the factory manager has to cut production. This means layoffs, and there is no guarantee that these layoffs will be modest, causing the subsequent recession to be shallow in nature and short in duration.

Thus, from the point of view of forecasting, the conditions necessary for a downturn in business to occur may not be sufficient to cause the downturn to occur. The system is resilient to correct for a certain degree of fluctuations in factory inventory in relation to orders from distributors. However, it is possible that declining distributor inventory and rising factory inventory cannot be corrected in time by price adjustments. Thus, the factory manager must hit the production throttle to keep factory inventory in line with vastly diminished orders from the distributors. He begins to lay off workers. The first wave of layoffs

Exhibit 7.23
Spending by Consumers

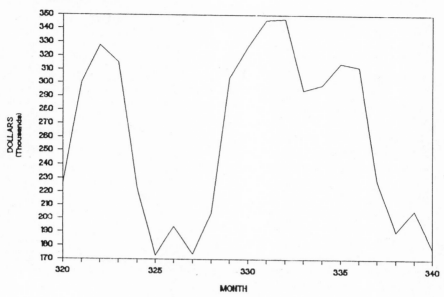

does not affect the state of mind of the workers. And maybe the second wave has only a nudging effect on savings rates. But at some point, the relentless pounding of successive waves of workers being laid off induces consumers to change their spending and saving behaviors. As good times change to bad, spending plummets, as illustrated in Exhibit 7.23. If, as the bad times start, consumers aren't spending, they must be saving. Exhibit 7.24 shows that saving is the consequence of not spending.

Declining spending by consumers worsens the situation. As sales plummet because of waning consumer confidence, distributors cut their orders to the factory. The factory manager, seeing little in the way of orders from distributors and skyrocking inventory in his warehouse, pulls back hard on both the pricing and the production throttles. If prices fall below the cost of production, the factory manager jams the production throttle into the stops, laying off workers as fast as he can. This adds to fear, the rate of saving goes through the roof, spending collapses, and the process of new layoffs inducing less spending repeats itself until the system is flat on its back.

And there it will sit either until the factory inventory level is restored to a more desirable balance with respect to incoming orders from distributors or until machinery capacity has decayed to the point that some builders have to be hired simply to keep production even with a depressed level of demand. No matter what the degree of anguish, no matter what the length of time, a depression

Exhibit 7.24
Saving by Consumers

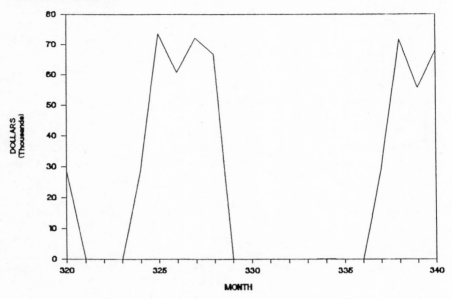

lasts until excess factory inventory or excess factory productive capacity has been liquidated.

And, at some point, liquidation ends because prices keep sinking when there is a high ratio of factory inventory to incoming orders. Liquidation can take a long time because spending has been drastically curtailed as a result of enhanced savings and reduced incomes as the unemployment lines lengthen. However, employment does not fall to zero because many government workers and the corporate overhead staff keep their jobs. There are always some machine operators taking home a paycheck. During the midst of the Great Depression, 75 percent of the people held onto their jobs.

But prices do have to fall to a level at which the total spending of those who have not lost their jobs and the withdrawals from savings of those who have lost their jobs can liquidate the excess inventories. The free market ensures that this will occur because factory managers cannot hold prices when goods are piled up to the ceiling. They are forced to cut prices, even when the price no longer covers the cost of manufacture.

The length, breadth, and depth of a depression are linked to the magnitude of spending, including the net effect of saving and dissaving, and to the rapidity with which prices are falling. As bad as depressions are, contrary to their seemingly endless nature for those who have lost their means of earning a livelihood, depressions do end. That is the lesson in Exhibit 7.5: the bad times do end.

When good times return, the savings rate plummets as man as consumer eagerly

Exhibit 7.25
Dissaving by Consumers

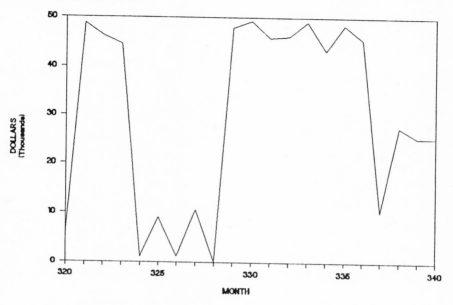

returns to his good times role of a spender. Dissavings, as illustrated in Exhibit 7.25, must be viewed from two different aspects. During the bad times, dissavings keep those who have lost their jobs alive. When good times are back in vogue, those who had not lost their jobs, but had been saving to the maximum practical extent during the bad times, now view their nest eggs as being more than adequate. The act of dissaving also refers to the spending of excess savings that were accumulated when the bad times mentality prevailed. The amount of dissaving adds to the strength of the recovery of business activity.

FLOW OF CASH DURING A BUSINESS CYCLE

It ought to be noted that the period under scrutiny had bad times that were fairly shallow in depth and fairly short in duration. Exhibit 7.5 shows that bad times can be much more severe in periods other than the one under scrutiny. During these depressions, all, or nearly all, of the builders lost their jobs. Exhibit 7.19 shows the degree of unemployment among the machine builders for the period under consideration. There were far worse times when the duration of the bad times was sufficiently long for all machine builders to lose their jobs.

Unemployment of machine operators was also rather shallow in scope. The utilization rate during severe business downturns was below 50 percent providing a good indication on how many machine operators lost their jobs. After such a severe contraction in business activity, the savings of the many who had lost

Exhibit 7.26
Cash Flow: Population

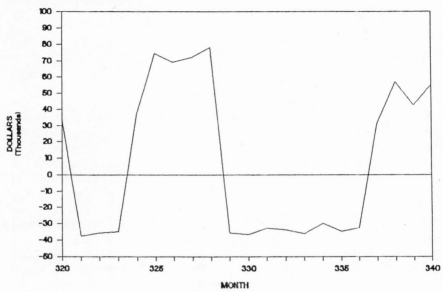

their jobs would have been drawn down to a considerable degree. During the next cycle of good times, the contribution of dissavings to the spending stream by those who had not lost their jobs would be reduced to the degree that others are rebuilding their depleted nest eggs. The nature of saving and dissaving after the bad times are over differs from cycle to cycle, depending on the length, breadth, and depth of the preceding bad times.

Exhibit 7.26 shows the cash flow of the whole population from the point of view of the bank. During the bad times, net deposits are being made into the banking system. Employed workers are saving at a greater rate than those who have lost their jobs are withdrawing funds to keep themselves alive. This, naturally, makes a bad condition worse because inventory liquidation is hard to achieve when all the big spenders are transformed into big savers. And the factory keeps on laying off its workers as long as it cannot get rid of its excess inventory.

During more severe contractions of business activity, dissavings can overwhelm savings as the legions of the unemployed swell, withdrawing funds at a faster pace than the employed are saving funds. This actually quickens the end of the bad times because unemployed machine operators are not adding to the excess inventory problem by producing goods, and they are still spending to the extent that they can withdraw funds from their savings. As the duration of such a severe business contraction increases, dissavings decrease because savings are being exhausted.

Therefore, the flow of savings and dissavings can vary widely from one business contraction to another, depending on the severity of the layoffs and the duration of the contraction. The pattern of saving and dissaving after the return of the good times also varies considerably from one cycle to another. Nevertheless, there is always dissaving because the government workers and those assigned to corporate overhead (who are exempt from layoffs, so to speak) and the workers who have not lost their jobs have nest eggs that are too large when the bad times are over. It is the relationship between savings and dissavings that counts in determining the spending power of consumers as business activity emerges from the doldrums.

Exhibit 7.26 differs from Exhibits 7.24 and 7.25 in that it includes the interest paid by the debtors—primarily the corporation and, at times, the government—to the savers, the people. This is part of the endless cycling of money. Money paid as interest by the corporation is not money that is lost forever. It is credited to the accounts of the savers. When the savers have nest eggs that are sufficient to tide them over the bad times—or at least perceive that they have nest eggs that are sufficient—the money paid by the corporation as interest flows back into the spending stream as dissavings. Thus, ultimately, the corporation receives as revenue all the money it pays to the workers to produce the wares and all the money it pays to the bank as interest. In a laissez faire society, all money is in constant circulation, with only differences in timing between paying the workers for their work, or paying interest to the workers for their savings, and receiving that money back in the form of revenue from wares sold.

To complete the banking picture, the cash flow of the corporation with regard to its bank accounts is shown in Exhibit 7.27. This is the net effect on the bank balance of the corporation, reflecting the purchase of all goods by the population, the payment of wages for its overhead staff and for its machine operators and builders, the payment of interest to the savers, and the liquidation and accumulation of inventory by both the distributors and the factory.

In general terms, the corporation deposits funds in the bank during the good times when prices are high and factories are buzzing with activity. The corporation withdraws funds from the bank during the bad times when prices have fallen and factories are partially idle. As previously mentioned, the downturns during the time period under investigation were not particularly severe in terms of the number of builders laid off. Severe layoffs of builders at the start of the downturn would have an impact on the amount of the funds being withdrawn from the bank. The quick cessation of capital projects reduces expenditures, and the quick liquidation of overhanging inventory is a source of cash. This could affect the nature of the corporate cash flow from one business cycle to another. This corporate cash flow might not follow the exact pattern shown in Exhibit 7.27 for every business cycle. In fact, all the exhibits are unique in some respect

Exhibit 7.27
Cash Flow: Corporation

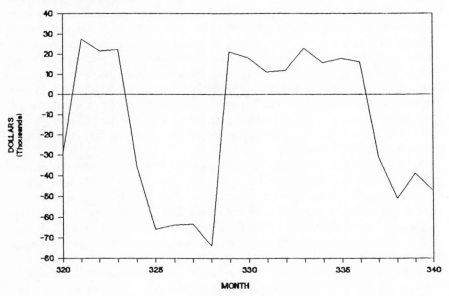

because each individual business cycle is itself unique. One would not expect patterns to repeat themselves in precisely the same manner. However, the general nature of the peaks and valleys of the business cycle would be similar from one cycle to the next.

Exhibit 7.28 shows the cash flow of the government with regard to its bank account. The government deficit during the bad times has nothing to do with relieving the plight of the distressed. It is a consequence of the fact that government revenue comes from a tax on spending and spending dries up during the bad times. Hence, the government's revenues fall, while its expenditures remain constant. The net result is a cash deficit, which is reduced by subsequent tax rate hikes during the good times. Government deficit spending during the bad times is part of a laissez faire economy. Only differences in degree and funding separate Exhibit 7.28 from the operation of a modern government.

SUMMARY OF FINDINGS

Forecasting is usually done with both eyes on the recent history of sales, with the forecast usually taking the form of an extrapolation of current trends. The marketing manager may contribute to the making of a forecast by introducing an alteration to the trend line, reflecting underlying changes in the market for a product. Forecasters do take the general level of business activity into consideration. The question being asked is, What signs should a forecaster consider

Exhibit 7.28
Cash Flow: Government

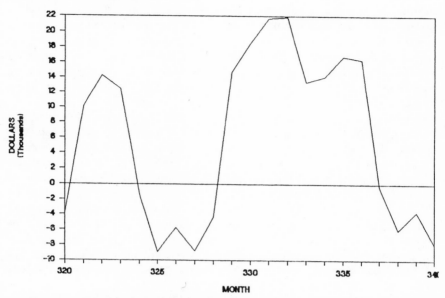

at the time of making a forecast that may presage a change in business activity during the forecast period?

The Transition from Good Times to Bad Times

The true nastiness of this task is that the underlying conditions that may induce a transition from good times to bad times need not result in the transition's actual occurrence. In other words, the twin signals of shrinking distributor and climbing factory inventory appear to be necessary, but not sufficient, conditions for good times to become bad times. Proper adjustment of the pricing throttle can reduce prices to a point at which the portion of goods that had been accumulating in inventory can be disposed of in the form of additional consumer purchases. Adjusting the pricing throttle properly means that good times do not necessarily have to become bad times.

However, once the transition from good times to bad times begins, anything from a short recession to a deep depression can occur. An economy can have a soft landing or a hard landing. No single party is responsible for either landing because business activity is the end result of many independent decisions. However, businessmen do have a penchant for copying one another. Drastic layoffs by one firm could well establish a pattern for others to emulate. The continual waves of layoffs have the potential to undermine consumer confidence—and once the confidence of the population has been shaken to its core, a short, mild recession can be transformed into a severe depression of much longer duration.

From the point of view of the model created herein, the divergent movements of decreasing distributor inventory and increasing factory inventory comprise the ominous sign that something adverse may happen during the forecast period, but not necessarily that it will happen. However, once the layoffs by man as producer trigger sharp reductions in spending by man as consumer, there is no way of predicting just how bad the landing will be. The descending airplane of business activity is suffering from a loss of fuel in the form of reduced purchasing by consumers and could make a soft landing in a field of grass or crash into a face of a cliff.

Another possibility for good times to turn to bad times occurs when some sort of shock immobilizes the spending pattern of the consumers. A national calamity, such as the loss of a leader or the collapse of the stock market, can cause consumers to shift from a spending to a saving mode. This, if not hastily corrected, could turn robust business activity into moribund business activity in short order. The 1929 Crash was singularly successful in bringing the Roaring 20s to a complete halt in a matter of months. The stock market crash in 1987 caused a sharp drop in big ticket purchases during the few short weeks of the market debacle. Not only did sales of big ticket items decline, but also there were home closings scheduled at which the buyers did not show up. Luckily for all concerned, the swing to saving swung back to spending, and business activity resumed its precrash level of activity.

A forecast made during good times should take into account whether the watershed of full employment has been passed. If so, then it is possible that there will be adjustments to distributor inventories that could perturb the system. Falling prices (in real terms), declining distributor inventory, and rising factory inventory are the perturbations that shake the system. A forecast made when business activity is subject to such perturbations ought to contain a greater element of caution than when distributor inventory is rising and factory inventory is falling. However, these perturbations do not necessarily mean that business activity will slump. And even if business activity does slump, it can rebound quickly with little damage to the general level of business activity. There is no iron-clad rule that a business recession must end up as a depression. But the danger of a depression does exist if layoffs reach the point at which the spending and saving habits of consumers are drastically altered.

With regard to forecasting shocks, which can send an economy into a tailspin, the forecaster is on his own. As implied in its definition, a shock cannot be anticipated. Perhaps the best advice that can be given to a forecaster is not to be overly complacent in practicing one's art. Or going one step further, too much complacency among forecasters is a warning sign in itself.

The Transition from Bad Times to Good Times

This is a more manageable situation from the viewpoint of the forecaster. The first, and foremost, rule for a recovery during a forecast period in which business is in the doldrums is that excess factory inventory must be liquidated. Get rid of the excess inventory, and a recovery can ensue. As soon as the excess inventory is liquidated, factory managers start hiring more workers. The very fact that unemployment is decreasing, despite what it is in absolute terms, has a salubrious effect on the economy. It starts to remove the element of fear that has paralyzed consumers, keeping them from spending their paychecks. This alone is sufficient to begin paving the road to recovery.

One other sign of an imminent recovery is the "decay" of existing plant capacity, reaching a point at which full utilization of the existing plant is necessary to satisfy depressed consumer demand. This can happen during unusually long recessions when building more plant productive capacity had longed since ceased with the dismissal of the last machine builder. Once a factory manager realizes that the full productive capacity of his existing plant is necessary to satisfy depressed levels of consumer demand, he will start hiring builders, even if only to prevent further deterioration of his plant capacity. This hiring of builders to keep the existing plant up to current production levels has the same effect as hiring more machine operators. The unemployment lines begin to shorten, people become less scared, they begin to spend a little more—which means they are saving a little less—and the first faltering steps to a recovery are taken.

A recovery can begin when either one of two conditions has been fulfilled. One is the liquidation of factory inventory so the factory manager can begin rehiring jobless machine operators. The other is the removal of productive capacity to the point that all the machines have to be used, even during the midst of depressed demand. As long as there is a modicum of profitability, a factory manager will hire a few builders just to keep his plant capacity from deteriorating further.

It is quite immaterial to the newly hired worker whether he is operating or building a machine. He is employed when yesterday he was unemployed. He takes a goodly portion of his pay and spends it. This adds to the spending stream for the buying of wares. His being employed takes some of the fear of being unemployed out of the system. Once these necessary steps are taken, it is fairly likely that the recovery will proceed to higher levels of business activity.

Therefore, a forecaster performing his task during depressed times—in sensing rising prices, expanding distributor inventory, and shrinking factory inventory—may well see a transformation from bad times to good times during the forecast period. This means that his forecast, embedded in past sales, will underestimate demand over the forecast period if such a recovery takes place.

APPENDIX

The simulation program described in this chapter, from which the exhibits were generated, is listed on the following pages.

Appendix 7.1

```
10 REM NAME OF PROGRAM IS CH7
20 DIM P(400,4):DIM U(20,8):DIM O(20):DIM R(40)
45 REM ARRAY U(I,J) CHANGES IN PRICE AND PRODUCTION FOR
46 REM WEEKS OF FACT ORDERS - U(I,1) & U(I,2) PRICE
47 REM CHANGES WO/W PROFITS - U(I,3) & U(I,4) PRODUCTION
50 FOR I=1 TO 20
52 FOR J=1 TO 8
54 READ U(I,J)
56 DATA 1.12,1.30,1.50,1.00,1.12,1.30,1.50,1.0
58 DATA 1.08,1.20,1.30,1.00,1.11,1.25,1.50,1.0
60 DATA 1.04,1.15,1.20,1.00,1.10,1.20,1.50,1.0
62 DATA 1.02,1.13,1.15,1.00,1.10,1.20,1.50,1.0
64 DATA 1.00,1.11,1.12,0.95,1.10,1.20,1.50,1.0
66 DATA 0.98,1.09,1.06,0.92,1.07,1.15,1.50,1.0
68 DATA 0.96,1.07,1.02,0.90,1.06,1.15,1.50,1.0
70 DATA 0.95,1.06,1.00,0.90,1.05,1.15,1.50,1.0
72 DATA 0.95,1.05,1.00,0.90,1.05,1.15,1.45,1.0
74 DATA 0.95,1.04,1.00,0.90,1.05,1.15,1.40,1.0
76 DATA 0.95,1.03,0.98,0.90,1.05,1.15,1.35,1.0
78 DATA 0.94,1.02,0.97,0.90,1.03,1.12,1.30,1.0
80 DATA 0.94,1.01,0.97,0.90,1.01,1.10,1.25,1.0
82 DATA 0.94,1.00,0.97,0.90,1.00,1.10,1.20,1.0
84 DATA 0.93,1.00,0.96,0.90,1.00,1.10,1.15,1.0
86 DATA 0.93,0.99,0.95,0.90,1.00,1.10,1.10,1.0
88 DATA 0.93,0.99,0.94,0.90,1.00,1.10,1.08,1.0
90 DATA 0.93,0.99,0.93,0.90,1.00,1.10,1.05,1.0
92 DATA 0.93,0.99,0.92,0.90,1.00,1.05,1.03,1.0
94 DATA 0.93,0.98,0.90,0.90,0.93,0.98,0.90,0.9
96 NEXT:NEXT
97 REM ASSIGNING CATEGORIES TO POPULATION
98 REM 1-GOV'T/BASIC SERVICES   2-CORP OVERHD   3-UNEMPLOYABLE
99 REM 4-UNEMPLOYED   5-MACHINE OPERATORS   6-MACHINE BUILDERS
100 FOR I=1 TO 40:P(I,1)=1:X=RND(X):Y=RND(Y)
102 P(I,2)=2000+X*6000:P(I,3)=3000+Y*9000:NEXT
104 FOR I=41 TO 60:P(I,1)=2:X=RND(X):Y=RND(Y)
106 P(I,2)=4000+X*4000:P(I,3)=5000+Y*12000:NEXT
108 FOR I=61 TO 80:P(I,1)=3:P(I,2)=0:P(I,3)=0:NEXT
110 FOR I=81 TO 150:P(I,1)=4:X=RND(X):Y=RND(Y)
114 P(I,2)=3000+X*12000:P(I,3)=3000+Y*12000:NEXT
118 FOR I=150 TO 300:P(I,1)=5:X=RND(X):Y=RND(Y)
120 P(I,2)=4000+X*10000:P(I,3)=4000+Y*10000:NEXT
122 REM PAYSCALES  1-0.8  2-1.0  3-0  4-0  5-1.0  6-1.2
125 FOR I=1 TO 6:READ B(I):DATA .8,1,0,0,1,1.2:NEXT
127 REM INITIAL MONTHLY PAY, PRICE/LB OF GOODS, DIST & FACT INV
129 REM WKS OF ORDERS TO FACT INV, STATE OF MIND
130 L=1000:P=7.5:V=70000!:V1=60000!:W=10:E=3:P1=P:N5=150:M5=N5
131 N6=0:M6=N6:N4=70:M4=N4:M=170:I2=.04:T=.16
132 REM OVERTIME AS A FUNCTION OF WEEKS OF FACT ORDERS
135 FOR I=1 TO 6:READ O(I):DATA 1.40,1.30,1.20,1.15,1.1,1.05:NEXT
137 FOR I=7 TO 20:O(I)=1:NEXT
140 F=0:FOR J=1 TO 300:F=F+P(J,2):NEXT:G=-.25*F:C=-.75*F
```

```
195 OPEN "O",#1,"CH7F"
200 FOR I=1 TO 520:S=0:A=0:B=0:Q=0:Q3=0:Q4=0:Q5=0
202 REM AGING OF POSSESSIONS BY 1%/MTH
205 FOR J=1 TO 300:P(J,3)=.99*P(J,3):NEXT
207 R(5)=0:FOR J=1 TO 300:R(5)=R(5)+P(J,3):NEXT:R(5)=R(5)/280
208 E3=(N5+N6)/(N4+N5+N6)
210 Z=0:FOR J=1 TO 40:Z=Z+P(J,2):NEXT:Z=Z/40
215 FOR J=1 TO 40:P3=L*B(P(J,1)):A=A+P3
217 X=RND(X):ON E GOTO 220,235,240
220 IF E3>.95 THEN 221 ELSE 228
221 IF Z>(.95+.1*X)*7*P3 THEN 224 ELSE 222
222 IF Z>(.95+.1*X)*6*P3 THEN 223 ELSE 228
223 X=RND(X):IF X<.5 THEN 224 ELSE 226
224 X=RND(X):D1=.03*X*P(J,2):S1=0:GOSUB 400:GOTO 245
226 X=RND(X):D1=0:S1=.04*X*P3:GOSUB 400:GOTO 245
228 X=RND(X):D1=0:S1=.02*X*P3:GOSUB 400:GOTO 245
230 D1=0:S1=(.02+.04*X)*P3:GOSUB 400:GOTO 245
235 D1=0:S1=(.04+.04*X)*P3:GOSUB 400:GOTO 245
240 D1=0:S1=(.08+.08*X)*P3:GOSUB 400
245 NEXT
250 Z=0:FOR J=41 TO 60:Z=Z+P(J,2):NEXT:Z=Z/20
255 FOR J=41 TO 60:P3=L*B(P(J,1)):B=B+P3
260 X=RND(X):ON E GOTO 265,285,290
265 IF E3>.95 THEN 270 ELSE 280
270 IF Z>(.95+.1*X)*7*P3 THEN 274 ELSE 272
272 IF Z>(.95+.1*X)*6*P3 THEN 273 ELSE 278
273 X=RND(X):IF X<.5 THEN 274 ELSE 276
274 X=RND(X):D1=.03*X*P(J,2):S1=0:GOSUB 400:GOTO 295
276 X=RND(X):D1=0:S1=.04*X*P3:GOSUB 400:GOTO 295
278 X=RND(X):D1=0:S1=.05*X*P3:GOSUB 400:GOTO 295
280 D1=0:S1=(.02+.04*X)*P3:GOSUB 400:GOTO 295
285 D1=0:S1=(.04+.04*X)*P3:GOSUB 400:GOTO 295
290 D1=0:S1=(.06+.04*X)*P3:GOSUB 400
295 NEXT
300 FOR J=61 TO 80:P3=L*B(P(J,1)):A=A+P3:D1=0:S1=0:GOSUB 400:NEXT
305 Z=0:FOR J=81 TO 300:Z=Z+P(J,2):NEXT:Z=Z/220
310 FOR J=81 TO 300:X=RND(X):IF P(J,1)=5 THEN 315 ELSE 320
315 P3=L*B(P(J,1))+1.5*L*B(P(J,1))*(O(W)-1):GOTO 335
320 P3=L*B(P(J,1))
325 IF P(J,1)=4 THEN 330 ELSE 335
330 A=A+P3:S1=0:D1=(.05+.05*X)*P(J,2):GOSUB 400:GOTO 395
335 B=B+P3:ON E GOTO 340,350,355
340 IF E3>.95 THEN 341 ELSE 349
341 IF Z>(.95+.1*X)*10*L THEN 344 ELSE 342
342 IF Z>(.95+.1*X)*9*L THEN 343 ELSE 347
343 IF X<.5 THEN 344 ELSE 345
344 X=RND(X):S1=0:D1=.03*X*P(J,2):GOSUB 400:GOTO 395
345 X=RND(X):D1=0:S1=(.02+.04*X)*P3:GOSUB 400:GOTO 395
347 X=RND(X):D1=0:S1=(.03+.05*X)*P3:GOSUB 400:GOTO 395
349 X=RND(X):D1=0:S1=(.05+.05*X)*P3:GOSUB 400:GOTO 395
350 D1=0:S1=(.075+X*.075)*P3:GOSUB 400:GOTO 395
355 D1=0:IF P(J,2)<Z THEN 360 ELSE 365
360 X1=.2+X*.2:GOTO 370
365 X1=.1+X*.2
370 X=RND(X)
375 IF N4>M4 THEN 380 ELSE 390
380 X1=X1+X*2*(N4-M4)/220:IF X1>.7 THEN 385 ELSE 390
385 X=RND(X):X1=.6+.2*X
390 S1=X1*P3:GOSUB 400
395 NEXT:GOTO 406
```

```
400  P(J,2)=P(J,2)-D1+S1:Q5=Q5+D1:S=S+S1
402  Q1=P3-S1+D1:Q2=T*Q1:Q1=Q1-Q2:Q3=Q3+Q2:Q4=Q4+Q1
405  Q1=Q1/P:Q=Q+Q1:P(J,3)=P(J,3)+Q1:RETURN
406  R(7)=S:R(8)=Q5:R(9)=Q4:R(10)=P:R(11)=Q
407  R(12)=200*N5*O(W):F=F-Q5+S
408  REM REVENUE EQUALS WORKERS PAY LESS SAVINGS PLUS DISSAVINGS
409  REM GOV'T REV IS A SALES TAX; CORP REV IS GROSS REV LESS TAX
411  REM ADD IN CURRENT PROD TO FACT INV
412  REM QTY OF GOODS SOLD COMPARED TO DIST INV
415  V1=V1+200*N5*O(W):V2=V-Q:IF V2<0 THEN 420 ELSE 435
420  Q1=Q-V:V=0:V2=V1-Q1:IF V2<0 THEN 425 ELSE 430
425  PRINT "ALL INVENTORY EXHAUSTED PERIOD ";I:END
430  V1=V1-Q1:GOTO 439
433  REM DIST INV REDUCED BY SALES
435  V=V-Q
438  REM DIST ORDERS INFLUENCED BY STATE OF MIND AND PRICE CHANGES
439  X=RND(X):IF E=3 THEN 442 ELSE 440
440  IF P>P1 THEN 444 ELSE 441
441  IF P<P1 THEN 442 ELSE 443
442  Q1=(4!+3!*X)*Q/4:GOTO 445
443  Q1=(6!+2*X)*Q/4:GOTO 445
444  Q1=(7+3!*X)*Q/4
445  R=Q1-V:IF R>0 THEN 455 ELSE 450
450  R=0:R(13)=V:R(14)=V1:R(15)=R:W1=W:GOTO 495
453  REM DIST ORDERS FILLED BY FACT
455  V2=V1-R:IF V2<0 THEN 460 ELSE 465
460  V=V+V1:V1=0:GOTO 470
465  V=V+R:V1=V1-R
468  REM WKS OF FACT INV TO DIST ORDERS
470  R(13)=V:R(14)=V1:R(15)=R:W1=W
475  W2=4*V1/R:W=INT((2*W2+W1)/3)
480  IF W<1 THEN 485 ELSE 490
485  W=1:GOTO 500
490  IF W>20 THEN 495 ELSE 500
495  W=20
497  REM PROFITABILITY OF FACTORY AND PAYBACK PERIOD
500  IF 200*P-L>0 THEN 505 ELSE 510
505  P2=1:P3=10*B(6)*L/(200*P-L):P4=P3/12
507  P3=P3*(1+I2)^P4:GOTO 515
510  P2=-1:P3=1000
512  REM ADJUST PRICE TO WKS OF FACT ORDERS & PROFITABILITY
513  REM AND POTENTIAL ADJUSTMENT TO MACHINE OPERATORS
515  P1=P:IF W<=W1 THEN 523 ELSE 517
517  IF P2=1 THEN 520 ELSE 522
520  P=P*U(W,1):D1=N5*U(W,3):GOTO 530
522  P=P*U(W,2):D1=N5*U(W,4):GOTO 530
523  IF P2=1 THEN 525 ELSE 527
525  P=P*U(W,5):D1=N5*U(W,7):GOTO 528
527  P=P*U(W,6):D1=N5*U(W,8):GOTO 530
528  IF N5>100 THEN 530 ELSE 529
529  D1=(20-W)*4+N5
530  X=RND(X):X1=X*.06:X=RND(X):IF X>.9 THEN 532 ELSE 534
532  X=RND(X):X1=X*2*X1
534  M=INT((1-X1)*M+N6/10):D1=INT(D1):M4=N4:M5=N5:M6=N6
535  IF D1>M THEN 536 ELSE 537
536  D1=M
537  D=D1-N5:IF D>0 THEN 540 ELSE 640
```

```
539 REM MUST ADD MACHINE OPERATORS
540 IF N4=0 THEN 595 ELSE 545
545 X=RND(X):IF X<.5 THEN 550 ELSE 554
550 Z1=81:Z2=300:Z3=1:GOTO 555
554 Z1=300:Z2=81:Z3=-1
555 FOR J=Z1 TO Z2 STEP Z3
560 IF P(J,1)=4 THEN 565 ELSE 585
565 P(J,1)=5:D=D-1:N4=N4-1
567 REM CHECK REMAINING UNEMPLOYED WORKERS OR NEED FOR OPERATORS
570 IF D=0 THEN 580 ELSE 575
575 IF N4=0 THEN 580 ELSE 585
580 IF Z3=1 THEN 582 ELSE 584
582 J=300:GOTO 585
584 J=81
585 NEXT
588 REM SWITCH BUILDERS TO OPERATORS TO MAN MACHINES
590 IF D>N6 THEN 592 ELSE 595
592 D=N6
595 IF D=0 THEN 597 ELSE 600
597 GOSUB 690:GOTO 710
600 X=RND(X):IF X<.5 THEN 602 ELSE 604
602 Z1=81:Z2=300:Z3=1:GOTO 605
604 Z1=300:Z2=81:Z3=-1
605 FOR J=Z1 TO Z2 STEP Z3
610 IF P(J,1)=6 THEN 615 ELSE 635
615 P(J,1)=5:D=D-1
620 IF D=0 THEN 630 ELSE 635
630 IF Z3=1 THEN 632 ELSE 634
632 J=300:GOTO 635
634 J=81
635 NEXT:GOSUB 690:GOTO 710
637 REM LAY OFF MACHINE OPERATORS
640 IF D=0 THEN 710 ELSE 645
645 D=-D:IF N5=0 THEN 648 ELSE 650
648 GOSUB 690:GOTO 790
650 X=RND(X):IF X<.5 THEN 652 ELSE 654
652 Z1=81:Z2=300:Z3=1:GOTO 655
654 Z1=300:Z2=81:Z3=-1
655 FOR J=Z1 TO Z2 STEP Z3
660 IF P(J,1)=5 THEN 665 ELSE 685
665 P(J,1)=4:D=D-1
670 IF D=0 THEN 680 ELSE 685
680 IF Z3=1 THEN 682 ELSE 684
682 J=300:GOTO 685
684 J=81:GOTO 685
685 NEXT:GOSUB 690:GOTO 710
```

Appendix 7.1 (continued)

```
689 REM DETERMINE NEW EMPLOYMENT FIGURES
690 N4=0:N5=0:N6=0
692 FOR J=81 TO 300
694 IF P(J,1)=4 THEN 700 ELSE 696
696 IF P(J,1)=5 THEN 702 ELSE 698
698 N6=N6+1:GOTO 705
700 N4=N4+1:GOTO 705
702 N5=N5+1
705 NEXT:RETURN
708 REM DETERMINING UTILIZATION
710 U1=U:U=N5/M
715 IF P2=1 THEN 716 ELSE 790
716 IF U>.95 THEN 717 ELSE 732
717 IF P3>80 THEN 718 ELSE 719
718 D=4:GOTO 760
719 IF P3>70 THEN 720 ELSE 721
720 D=5:GOTO 760
721 IF P3>60 THEN 722 ELSE 723
722 D=7:GOTO 760
723 IF P3>50 THEN 724 ELSE 725
724 D=9:GOTO 760
725 IF P3>40 THEN 726 ELSE 727
726 D=12:GOTO 760
727 IF P3>30 THEN 728 ELSE 730
728 D=15:GOTO 760
730 D=20:GOTO 760
732 IF P3>40 THEN 790 ELSE 735
735 IF U>.85 THEN 740 ELSE 790
740 IF U>=U1 THEN 744 ELSE 790
744 IF P3>30 THEN 870 ELSE 746
746 IF P3>20 THEN 752 ELSE 754
752 D=10:GOTO 760
754 D=15
760 IF N4=0 THEN 870 ELSE 762
762 IF D>N4 THEN 764 ELSE 766
764 D=N4
766 X=RND(X):IF X<.5 THEN 768 ELSE 770
768 Z1=81:Z2=300:Z3=1:GOTO 772
770 Z1=300:Z2=81:Z3=-1
772 FOR J=Z1 TO Z2 STEP Z3
774 IF P(J,1)=4 THEN 776 ELSE 785
776 P(J,1)=6:D=D-1
778 IF D=0 THEN 780 ELSE 785
780 IF Z3=1 THEN 781 ELSE 783
781 J=300:GOTO 785
783 J=81
785 NEXT:GOTO 870
```

```
788 REM LAYING OFF BUILDERS
790 IF N6=0 THEN 870 ELSE 791
791 IF P3>40 THEN 820 ELSE 792
792 IF P2=-1 THEN 800 ELSE 795
795 IF U<.7 THEN 800 ELSE 815
800 IF N6>10 THEN 805 ELSE 801
801 FOR J=81 TO 300:IF P(J,1)=6 THEN 802 ELSE 803
802 P(J,1)=4
803 NEXT:GOTO 870
805 FOR J=81 TO 300
807 IF P(J,1)=6 THEN 808 ELSE 810
808 X=RND(X):IF X<.3 THEN 809 ELSE 810
809 P(J,1)=4
810 NEXT:GOTO 870
815 IF U<U1 THEN 820 ELSE 870
820 IF P3>30 THEN 822 ELSE 824
822 X=RND(X):X1=.1+X*.1:GOTO 835
824 IF P3>20 THEN 826 ELSE 830
826 X=RND(X):X1=.05+.05*X:GOTO 835
830 X=RND(X):X1=.1*X
835 D=INT(X1*N6)
840 IF D<1 THEN 842 ELSE 843
842 D=1
843 IF N6<10 THEN 845 ELSE 847
845 D=N6
847 Z1=81:Z2=300:Z3=1:GOTO 850
848 Z1=300:Z2=81:Z3=-1
850 FOR J=Z1 TO Z2 STEP Z3
852 IF P(J,1)=6 THEN 854 ELSE 865
854 P(J,1)=4:D=D-1
855 IF D=0 THEN 857 ELSE 865
857 IF Z3=1 THEN 858 ELSE 860
858 J=300:GOTO 865
860 J=81
865 NEXT
868 REM WAGE RATE ADJUSTMENTS
870 GOSUB 690:U2=N4/(N4+N5+N6):IF U2<.01 THEN 875 ELSE 880
875 L=1.00075*L:GOTO 890
880 IF P3=-1 THEN 886 ELSE 882
882 IF U2>.2 THEN 883 ELSE 890
883 L=.999*L:GOTO 890
886 L=.998*L
```

```
888 REM DETERMINE STATE OF MIND
890 R(16)=W:R(17)=P3:R(18)=L:E2=M5+M6:E3=N5+N6
891 R(19)=N4:R(20)=N5:R(21)=N6:IF E=3 THEN 895 ELSE 905
895 Z8=Z8+1:IF Z8=2 THEN 900 ELSE 925
900 Z8=0
905 IF E3<.5*220 THEN 924 ELSE 910
910 IF E3>.95*220 THEN 920 ELSE 912
912 IF E3>.9*220 THEN 922 ELSE 914
914 IF E3>E2 THEN 916 ELSE 924
916 IF E3>.6*220 THEN 922 ELSE 924
920 E=1:GOTO 925
922 E=2:GOTO 925
924 E=3
925 G1=G:G=G1+Q3-A
930 IF G>0 THEN 932 ELSE 938
932 IF G>G1 THEN 934 ELSE 950
934 T=T-.01:IF T<.06 THEN 936 ELSE 950
936 T=.06:GOTO 950
938 IF G<G1 THEN 940 ELSE 950
940 IF E=1 THEN 942 ELSE 950
942 IF N4/(N4+N5+N6)<.1 THEN 943 ELSE 950
943 T=T+.01:IF T>.3 THEN 945 ELSE 950
945 T=.3
948 REM CORPORATE AND POPULATION ACCOUNT
950 C1=C:C=C1+Q4-B:F1=F
951 R(22)=E:R(24)=Q3:R(25)=A:R(27)=B
959 REM IF GOOD TIMES AND PRICES RISING, INC INT TO 10% MAX
960 IF E=1 THEN 962 ELSE 970
962 IF P>P1 THEN 964 ELSE 970
964 IF I2>=.1 THEN 966 ELSE 978
966 I2=.1:GOTO 1030
969 REM IF PRICES CONSTANT, KEEP INTEREST AROUND 4%
970 IF P<P1 THEN 990 ELSE 974
972 IF I2>.04 THEN 982 ELSE 974
974 IF I2<.04 THEN 978 ELSE 1030
978 I2=I2+.0025:GOTO 1030
982 I2=I2-.0025:GOTO 1030
989 REM IF PRICES FALLING, LOWER INT RATES TO 2%
990 IF I2<.02 THEN 978 ELSE 995
995 IF I2>.02 THEN 982 ELSE 1030
```

```
1028 REM INTEREST ON DEBTORS PAID TO SAVERS
1030 A=0:B=0:IF G<0 THEN 1032 ELSE 1034
1032 A=A-G:B=B-G*I2/12:G=G*(1+I2/12)
1034 IF C<0 THEN 1036 ELSE 1050
1036 A=A-C:B=B-C*I2/12:C=C*(1+I2/12)
1048 REM B IS TOTAL INTEREST TO BE PAID TO SAVERS
1050 A1=0:IF G>0 THEN 1052 ELSE 1054
1052 A1=A1+G
1054 IF C>0 THEN 1056 ELSE 1060
1056 A1=A1+C
1060 IF F<0 THEN 1064 ELSE 1070
1064 PRINT "POPULATION NET DEBTORS:END PROGRAM":END
1070 A1=A1+F:B1=0:B2=0:B3=0
1072 A1=A1+Y:B5=(Y/A1)*B:Y=Y+B5
1078 REM INTEREST TO BE SPREAD AMONGST SAVERS
1080 IF G>0 THEN 1082 ELSE 1084
1082 B1=(G/A1)*B:G=G+B1
1084 IF C>0 THEN 1088 ELSE 1095
1088 B2=(C/A1)*B:C=C+B2
1095 B3=B-B1-B2-B5:IF B3<0 THEN 1097 ELSE 1100
1097 PRINT "INT TO POPULATION NEGATIVE":END
1100 FOR J=1 TO 300:B4=P(J,2)*B3/F:P(J,2)=P(J,2)+B4:NEXT:F=F+B3
1105 R(30)=100*I2:R(31)=100*T:R(32)=M:R(33)=100*U
1110 R(34)=B:R(35)=B1:R(36)=B2:R(37)=B3:R(23)=G:R(26)=C
1115 R(28)=F:R(6)=Y:R(38)=R(23)+R(26)+R(28)+R(6)
1117 PRINT "POSSESSIONS ";R(5)
1120 PRINT "SAVINGS ";R(7),"DISSAVINGS ";R(8)
1125 PRINT "TSPEND ";R(9),"PRICE ";R(10):PRINT
1130 PRINT "GOODS MADE ";R(12),"GOODS BOUGHT ";R(11)
1135 PRINT "DEALERS INV ";R(13),"FACT INV ";R(14),"ORDERS ";R(15)
1137 PRINT "DEALERS INV/SALES ";4*R(13)/R(11)
1140 PRINT:PRINT "WEEKS ";R(16),"PAYBACK ";R(17),"WAGE ";R(18)
1150 PRINT "UNEMPL ";R(19),"OPERATORS ";R(20),"BUILDERS ";R(21):PRINT
1155 PRINT "STATE ";R(22),"MACHINES ";R(32)," ","UTILIZATION ";R(33)
1165 PRINT "INTEREST ";R(30),"TAX RATE ";R(31)
1170 PRINT
1175 PRINT "GOVT ACCT ";R(23),"G RECEIPTS ";R(24),"G OBLIGS ";R(25)
1180 PRINT "CORP ACCT ",R(26),"C OBLIGATIONS ";R(27)
1185 PRINT "POP ACCT ";R(28),"FOR ACCT ";R(6),"TOT ACCT ";R(39):PRINT
1190 PRINT "TOT INT ";R(34),"INT TO GOVT ";R(35),"INT TO FOR ";R(38)
1195 PRINT "INT TO CORP ";R(36),"INT TO POP ";R(37)
1200 IF I<11 THEN 1220 ELSE 1205
1205 WRITE #1,I-10,R(5),R(7),R(8),R(9),R(12),R(11),R(10),R(13),R(14),R(16),R(15)
,R(17),R(18),R(19),R(20),R(21),R(22),R(32),R(33),R(30),R(31),R(28),R(23),R(26),R
(38),R(6)
1220 X=INT(70*(N5+N6)/220):PRINT I TAB(X) "X":PRINT
1230 NEXT:CLOSE#1:END
```

8

Forecasting in a Free Market Society

One would expect that forecasting in a laissez faire society and in a free market society would be similar in nature. Both societies are marked by freedom for individuals to make decisions with regard to the nature of the goods and services to be supplied to the marketplace. Both are associated with a democratic form of government. It might be unsettling to realize that forecasting in a free market society might be applicable where the form of government is less than democratic in the American context of the word. For instance, a free market economy can operate in a monarchy with no formal representative body of the people. What matters is not so much the political structure of the government but the manner in which a society organizes itself from the point of view of producing goods and providing services.

The free market society, for purposes of this chapter, is any society that permits new firms to be formed for the intent of addressing the needs of the marketplace. Existing firms are given no monopolistic rights, nor can they unduly restrict the introduction of new products, or modifications to existing products, by newly formed or existing competitive firms. A free market society is one in which there is freedom for individuals and companies to introduce new products and services to satisfy the real, or perceived, demands of the market. Inherent in this definition is the concomitant risk of bankruptcy if these needs are not adequately satisfied, or if others meet these needs more satisfactorily, or if perceived needs never materialize. The essence of the free market includes risk and reward, free choice, and a disinterested government from the point of view of making any serious incursion on the decision making process of businessmen, corporate managers, and entrepreneurs.

In any society, the government sets the rules by which the game is played. In a free market society, the government may establish laws with respect to minimum standards on working conditions in terms of pay and hours, the risk of exposure to occupational hazards, and the degree of pollution of the environment. These then become the costs of doing business that enter into the economic analysis portion of the decision making process. Government taxation of corporate profits is simply another cost. There is no question that these costs affect decisions made by businessmen, but the decision making process, and the decision itself, is left in the hands of businessmen. If the costs of paying the minimum wage, of protecting a workman from mutilation, of not polluting a river, and of paying taxes for building a new plant are too high in relation to revenue for a businessman to enter into an endeavor, then his decision not to proceed is one of free choice. In today's global economy, he may simply decide to build his plant in another location where these costs are less onerous. If he doesn't, someone else will do the same economic calculation for a more "congenial" location and build the plant.

The essential difference between a laissez faire society and a free market society, as interpreted herein, lies in the nature of government intervention in the running of the economy. In a laissez faire society, there is no government intervention—the role of government is limited to providing vital services that are paid for in full by taxation and user fees. In principle, the unemployable and the unemployed receive no public support. One can argue whether laissez faire government is as heartless as it appears—certainly education is provided to those who might one day be numbered among the ranks of the unemployable. However, all this is a moot point because a laissez faire society does not exist—and it might be arguable that it never existed.

GOVERNMENT INTERVENTION

Government intervention has always been present in the running of societies, especially in the conduct of business. Many of the so-called robber barons of the nineteenth century made their fortunes by building railroads. Their fortunes might not have been possible had not the government actively supported their endeavors by granting them rights of way, by providing inducements in the form of land rights and ownership for something more than a few feet of necessary right of way. The government wanted the railroads built, and the most efficient way to do so, in the minds of those in power, was to let it be done by private enterprise. The cost to the government was to give away large tracts of unsettled land that no one wanted because of a lack of transport. Once railroads were built to transport goods and commodities, the land could be settled and developed. Much of the wealth of the robber barons was accumulated when the worthless land holdings, given to them as an inducement to build the railroads, became valuable once the railroads were built. The enormous real estate holdings of railroads today are the result of nineteenth century "laissez faire" government intervention on behalf of private industry. "Laissez faire" may be interpreted to mean no government intervention, but it really means government intervention on behalf of commerce and industry.

There is nothing wrong with a government being pro-business. There is nothing wrong with society having a few robber barons. After all, no matter how harshly the robber barons may be criticized, they, and not their critics, are responsible for some portion of the development and industrialization of the United States. Railroads opened up the vast regions of North America to settlement and development. It would not be practical, or perhaps even possible, to grow wheat on the Great Plains and market the grain in Chicago or New York without the railroads. Government support of commerce and industry means that jobs are created for people to earn their livelihoods. In turn, their earnings can be taxed to support education, medical care, and anything else deemed beneficial to society.

The most ardent supporters of government intervention are not those speaking for the social outcasts, the indigent, those handicapped in one way or the other who cannot participate in the workings of modern day society. The most ardent, although not the most vociferous, supporters are the advocates and the chief beneficiaries of the free market system. The free market, in all its variant forms, is not a haven for fun and frolic. It is a system in which managers of private concerns must be forever on their toes. The customers show no loyalty. Someone else comes out with a superior product in terms of performance or quality, or the same product at a lower price or with a higher level of service, and blotto—the cadre of happy, satisfied, loyal customers melts faster than a snowball in a fiery inferno.

A manager in a free market environment cannot rest on his oars at any time. Nor can he depend on the laurels of past achievements to keep him in business. The enemy, under the name of competition, can strike at any time. Or more to the point, the enemy will strike at the first opportunity. Managers also are aware of the fact that companies that have depended on their past achievements to guarantee their position in the future are no longer in existence. Nothing demonstrates the challenge of the free market environment more than the fact that managers themselves are forced to be agents of change.

COMPETITION AS AN AGENT OF CHANGE

Isn't it strange that a company that dominates its industry is the company most apt to improve its own product? The company that dominates the computer industry is the company most apt to bring out a new model line that makes its old model line obsolete. The company that dominates the aircraft industry is the company most apt to bring out a new series of aircraft with performance characteristics superior to those of its existing line of aircraft. The company that dominates the chemical industry, the drug industry, the you-name-it industry, is the company spending about 5 percent of its gross revenues on research and development to bring out products that make its existing line of products, which already dominates the market, obsolete.

Some say that the reason for this behavior is the quest for profit maximization. If profit maximization were the objective, then after-tax profits could be greatly enhanced by eliminating research and development and letting the existing line of products, which already dominates the market, continue to dominate the market. That is profit maximization. Spending millions in the quest to put out a better potato peeler when the existing potato peeler has an 80 percent share of the market is a testament to the insecurity of management in a free market environment.

Management knows that if they don't put in the effort to make a better potato peeler, someone else will. Sooner or later, a competitor will develop a better potato peeler, and the dominating company will no longer dominate the industry. To thwart a potential competitor, the company becomes its own competitor, so to speak, by developing better products that consign its product line to the junk heap.

One can describe this behavior as profit maximization, but there is a defensive aspect to all this. The company that introduces change also manages change, and, by being at the forefront of change, the company becomes a leader in its industry. The company that copies change will find itself reacting to change— and a company that reacts cannot lead.

After all, it takes time to react to the introduction of a new product by the market leader in an industry. During that time, the market leader is continuing to expand its share of the pie. By the time a competing company can copy the change and bring it to market, the market leader may already be introducing an improved version of what the copier has copied. Then the copying company finds itself behind the eight ball again. The graveyard of corporations is full of companies that could not keep up with the innovations introduced by the survivors. The survivors are those who manage their destiny by initiating and controlling change. Managers who wish to work for surviving companies must foster change.

This discussion should serve to illustrate the discomfiture of running a company in a free market environment. The easiest course of action for a manager is to spend his career doing nothing that upsets the corporate applecart. The most comfortable way of life for businessmen is "business as usual." The free market does not permit this form of indolence. Businessmen welcome government intervention if some degree of discomfiture can be removed from the running of companies in a free market environment. The support can be in the form of import duties or quotas or other forms of barriers to trade, protection from competition in the form of exclusive rights, patents, and monopolies, and any involvement by the government to make the conduct of business a bit more comfortable. And, of course, obtaining government contracts with essentially no competition once the contract has been awarded provides a nice, comfortable corporate lifestyle away from the hurly burly of the free marketplace.

CALLS FOR GOVERNMENT INTERVENTION

Calls for government intervention in the form of protection during normal times pale in comparison to the hues and cries for government intervention once the onslaught of bad times takes two or three turns for the worse. Nothing can get a businessman to purchase a ticket to Washington, or any other capital, faster than a good old laissez faire dip into the worst of the bad times of a business cycle.

However, laissez faire economic theory calls for minimum government expenditures overall and a balanced budget to boot. Theory says that the government is to do nothing during a severe recession because recessions are supposed to test the financial resilience of companies. Those who don't pass the test file for bankruptcy. The destruction of equity and the elimination of debt of companies found wanting are supposed to be good for the corporate immortal soul and, ultimately, good for society. This sounds fine as a lecture delivered from the podium by a tenured professor. It is palatable to those associated with surviving companies as shareowners, debt holders, managers, or workers. However, it is hardly solace to those wondering how they are going to feed their families because the financial resilience of their firms was found wanting.

A recession is a recession when most companies pass the financial resilience test. A recession becomes a depression when most companies feel that they may fail the test. If there is one lesson in Chapter 7, it is that there is no way to tell how bad the bad times will be once the good times turn to bad. Bad times can range from a case of sniffles to pneumonia. While it is true that bad times eventually turn to good—that is, the pneumonia is not fatal to society as a whole—business depressions are fatal to many individual firms. Businessmen can live with the ups and downs of the business cycle, but a jump into the abyss of a depression is a downer that few view as a desired course of action for purging past excesses.

A depression, the continuance of which threatens the existence of every company, can transform the most rabid free marketeer into a doctrinaire socialist overnight. He will add his voice to the chorus of cries for the government to do something about the situation. The situation is now a depression that threatens the existence of not *every* company, but *his* company. And why shouldn't he act this way? Sensing the ever-increasing chances of ultimate liquidation, a businessman feels no different than an individual who has become unemployed and is fast becoming unemployable. Faced with the prospect of losing all, the prospect of government intervention doesn't look that bad. The businessman is acting true to his character: he will do what is best for his interests.

The businessman has already performed all the acts in his repertoire. He has already jammed the pricing and production throttles into the stops, and nothing is happening. The warehouse is still filled with unsold goods. The price of goods does not compensate for the cost of production. He has laid off much of his work force; he has closed some factories, and the rest are limping along at a low rate of productivity. He knows that there can be no hope of a recovery until the excess inventory is liquidated, and the warehouse remains full. Bankers and creditors are breathing down his neck.

The businessman is a victim of behavior patterns that he himself has triggered by playing his role as man as producer. Man as consumer is holding spending to an absolute minimum because he is afraid of being laid off. This prevents the businessman from reducing his unsold inventory so he acts out his role as man as producer and lays off more workers. The cycle repeats itself until man as producer and man as consumer no longer have the strength to continue beating one another about the face and brow. During really bad times, there is no difference, other than in timing, between man as consumer and man as producer. They both end up standing in the same unemployment line. The unemployment line, not the marketplace, becomes the common meeting ground for man as consumer and man as producer.

FORMS OF GOVERNMENT INTERVENTION

During this nation's worst depression, the man of the hour was Franklin D. Roosevelt. He dealt out a new hand of cards called the New Deal. The economist who espoused the idea of government intervention in the form of public spending during times of an absence of private spending was John Maynard Keynes (1883–1946). The New Deal was Keynes' thoughts put into practice. Keynes communicated his thoughts to Roosevelt by word of mouth. He communicated his thoughts to the rest of the world in his book entitled *The General Theory of Employment, Interest, and Money,* published in 1936. Quoting from the 1972 edition of the *Encyclopaedia Britannica*:

Seeking to analyze the causes of the recession of the 1930's, [Keynes] showed how demand in total was determined by expenditures and how an equilibrium short of full employment might emerge without automatically setting in operation forces of recovery. Full employment, according to his theory, could be achieved only if governments and central banks deliberately encouraged investment in new capital goods and maintained a cheap money policy and public investment during a recession.

Concentrating on the concept that demand in total is determined by expenditures (and expenditures are the total spending by a society), one can easily analyze the impact of Keynes' thoughts on Adam Smith's island society by making two minor changes to the simulation in Chapter 7.

The first change is not important from the point of view of hastening the end of a recession or a depression. It is simply a matter of what might be considered social justice: the unemployables should have some form of public support. The simulation can be easily adapted to support the unemployables in some proportion to the take-home pay of the machine operators. This can be shown to have no real impact on the ups and downs of the business cycle. One can interpret supporting the unemployables as enlarging the government worker category—those providing vital services—except that this subgroup does not provide any services.

A few caveats are in order. One is that a society in which most of the citizens are contributing to the functioning of society in the form of producing goods or providing services can support the relatively few who can't, or won't. The many can support the few, but the few cannot support the many. Another point is that the degree of support cannot be equivalent to the earnings of those who do contribute to the workings of society. There has to be an inducement for individuals to spend a large portion of their lives tied to a machine stamping out parts or tied to a desk pushing paper to make the system work. If there is no inducement for individuals to participate in society, they may tend to remain home, content to be numbered among the idle. Having accepted the premise that the many can support the few, but not vice versa, the only way to ensure that there is an incentive for individuals to contribute to the workings of society is to make the compensation for those who can't, or won't, a small fraction of the compensation for those who can, and do.

However, there are some who cannot participate in the workings of society, regardless of the magnitude of the incentive to do so. Their being supported by society falls under the rubric of social justice. If the government is committed to a balanced budget over the long haul, social justice means higher taxes. Higher taxes mean less take-home pay and less goods to be purchased by those who produce the goods and by those who provide the services of a functioning society. A society can provide minimum income maintenance to those incapable, and perhaps unwilling, with the recognition that the living standards of those who do provide the services and produce the goods will decline proportionally.

Modern-day societies may argue over the degree of equalization of standards of living, but most provide some sort of safety net for those who cannot participate in the functioning of society. Any society can afford to have 90 percent of its working members support, to some degree, the 10 percent who cannot work. The real problem comes in with the attitude that an individual has a right not to contribute to the functioning of society, and that were he to exercise that right, he has another right to receive compensation equivalent to those who do contribute to the functioning of society.

The safety net under the unemployables does not change the nature of the ups and downs of the business cycle. What is critical in modifying the swings of the business cycle is unemployment benefits. Money paid to workers who have lost their jobs adds to the spending stream at a time when total spending, or expenditures in Keynes' terminology, is collapsing. Unemployment benefits, in conjunction with dissavings, means that more goods can be purchased during the bad times. More goods being purchased means that the liquidation of excess inventories can be hastened. The hastening of the process of inventory liquidation then hastens the beginning of a recovery. Recovery means that the liquidation of overhanging inventory has reached a point at which factory managers can begin rehiring machine operators. Rehiring machine operators eventually promotes a change in saving patterns that favors spending over saving. This increases total spending (expenditures), which takes goods out of the factory warehouse and puts them into the hands of consumers. This, in turn, induces managers to hire more workers to restock the warehouse. Finally, when utilization of machine capacity nears its limits, managers start hiring machine builders. In the most succinct terms, government deficit spending compensates for the excess savings of the population.

Two variants of Keynes' thinking can be tested. For both variants, the unemployables receive benefits equivalent to 25 percent of the pay of machine operators. For the first variant, the unemployed also receive 25 percent of the pay of machine operators. This is a government benefit that lasts for as long as they are unemployed. It is presumed that the unemployed stay at home until the factory calls them back to build or operate machines. It is also presumed that the workers heed the call, trudging on down to the factory rather than choosing to remain idle at home living off their unemployment benefits. Some may be satisfied to remain home and be numbered among the idle—but this does not benefit society. To correct for this nonaltruistic attitude on the part of some, unemployment benefits cease when there is an available job offering. To this extent, the unemployables have an advantage over the unemployed.

For the second variant, the government doubles the unemployment benefits to 50 percent of the regular pay of the machine operators and puts the unemployed to work. This work can take on many different forms: repairing roads, draining swamps, building schools and hospitals, and doing anything else that can provide value for the money expended on unemployment benefits. It could also be in the form that benefits industry: for instance, replacing ties in railroad track at a time when railroad managers have had to cut maintenance expenditures to the bone or building electricity-generating dams, the output of which will not be in demand for years. Industry cannot be expected to make these investments because the economic calculation of revenue less cost cannot justify the expenditure. Railroad ties cannot be replaced when revenue from moving goods less the cost to move the goods leaves little to be spent on such frivolous things as maintenance. Electricity-generating dams cannot be built when present capacity is more than ample to meet current demand. It is better to wait until there is an inkling of a developing shortage of electric power—say, brownouts and blackouts. Then the economic calculation will support the decision that it is the appropriate time to add to capacity.

Another method of employing the unemployed to the benefit of industry might be a ''scrap and build'' program. Workers without regular jobs are employed building new plant capacity incorporating the latest technology, while at the same time scrapping obsolete plants. All this is done at government expense: the corporations are not in a position to expend funds for such purposes.

In the simulation, the unemployed work for the benefit of industry, building machines at a rate of one machine per thirty man-months of unemployed effort. This is compared to ten man-months of effort required from machine builders to complete one machine. The lower productivity of the unemployed reflects that some work may be oriented to public service. The unemployed are not being employed solely for the benefit of industry. Because the unemployed are working to receive their unemployment benefits, it is presumed that they will switch over to industry at double their unemployment pay without any further coaxing by the government. The machines built by the unemployed are simply given to the corporation. The government is eventually compensated for the expense of providing employment to the unemployed during the bad times by increasing taxes during the subsequent good times. Perhaps, in a more realistic setting, the government would receive shares of stock in the companies that benefit from the building of capacity at times when private industry itself cannot economically justify capital expenditures.

IMPACT OF GOVERNMENT INTERVENTION

The following table summarizes the average values of the various parameters describing economic activity for a laissez faire society and for two variants of a free market society in which there is some form of government intervention in the workings of society beyond providing required services. Both variants of a free market society provide income maintenance to the unemployables amounting to 25 percent of the base wage of workers. The first variant provides unemployment benefits of 25 percent of the base wage, with no responsibility on the part of the recipient other than accepting an offer of employment when better times are at hand. The second variant provides unemployment benefits of 50 percent of the base wage, with society and industry benefiting because the unemployed are put to work building machine capacity and doing other useful tasks. The minor modifications to the simulation set up in Chapter 7 are described in the appendix.

According to nearly all measures of economic performance, the second variant on the free market society—in which higher unemployment benefits are paid to the unemployed who are then provided with jobs advantageous to society—is the best of the three. The average amount of goods bought, which is an indication of the output of the factories, is highest for this alternative. Prices for all three alternatives are about the same, as are wages, profitability as measured by the payback period, interest rates, and the respective bank account balances for the three constituencies of the island economy.

Higher productivity in the form of goods bought per month by the entire island population is not the only measure on which the second variant of the free market society is outperforming the laissez faire society. Other indications of better times for all concerned can be seen in the lower overall number of those unemployed, which reflects shorter times to liquidate excess inventories, a greater number of machines, higher utilization rates on machines, and more machine operators. The lower average state of mind means more months of a good times

NATURE OF SOCIETY

	Laissez Faire	Free Market I	Free Market II
Unemployable benefits as a % of base wage	None	25%	25%
Unemployment benefits as a % of base wage	None	25%	50%
Unemployment benefits of advantage to industry	—	No	Yes
Average over 500 months of simulation			
Good bought (lbs.)	29,932	31,180	32,182
Price	$8.51	$8.69	$8.63
Payback period (months)	27.7	24.5	27.8
Wage (per month)	$1,043	$1,076	$1,090
Number of unemployed	25	16	13
Number of operators	143	150	155
Number of builders	52	54	52
Number of machines	156	163	166
Utilization	92%	93%	94%
State of mind	1.75	1.68	1.64
Interest rate	4.3%	4.4%	4.5%
Tax rate	12.1%	14.5%	15.0%
Balance in population account ($1,000s)	$2,957	$3,013	$3,057
Balance in government account ($1,000s)	−$154	−$196	−$149
Balance in corporation account ($1,000s)	$2,803	$2,817	$2,908

mentality, which is given a value of 1, as compared to a bad times mentality value of 3. The cost of all this is in the tax rate, which, in the simulation, takes the form of a national sales tax. The tax rate increased from 12 to 15 percent, an increase of 25 percent. Whether the tax hike is worth the reduced cyclicality should be put to the utilitarian test of John Stuart Mill. On that basis, or by simply being pragmatic about the situation, it appears that government intervention during the bad times in the form of enhanced deficit spending to provide employment to the unemployed is better than "business as usual" of a laissez faire society.

It should be noted that Keynes was somewhat silent on the subject of how government deficit spending during recessions was to be repaid during the subsequent good times. His followers, generally speaking, were not. Deficit spending was to be the control throttle for setting the level of economic activity of a society at all times—good times and bad times. Or put another way, Keynesian economists would run society.

The free market system simulated herein has the government backing off from deficit spending during the good times. That is the advantage of unemployment benefits—there aren't any when times are good. Taxes are raised during the good times to generate surpluses to begin liquidating the deficits accumulated during the bad times. Deficit spending by the government during the bad times is necessary to offset the excessive rate of saving by the population and to maintain constant expenditures (spending). Tax increases when the population is in a dissaving mode dampen pressures for increasing the price of goods because purchasing power is being reduced by the extent of the tax increases. Government deficit spending during the bad times and tax increases during the good times act as a counterweight to the population's saving more during the bad times and saving less during the good.

The adaptation to the simulation does not include all of Keynesian thought, but it does incorporate a key element of Keynesian thinking in that it is the duty of the state, so to speak, to maintain spending when man as consumer is not. The model does not suggest that deficit spending by the government during the good times is a necessary consequence of deficit spending during the bad. In fact, the model suggests that long-term stability can be achieved when the government is intent on repaying the debts accumulated during the bad times. "Laissez faire" thinking that a balanced budget over the long haul is good for society seems to be confirmed with or without government intervention. Deficit spending during the good times cannot enhance employment when employment is already at high levels. Deficit spending during the good times simply adds to inflationary pressures of too much money chasing too few goods.

CHEAP MONEY

The impact of government deficit spending during the good times could be tested in the simulation with some adjustments to the program. However, the testing of whether cheap money would assist in a recovery from a recession by inducing managers to expand productive capacity would fail, were this incorporated into the simulation. The failure would have nothing to do with whether the assertion of the beneficial aspects of cheap money is true. The failure would have to do with the simulation itself. The simulation contains specific rules about the behavior of man as producer that go something like this. Man as producer is interested in profit maximization. Profit maximization is a balance between production cost and price in which price, hopefully, exceeds the cost of production. Price determines the volume of goods sold for a given level of spending. The higher the price, the less the volume for a given level of spending. The lower the price, the greater the volume. Man as producer keeps his eye on the amount of inventory in his warehouse. He touches his pricing and production throttles to keep the volume of factory inventory in line with incoming orders.

When factory inventory is too large with respect to incoming orders, the manager's first reaction is to cut the price to liquidate his inventory. If that isn't effective, he pulls back on the production throttle and starts to lay off workers. If the saving habits of the population change because the extent of the layoffs has undermined consumer confidence, then the recession worsens as the vicious cycle of enhanced saving encourages further layoffs, which encourage more saving. Man as consumer destroys man as producer by not spending his paycheck. Man as producer destroys man as consumer by not giving him any more paychecks. Both kneel before one another and commit hari-kari.

During a recession, prices are low, and there is plenty of spare capacity. Man as producer is worried about his solvency. He is thinking in terms of survival. Keynes says that man as producer can be enticed to enter into capital projects— that is, build more plant capacity—if he is offered cheap sources of credit. The simulation model is built on the perception of man's behavior that he will not expand productive capacity when his factory is half idle and prices may or may not cover the cost of production. The model contains instructions to the effect that man as producer isn't going to expand production until his current plant is fairly busy and prices at least cover the cost of production. Testing Keynes' theory on the ability of cheap money to induce capital spending during a recession is doomed to failure because the simulation model is constructed on the basis that man as producer does not behave in this fashion. As some have observed, low interest rates (i.e., cheap money) are as effective in resuscitating an economy in the doldrums as "pushing on a string."

During bad times, private companies face the risk of bankruptcy. When prices are low and factories are idle, managers think in terms of survival first. Survival means husbanding resources, and building more factories when the existing ones are idle means squandering resources. Whether money is cheap or expensive does not enter into the thinking of managers. However, this does not prevent the government from building plant capacity for its own account, so to speak, and transferring ownership of, or selling, the new factories to a corporation when the managers of that corporation perceive that it is the correct time to expand capacity.

GOVERNMENT INTERVENTION AND FORECASTING

Forecasting in a free market society remains unchanged for the two variants under consideration. There is little or no chance that a recession will occur when distributor inventories are expanding and factory inventories are contracting. There is a chance that a recession will occur when distributor inventories are contracting and factory inventories are expanding. However, judicious or fortuitous price adjustments by factory managers can avert a recession. Then the cycle of expanding and contracting inventories can repeat itself with relatively few layoffs and little disruption to production. However, if the layoffs reach a level that triggers a shift in spending patterns by the population, then a recession of unknown depth and duration can occur. The turning point from good times to bad times remains unchanged, regardless of the nature of government intervention under consideration because the interventionist policies under scrutiny deal with the reactions of a government to the bad times. Whether government deficit spending during the good times would avert a turn for the worse is left unanswered.

Without running the simulation to examine this possibility, all one can do is speculate on the results. Second-guessing the results of a simulation isn't recommended. On the surface, because the change from good times to bad times is predicated on adverse inventory adjustments by distributors and factory managers, and because these adverse inventory adjustments are influenced by falling prices, the simulation might end up supporting those who believe that deficit spending can be used as a throttle to control the general level of economic activity for a society. The cost of this policy would probably take the form of unending inflation. What the effect of rising prices would be on savings and spending patterns, or the effect of increasing government deficits on economic activity, is unclear. It is better to perform an actual run of the simulation and examine the results than to try to imagine a run of the simulation and speculate on the results.

The purpose of this book is not to evaluate economic theories but to forecast. However, forecasting is affected by the particular economic theory adopted by a society. The economic theory practiced in a society determines the rules of the game. The reactions of businessmen to a given situation are influenced by the nature of the rules of the game because businessmen are playing the game in terms of what is of greatest benefit to themselves. Therefore, forecasting on the basis of changes in human behavior cannot be done without an understanding of the rules of the game. And because the rules of the game are largely determined by the economic theory that a society is following, or is attempting to follow, the subject of economics is dragged into the picture, despite all attempts to leave it out.

Forecasting during the midst of a recession does not change because of the nature of government intervention under consideration. A recovery cannot ensue until excess inventories are liquidated. The fact that government intervention may be speeding up the process of inventory liquidation does not change the necessity of clearing out the factory warehouse before the factory manager orders more production. Once he orders more production, then he hires more machine operators. Once he begins to fully utilize his plant capacity, then, and only then, does he begin to hire machine builders. Thus, a forecaster practicing his art during a recession should be, or would be, mindful of both the size of the inventories and the rate of their liquidation. Government intervention affects the rate of liquidation, and, presumably, the forecaster should be, or would be, aware of the implications of government deficit spending during the bad times for inventory liquidation.

FORECASTING WITH A LEAKY BUCKET ECONOMY

A leaky bucket economy is one in which the money paid to workers does not all come back to the manufacturers as revenue for goods sold to the population. Up to this point, leaky buckets were transient in nature. During times of net saving, money paid to the population does not all flow back to the factory owners in the form of purchases of goods. A portion of the paychecks is being saved. However, with time, the nest eggs grow to the requisite size, and the population is no longer in a net saving mode of thinking. Once the nest eggs are established, the leaky bucket in the form of continual net saving no longer leaks. The hole has been sealed, and the manufacturers see all their workers' pay return as receipts for goods sold.

If the net saving occurs during a recession, and if the recession lasts long enough, the working population will accumulate a substantial amount of savings. Once the good times return, the population as a whole may become net withdrawers from the bank. They are dissaving because their collective nest eggs are now viewed as being a bit too adequate for the circumstances. Thus, between good and bad times, the population shifts between being net spendthrifts and net savers. Sometimes the bucket has a leak in it in the sense that remuneration paid to workers is not coming back in its entirety to the factory owners in the form of goods sold. The bucket may have a hole in it or a hose attached to it with a spigot. Turning on the spigot occurs when remuneration

Exhibit 8.1
Account Balances

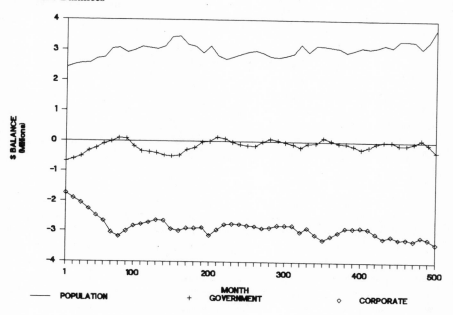

paid to workers comes back in its entirety, and then some, from net dissaving on the part of the population. Overall, the money paid to workers, be it in the form of pay for work or interest on savings, comes back as goods sold to the workers or to those whose paychecks depend on taxes paid by the workers.

The stability in the continual recycling of money during good and bad times can be seen in the nature of the volatility of the bank accounts of the population, the government, and the corporation over many business cycles, as shown in Exhibit 8.1. In viewing this exhibit, one can sense that the free market economy can go on forever, despite its oscillations between good and bad times.

Exhibit 8.1 is the second variant on the free market society in which the unemployed are provided with jobs that are beneficial for society as a whole, including the factory owners themselves. This will serve as the base case for the comparison with a leaky bucket economy.

There are a number of ways to obtain a leaky bucket economy. Never-ending saving would be one method. Because the population never finds a satisfactorily sized nest egg, it saves and saves and saves. This is a leaky bucket in that the manufacturers do not see receipts from selling goods equal to the expenses being paid to the work force to make goods and to make the machines used to make the goods. The "shrouds have no pockets" thinking of the religious and the irreligious can eventually end oversaving when one realizes that there is a finite-sized nest egg that can carry one over the bad times. For instance, a nest egg equivalent to twenty years of unemployment, though large, and probably excessive, is still finite. Once that is achieved, the leaky bucket is sealed. For those who die with twenty years' savings in the bank, the heirs are spared some of the effort of accumulating so much in savings. At some point, an equilibrium point is reached at which spending by the workers equals income received by the workers. The leaky bucket is eventually sealed.

Another way to have a leaky bucket economy is hoarding. This can occur when gold and silver are money. Each month a portion of the population buries a few gold coins in the family garden. The coins are never dug up—each month the tulip bed gets richer, and the manufacturers are experiencing trouble selling their wares. People are less apt to hoard when paper is money and deposits are guaranteed by the government. Besides, paper rots in a tulip bed.

Another source of a leaky bucket economy is the creation of a class of rich folk so rich that they are unable to spend the interest being paid on the interest on their fortunes. The superrich of the nineteenth and early twentieth centuries had this problem. Their fortunes were oftentimes built on the idea of selling dear and paying cheap—that is, high profit margins on goods sold and low pay for workers who produced the goods. Income taxes and inheritance taxes have more or less sealed this leak, along with the mass marketing and mass production ideas of Henry Ford.

The leaky bucket deserving of scrutiny in today's world is a perpetual trade imbalance. The population buys domestically made goods with 99 percent of its spending. One percent of total spending is on foreign-made goods. This is a deficit in that there is no countervailing expenditure by the exporter in the island marketplace. The exporting nation is therefore accumulating liquid funds by virtue of the fact that it is selling more goods in the island market than it is buying goods produced in the island's factories.

There is continual buying and selling, or an exchange of goods, between the two nations, but there is always an imbalance in trade equivalent to 1 percent of total spending by the island population. The following table illustrates the relative performance of the island economy with and without a perpetual trade deficit. The base case for comparison purposes is the second variant of the free market society. "Deficit-I" denotes that the leaky bucket is in the form of a trade deficit equivalent to 1 percent of all spending by the population.

On the surface, the workers are benefiting to some extent from the presumably higher-quality or lower-priced products being purchased overseas. However, the workers are bearing a cost in the form of a higher rate of unemployment. In addition, the higher value of the state of mind indicates that good times are not

AVERAGE OVER 500 MONTHS OF SIMULATION	NO LEAKY BUCKET (BASE)	LEAKY BUCKET (DEFICIT–I)
Goods bought (lbs.)	32,182	32,172
Price	$8.63	$8.28
Payback period (months)	27.8	39.4
Wage (per month)	$1,090	$1,069
Number of unemployed	13	14
Number of operators	155	156
Number of builders	52	50
Number of machines	166	166
Utilization	94%	94%
State of mind	1.64	1.68
Interest rate	4.5%	4.5%
Tax rate	15.0%	15.6%
Balance in population account ($1,000s)	$3,057	$3,151
Balance in government account ($1,000s)	−$149	−$207
Balance in corporation account ($1,000s)	−$2,908	−$4,379

quite as prevalent as before. Overall, there does not seem to be an enormous difference in the performance of the two economies, measured in terms of physical output. However, a much more serious situation is occurring in the banking system.

Exhibit 8.2 shows that the corporation is marching off to bankruptcy. The reason for this is that the foreign bank account, representing the trade deficit, is growing. For the foreign bank account to grow, something has to come up short. The population is saving at its usual rate, so that its aggregate nest egg remains unchanged. Government conducts its fiscal policy of maintaining a balanced budget over the long haul, while pursuing a course of deficit spending during the bad times.

People can determine what they consider to be a desired level of savings and set aside money, by not spending all their paychecks, to satisfy their objectives. The government has the tool—taxes on sales and income—to do whatever it wants from the point of fiscal responsibility. The corporation is left with no control over its revenue, which is the after-tax dollars not being saved. Its

Exhibit 8.2
Account Balances: Deficit–I

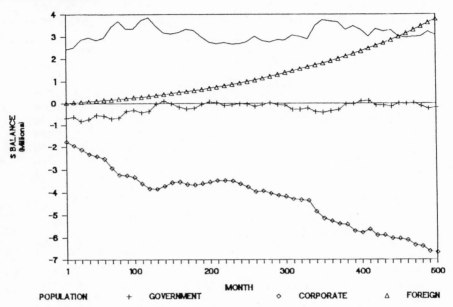

POPULATION   + GOVERNMENT   ◇ CORPORATE   △ FOREIGN

expenses in terms of salaries paid to machine builders and operators cannot be controlled because the number of those employed making machines and making goods is the result of decisions based on the level of prices and the size of the inventory in the factory warehouse.

Viewed from this perspective, a corporation cannot dictate the size of its bank account. The size of its bank account is the difference between revenue and costs, which, for the most part, are beyond the control of management. Because the population, by virtue of individual decisions on what not to spend, and the government, by virtue of its ability to tax, can determine the size of their bank accounts, the corporate bank account is the one that must be depleted as the foreign bank account grows. Exhibit 8.2 presumes that the foreign merchants are depositing their trade surpluses in the banking system of the island economy. Were this not so, then a phony bank account, called bank credit, would have had to be created to keep the banking system solvent.

The reason why the corporation is descending ever deeper into debt with a leaky bucket economy can be seen both in the price of goods and in the payback period. Without a leaky bucket, which would be equivalent to an island economy with no lasting trade deficits or surpluses, the price of goods averages $8.63 with a payback period of 27.8 months. This is the "invisible hand" of Adam Smith visibly at work. The 27.8 months are adequate to recoup an investment in machinery that decays at an average rate of about 3 percent per month with a cost of capital on the order of 4 percent. Thus, the price of goods is high

Exhibit 8.3
Price

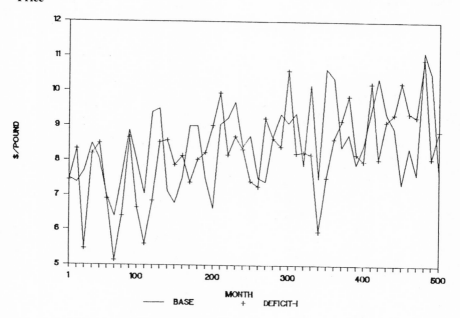

enough for the corporation to recoup its entire investment in plant capacity, and interest on that investment, during the physical lifetime of the capital investment.

For the leaky bucket situation, which represents a perpetual drain of financial resources in the form of a balance of trade deficit, the average price of goods is $8.28 with an associated payback period of 39.4 months. The lower price of goods, which on the surface looks good for consumers, is bad for industry. As the factory manager adjusts his pricing throttle to keep his factory inventory within an acceptable number of weeks in relation to orders from distributors, he must also maintain lower prices when his workers are not spending all their paychecks on domestically produced goods. The workers may seem to be benefiting by lower prices—which might not be true when unemployment is taken into consideration—but the factory owners are suffering. They are, in effect, throwing away a machine that has been exhausted of any further productivity, but that has not produced the amount of goods necessary to earn sufficient revenue to recoup its initial investment including interest costs. This is the reason why the corporation is forever sinking into debt.

Exhibit 8.3 compares the price of goods between the base case (no leaky bucket in the form of an imbalance of trade) and the Deficit-I case (a leaky bucket because of an imbalance of trade).

While prices seem to be peaking at around the same level, there is a marked lowering of prices during the bad times of the business cycle. This means that

Exhibit 8.4
Number Unemployed: Base Case

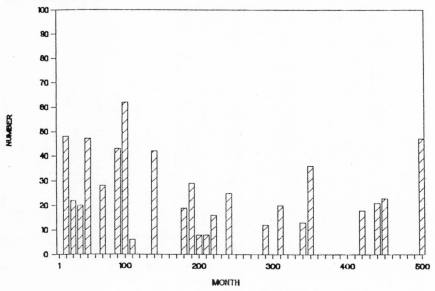

slumps in business are worse for an economy with a deficit in trade than for one that maintains a balanced exchange with its trading partners. A comparison of the numbers unemployed shows in more poignant terms that the trade imbalance is making bad times worse. The average number unemployed without a trade deficit is 13, actually 12.98, as shown in Exhibit 8.4. With a trade deficit, the average number unemployed climbs to 14, actually 14.29, as shown in Exhibit 8.5.

Although the price differentials in Exhibit 8.3 do not appear to be particularly significant, the impact on the payback period is quite adverse, as illustrated in Exhibit 8.6. The payback period is not much different between a balance of trade and a deficit in trade during the good times. But the payback period is much greater during the bad times, reflecting the fact that the bad times are worse when there is a trade imbalance. This can be seen in the exhibits concerning the number unemployed, prices, and the payback period, even though there is substantial government intervention in both cases in the form of unemployment benefits.

The worst aspect of the deficit of trade situation has not yet been addressed. With a balance of trade, the island economy can go on indefinitely bouncing between goods times and bad times. This is the lesson in Exhibit 8.1. The lesson in Exhibit 8.2 is that the island economy must one day collapse if there is a perpetual balance of trade deficit. The reason for this is that the corporation, representing a fixed amount of assets, is forever sinking into the quagmire of

Exhibit 8.5
Number Unemployed: Deficit–I

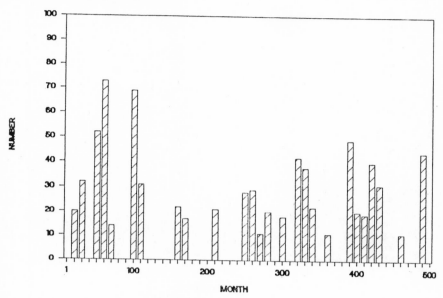

debt. There must be a point at which the ratio of asset coverage to underlying indebtedness affects the quality rating of industrial bonds. There must be a magnitude of indebtedness at which a corporation begins issuing bonds of questionable security to support its capital structure.

A fitting analogy in describing the plight of corporations sinking further and further into debt is found by examining what happens to individuals who become overburdened with debt. No one would argue with the fact that the chance of repayment of a $1,000 debt by an individual earning $10,000 per year is considerably higher than the chance of repayment of a $100,000 debt by an individual with the same $10,000 income. A corporation is no different than an individual. When overburdened with debt, a corporation can have the same difficulties an individual does in servicing its obligations. Perhaps a sign that corporations are becoming overextended in debt is when their bonds are being sold as "junk."

At some point, the corporation cannot borrow more money from the liquid assets being accumulated by the foreigners to sustain its ever-weakening financial structure. The foreigners will be asking for more security than it has security to give. Universal bankruptcy would follow, were there no government intervention. But that bridge has already been crossed. The government is expected to intervene to save the maiden from the dragon of bad times. Intervention can be in the form of government payments to corporations to prevent their sinking further into debt.

Exhibit 8.7 shows the balances in the various bank accounts, with the proviso

Exhibit 8.6
Payback Period

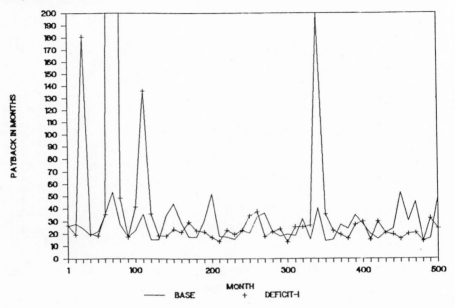

that the government has elected to bear the obligation to prevent industry from sinking more than $3 million into debt. "Deficit-II" denotes that the government is limiting the extent of the total indebtedness of the corporation by a direct cash payment from the government to the corporation. The corporation is being subsidized by the government.

The foreign account still shows its unremitting growth. The people save—that is, they do not spend—to accumulate a sufficiently sized nest egg. The corporate account cannot sink more than $3 million into debt because the government is now obligated to underwrite the corporation. As described in the appendix, only a few programming statements are necessary for the government to assume the obligation of transferring funds to the corporation when the amount of debt reaches a predetermined point. Exhibit 8.7 shows that the net result of the government's supporting the corporation to prevent it from sinking further into debt is that the government sinks further into debt. As the saying goes, if you squeeze a snake in one spot, it balloons in another.

For this particular society, supporting industry is not an optimal government policy. Exhibit 8.8 shows the price of goods associated with this policy.

A comparison of Exhibit 8.8 with Exhibit 8.3 shows that there are significantly lower prices. Offhand, this appears to be in the consumers' interest in that there are plenty of bargains. However, there are plenty of bargains because the manufacturers are having a great deal of difficulty keeping their inventories in line

Exhibit 8.7
Account Balances: Deficit–II

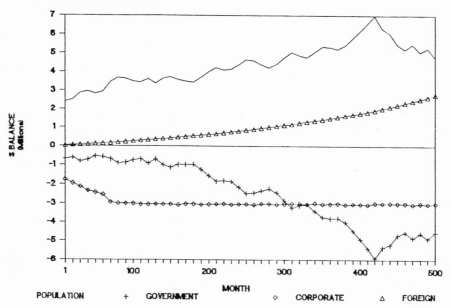

with demand. In fact, because the pricing throttle is not sufficient to keep inventories at bay, factory managers are grabbing the production throttle much more frequently, as seen in Exhibit 8.9.

Layoffs are much more commonplace in Exhibit 8.9 where there is a policy of government intervention to support industry than in Exhibits 8.4 and 8.5 where industry is not being supported by the government. However, it must be noted that when there is a perpetual trade deficit, the continual sinking into debt by the corporations will eventually force the government to support the financial underpinnings of the corporations. The general distress of the corporations, even with the government backing their survival, can be seen in Exhibit 8.10.

The question of why this particular government interventionist policy is hurting the economy can be answered by looking at Exhibit 8.11. The rule incorporated in the simulation is that the government is to raise taxes when there is a growing government deficit during the good times. From Exhibit 8.11, a 30 percent tax rate is sufficient to prevent the deficit from becoming worse during good times. However, the deficit expands during bad times to help the unemployed and to ensure that the corporation does not sink further into debt. Such high tax rates take away from the spending stream of the population. Reduced spending, in relation to the money being paid out in the form of worker salaries, means hard times for the factory managers. They are pulling back on both the pricing and the production throttles in their attempt to keep factory inventory under control.

Exhibit 8.8
Price

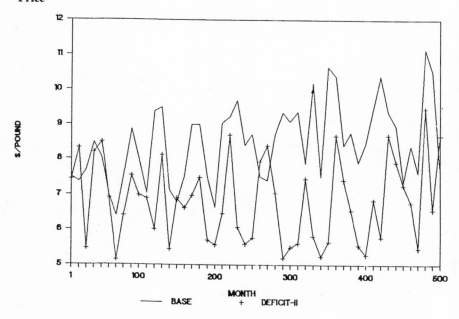

MONTH
——— BASE   +   DEFICIT–II

GOVERNMENT INTERVENTION AND ECONOMIC ACTIVITY

The point of this discussion is to show that government policies do affect economic activity. In particular, government policy might cause an equilibrium short of full employment to emerge. Indeed, in watching this simulation, an equilibrium short of full employment does occur during the recovery phase from the bad times. Prices are not sufficiently high to recover the full investment in new capital equipment. With so much of the spending stream being taxed to support the financial underpinnings of the corporation, the factory managers are not able to raise prices to a point at which the expansion of plant capacity can be economically supported to any great degree.

Low prices are necessary to keep the factory warehouse inventory in line with incoming orders, even during the recovery from the previous bad times. Low prices do not motivate managers to hire machine builders to expand capacity to any great extent, even though the existing plant capacity is being fully utilized. The price/cost calculation cannot justify expansion other than on a very subdued level because the payback period is far beyond the point necessary to recoup the investment in new plant capacity. Keynes' contention that cheap money promotes economic activity does play a positive role in management investment decisions under these circumstances because the payback period in the simulation was

Exhibit 8.9
Number Unemployed: Deficit–II

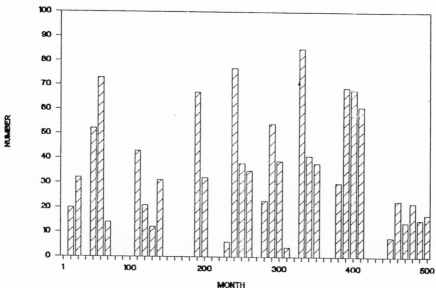

sensitized to interest rates. Higher interest rates would have exacerbated the situation.

Regardless of the level of interest rates, this particular government interventionist policy left a substantial number of people on the unemployment rolls. The workers' state of mind remained cautious for a longer period of time, and, thus, savings accumulated to a greater extent, which can be seen by comparing Exhibits 8.1, 8.2, and 8.7. For the Deficit-II case, with the government funding the corporations, the good times did not last long enough for the excess savings to be liquidated. This enlarged the opening in the leaky bucket. The spending stream was reduced by the perpetual balance of trade deficit, growing savings on the part of the population because of the extended length of the recovery from bad to good times, and high taxation rates to keep the corporations solvent.

Forecasting during the bad times for the Deficit-II leaky bucket economy is not the same as for the base and the Deficit-I economies. In the Deficit-II leaky bucket economy, recovery of the economy is dependent not only on the liquidation of excess inventory but also on the increase of the price of goods to a point that will induce factory managers to add to plant capacity, not just maintain plant capacity at current levels.

Substantial unemployment exists during the recovery phase from bad to good times in the Deficit-II leaky bucket economy because prices are high enough for factory managers to hire operators to man all the machines—but not high enough to expand capacity by hiring machine builders. Unemployment exists because

Exhibit 8.10
Payback Period

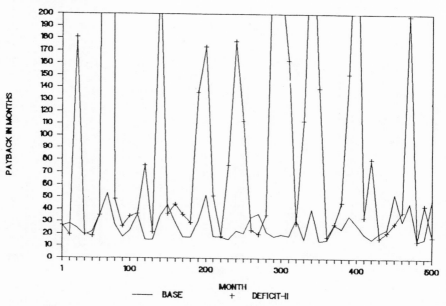

the number of machine operators far exceeds the number of machines. Were demand for goods more robust, then there would be price hikes of sufficient magnitude to induce factory managers to hire substantial numbers of machine builders to expand plant capacity.

However, the government is taxing such a large portion of the workers' pay and is expending the monies in a way that does not create any employment opportunities. The money is not being spent to provide jobs; it is being paid directly to the corporation to save it from going bankrupt. Thus, the spending stream (the revenue from the sale of goods) is being reduced by the amount of the money being taxed by the government and not being recirculated into the spending stream in terms of salaries or benefits to the population. To move whatever goods are being produced from the warehouse to the marketplace, the managers are forced to cut prices. Although prices are not less than the variable cost of production, they are lower than the price necessary to economically justify capital expenditures. Thus, the factory managers are reluctant to invest in new plant capacity because the price of goods cannot financially support new investment, even though the existing plant capacity is being fully utilized.

Keynes' contention that economic activity can level out at something less than full employment is true. His conclusion that government deficit spending can cure this situation must be viewed from the point of view that government deficit

Exhibit 8.11
Tax Rate

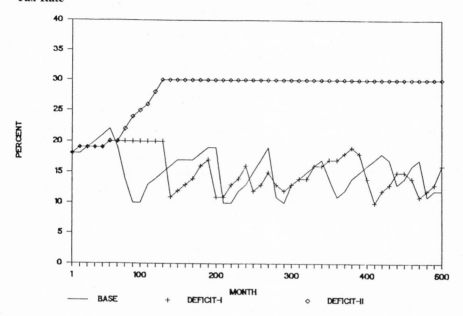

spending is causing the less-than-optimal performance of the economy. In other words, for the situation under scrutiny, Keynes' cure appears to be the cause of the malaise.

The problem is not in Keynes' thinking but in the existence of a leaky bucket economy. Leaks in the bucket can be handled if they are transient in nature. Perpetual leaks lead to a degenerating situation that results in uncontrollable deficits, either for the corporation or the government, or both. In today's world, uncontrollable deficits seem to occur on all levels of society: personal, corporate, and governmental. Forecasting of business conditions has to take into consideration how people are reacting to this situation of growing debt in all phases of society. This can be done using simulation. Perhaps the simulation can answer the question of where the source of credit is to support the growth in debt. That is one of the benefits of simulation—no question can go unanswered. Without too much ado on the subject, another benefit of simulation is that it can be used as a bloodless method of evaluating different government interventionist policies.

ECONOMIC STABILITY OF A SOCIETY

A perpetual imbalance of trade destabilizes a national economy. An imbalance in trade generates a deficit of payments which acts as a hole in a bucket in the sloshing back and forth of money paid to workers to make goods and money collected from workers in selling them the goods that they have made. This leaky bucket weakens the financial structure of a nation that suffers from a chronic trade deficit.

The situation can also describe a chronic deficit in the balance of payments between two nations. The discussion assumed that the deficit was caused by an imbalance of trade. However, the deficit could also be caused by perpetual indebtedness such that financial payments in the form of interest are forever causing a drain on the national economy. If anything is learned from all this, it is that perpetual drains on a national economy in the form of an outflow of capital, whether caused by an imbalance in trade or by financial payments on gross indebtedness, will depress that economy to some suboptimal level of performance.

If two nations are imbalanced with respect to trade, the bankruptcy of one does not help the other because its financial resources are most probably invested in the defaulting nation. Indebtedness of this magnitude would lead to the uniting of the two economies. Then what was an imbalance of trade yesterday would no longer be an imbalance today. For example, the state of Massachusetts probably suffers from an imbalance of trade with other states in that it must "import" oil from Texas and "import" grain from Nebraska without countervailing "exports" to pay for these commodities. But within the context of the United States, Massachusetts is not suffering from its imbalance of trade with Texas and Nebraska. The imbalance of trade between the United States and Japan would not be an imbalance if both were one and the same nation united by a common currency and, consequently, common political institutions.

But there is an imbalance of trade between the United States and Japan which is adversely affecting the United States. The American worker who drives a Japanese-made car might wonder why there are so many idle factories, the so-called Rust Belt of the Middle West. He really shouldn't wonder why; nor should he marvel at the fact that his company has been sold to a Japanese firm and he is now working for a Japanese boss. It is the consequence of a perpetual leak in a bucket.

This same story is being repeated in many third world nations. These nations cannot seem to get their economies moving because they are weighed down with interest payments of such magnitude that the leaky bucket could be better described as a bucket with no bottom. The problem begs for a solution, and a solution will be found. Part of that solution may be imbedded in the continual trend toward globalization of the world economy.

This discussion has strayed somewhat from the intent of the book on forecasting business conditions. On the other hand, in attempting to forecast business conditions, one is forced into thinking about the rules of the game because businessmen react according to these rules—that is, they make decisions in their best interests in accordance with these rules. Without understanding the rules of the game, which may more formally be addressed as the economic system by which a nation operates with regard to producing goods and providing services, one can hardly be in a position to forecast changes in business activity. The micropicture of how a factory manager will react to changing conditions in his warehouse and to changing prices and costs as he plans his production goals cannot be divorced from the macropicture of how government policies affect economic activity. The two are intertwined. As the forecaster tries to assess the impact of changing business conditions over a forecast period, he cannot deal exclusively with the micropicture. The author would have been remiss to stress the micropicture without a casual mention of the macropicture.

APPENDIX

Statement 125 in the program listed in Chapter 7 determines the pay for all six categories of the population in relation to the base pay:

125 FOR I = 1 TO 6:READ B(I):DATA .8,1,0,0,1,1.2:NEXT

Providing the unemployables and the unemployed with an income equal to 25 percent of the base pay received by machine operators can be done by changing this statement to read as follows:

125 FOR I = 1 TO 6:READ B(I):DATA .8,1,.25,.25,1,1.2:NEXT

The original program was set up with these two categories being paid by the government. Adapting the simulation to permit the unemployed to receive 50 percent of the base pay is shown below:

125 FOR I = 1 TO 6:READ B(I):DATA .8,1,.25,.5,1,1.2:NEXT

The unemployed can be made to contribute to the benefit of industry by building machine capacity at a rate of thirty man-months of unemployed effort by inserting + N4/ 30 into the beginning portion of statement 534.

A leaky bucket economy where 1 percent of all spending is lost to the domestic economy can be accomplished by incorporating the following changes. Add Y8 = 0 at the end of statement 200 and rewrite statement 402 as follows.

402 Q1 = P3 − S1 + D1:Q2 = T*Q1:Q1 = Q1 − Q2:Q3 = Q3 + Q2
403 Y8 = Y8 + .01*Q1:Q1 = Q1 − .01*Q1:Q4 = Q4 + Q1

Add Y1 = Y:Y = Y + Y8 to statement 950. The calculation of interest for the foreign bank account, and the recording of results, have already been included in the program listed in the appendix to chapter 7.

The following statement modifications force the government to pick up the tab when the overall indebtedness of the corporation increases above $3 million:

926 IF C< − 3000000 THEN 927 ELSE 930
927 Y9 = C + 3000000:G = G + Y9:C = C − Y9

Index

About the Author

ROY L. NERSESIAN is Chair of the Management Department at the School of Business Administration, Monmouth College, and the author of *Computer Simulation in Business Decision Making*, also published by Quorum Books.